Maheen class 5

CW01333173

Juz 'Amma

For School Students

Husain A. Nuri and Mansur Ahmad

ISBN 13: 978-0-9818483-0-3

First edition: 2008
First color edition: 2010

Cover Design: Mansur Ahmad
Graphics and layout: Mansur Ahmad, Shabnam Mansur

WeekendLearning Publishers
5584 Boulder Crest St
Columbus, OH 43235
www.weekendlearning.com

Printed in China

Price: US $12.00

Preface

This book is compiled to help the children in learning, memorizing and understanding Juz 'Amma. We have aimed this book at children of different ages. Therefore, some sections of the book may be too difficult or too easy for some children. A child just starting to learn Arabic may find the transliteration section very important, while a mature student may find the transliteration section unnecessary. The teacher is requested to use different parts of the book as appropriate for the level of the student. We expect that, insha-Allāh, the book will be helpful to all children from elementary to senior grades.

We have attempted to make the book as useful as possible. Large and clean Arabic fonts used in the book should be easier to read. We sincerely acknowledge the generosity of Dr. Zohurul Hoque for allowing us to use his transliterations. We feel that, with a little practice, a child will be able to use this transliteration system for good pronunciation. We have adopted Zohurul Hoque's translation of the Qur'ān, because it follows the Arabic quite literally. We have taken the liberty of modifying some of his translations for easier reading by the children. Translation of the Qur'ān is indeed a huge challenge, and is truly considered impossible. Words of the Qur'ān often carry different shades of meaning. When translated, it may reflect only one meaning, or may deviate from the meaning intended in the Qur'ān. With this limitation, our effort is to provide a simple, single and as close as possible meaning of the words.

The explanation is not exhaustive, but is short and simple to benefit school children. We based our explanations on works by Syed Qutb, Ibn Kathir and Yusuf Ali. In case there is a need for further elaboration, an authoritative commentary should be consulted.

The "Words to Know" section is to help non-Arabic speaking students to learn a few words arising from the same Arabic root.

For the "Word-to-Word meaning" section, we have frequently consulted the works of Dr. Zohurul Hoque, and a translation by Sr. Zaheen Fatima Baig. We have also extensively used the "Dictionary of the Holy Qur'ān" by Abdul Mannān Omar, and "A Dictionary and Glossary of the Koran" by John Penrice. We also acknowledge the help that we received from the translations of Abdullah Yusuf Ali and M. A. S. Abdel Haleem. May Allah (swt) bless all of them, Amin.

A major part of formatting the Arabic text, graphics and layout of this book was done by Shabnam Mansur, a 12-year old girl. We sincerely acknowledge her help. May Allah (swt) bless her, Amin.

We are thankful to Allah for giving us the ability to compile this book. We pray to Allah to accept our effort in communicating the message of Islam. Any mistakes or errors in the book are our fault. We appreciate receiving meaningful comments and suggestions to improve this book.

رَبَّنَا تَقَبَّلْ مِنَّآ ۖ إِنَّكَ أَنتَ ٱلسَّمِيعُ ٱلْعَلِيمُ ﴿١٢٧﴾

"Our Rabb! Accept from us, you indeed are the all-Hearing, all Knowing." (2:127)

Eid-ul-Fitr, 1429
October 1, 2008

Husain A. Nuri
Mansur Ahmad

Guide to transliteration

ا	Alif	a	ط	Ṭā	ṭ
ب	Bā	b	ظ	Ẓā	ẓ
ت	Tā	t	ع	'Ain	'
ث	Thā	t͟h	غ	Ghain	gh
ج	Jīm	j	ف	Fā	f
ح	Ḥā	ḥ	ق	Qāf	q
خ	Khā	kh	ك	Kāf	k
د	Dāl	d	ل	Lām	l
ذ	Dhāl	d͟h	م	Mīm	m
ر	Rā	r	ن	Nūn	n
ز	Zā	z	ه	Hā	h
س	Sīn	s	و	Wāw	w
ش	Shīn	sh	ي	Yā	y
ص	Ṣād	ṣ	ء	Hamzah	'
ض	Ḍād	ḍ			

Long vowels: ā, ī, ū
Nūn joined with next letter, and Tanwin: ṅ

Table of Contents

Sūrah 1.	Al-Fatihah	7
Sūrah 114.	An-Nās	11
Sūrah 113.	Al-Falaq	14
Sūrah 112.	Al-Ikhlās	17
Sūrah 111.	Al-Masad/Al-Lahab	20
Sūrah 110.	An-Nasr	23
Sūrah 109.	Al-Kāfirūn	26
Sūrah 108.	Al-Kawthar	29
Sūrah 107.	Al-Mā'ūn	32
Sūrah 106.	Al-Quraish	36
Sūrah 105.	Al-Fīl	39
Sūrah 104.	Al-Humazah	42
Sūrah 103.	Al-'Asr	47
Sūrah 102.	Al-Takāthur	50
Sūrah 101.	Al-Qāri'ah	54
Sūrah 100.	Al-'Adiyāt	59
Sūrah 99.	Az-Zalzalah	63
Sūrah 98.	Al-Bayyinah	67
Sūrah 97.	Al-Qadr	74
Sūrah 96.	Al-'Alaq	78
Sūrah 95.	At-Tīn	84
Sūrah 94.	Al-Inshirah	88

Sūrah 93.	Ad-Duhā	92
Sūrah 92.	Al-Lail	96
Sūrah 91.	Ash-Shams	102
Sūrah 90.	Al-Balad	107
Sūrah 89.	Al-Fajr	114
Sūrah 88.	Al-Ghāshiyah	123
Sūrah 87.	Al-A'lā	130
Sūrah 86.	At-Tāriq	136
Sūrah 85.	Al-Burūj	142
Sūrah 84.	Al-Inshiqāq	150
Sūrah 83.	At-Mutaffifīn	158
Sūrah 82.	Al-Infitār	168
Sūrah 81.	At-Takwīr	174
Sūrah 80.	'Abasa	182
Sūrah 79.	An-Nazi'āt	191
Sūrah 78.	An-Naba'	202

Sūrah 1

Revealed in Makkah

Al-Fātihah

The Opening

Introduction:

Sūrah Al-Fātihah is not part of Juz 'Amma, but it is included in this book as this sūrah is most frequently recited. We must recite this sūrah in every rakah of a salāh. This is the first sūrah in the Qur'ān, and is a prayer to Allāh. By reciting this sūrah, we establish our relationship with Allāh. He is the Lord of the whole universe. He provides us with everything that we need, and rewards our good efforts. We are His servants, and we pray only to Him for any help. Allāh shows us the Right Path—the path that is favored, and not the misleading path.

بِسۡمِ ٱللَّهِ ٱلرَّحۡمَٰنِ ٱلرَّحِيمِ ١	Bismi-llāhi-r raḥmāni-r raḥīm	1. In the name of Allāh, the most-Kind, the most-Rewarding.
ٱلۡحَمۡدُ لِلَّهِ رَبِّ ٱلۡعَٰلَمِينَ ٢	Al-hamdu li-llāhi rabbi-l 'ālamīn.	2. The Praise belongs to Allāh, the Lord of all the worlds
ٱلرَّحۡمَٰنِ ٱلرَّحِيمِ ٣	Ar-raḥmāni-r raḥīm.	3. Most-Kind, most-Rewarding
مَٰلِكِ يَوۡمِ ٱلدِّينِ ٤	Māliki yawmi-d dīn.	4. Master of the Day of Judgment
إِيَّاكَ نَعۡبُدُ وَإِيَّاكَ نَسۡتَعِينُ ٥	Iyyāka na'budu wa iyyāka nasta'īn.	5. You alone we do serve, and to You alone we seek help.
ٱهۡدِنَا ٱلصِّرَٰطَ ٱلۡمُسۡتَقِيمَ ٦	Ihdina-ṣ ṣirāta-l mustaqīm.	6. Guide us to the Right Path,
صِرَٰطَ ٱلَّذِينَ أَنۡعَمۡتَ عَلَيۡهِمۡ غَيۡرِ ٱلۡمَغۡضُوبِ عَلَيۡهِمۡ وَلَا ٱلضَّآلِّينَ ٧	ṣirāta-l ladhīna an'amta 'alaihim, ghairi-l maghdūbi 'alaihim wa la-d dāllīn.	7. the path of those on whom You have granted favors, not of those on whom wrath is brought down, nor of those who are lost.

Explanation:

1. The first verse of Sūrah *al-Fātihah* is the beginning of the Qur'ān. This verse is recited before starting any good work. This verse has two of the most beautiful names of Allāh—*ar-Rahmān* and *ar-Rahīm*. *Ar-Rahmān* means the most-Merciful. This name tells us Allāh is full of mercy and kindness towards everything. The name *ar-Rahmān* shows we get mercy of Allāh even if we do not ask for it. *Ar-Rahīm* means extremely loving and merciful. This name is very similar to Ar-Rahmān. This name shows the quality of Allāh's mercy that we get as a result of our good work, and the mercy that we will get in the Hereafter based on our good deeds.
2. All praise belongs to Allāh. He is the *Rabb* or Lord of all the worlds. *Rabb* is one who not only creates us, but also feeds us, takes care of us, perfects us, preserves us, maintains us, and controls us. He does many other things for us so that we can survive in this world. He is not only our Rabb, but also the Rabb of the entire universe. Whatever He does to us, He also does to the Universe.
3. We again remember Allāh by using His two beautiful names—*ar-Rahmān* and *ar-Rahīm*. The meaning of the names is explained above.
4. Allāh is the Master of the Day of Judgment. He is the Master because on that Day He will give us our dues based on how we worked in this life.
5. In this verse we confirm that He is the only One we worship. As we say this, we are making sure that we do not worship any idols, stones, people, sun, moon, animals or anything. Since we do not worship anything or anybody other than Allāh, we depend upon Him for all help. Then, in the verse, we respectfully mention that Allāh is the only one from whom we seek help.
6. We ask Allāh to guide us on the Straight Path. This straight path is the Right Path. This is the path of Islam. The path does not have any twists or surprises on it. It is the perfect path for our survival. This path will lead us to the best result in the Hereafter.
7. The path that we want to follow is the path of the past prophets and good people. Allāh blessed these people who walked on this path. We want to be blessed like them, therefore, we pray to Allāh to help us walk on the path. Any other path is a wrong path. Those who walked on the wrong path earned anger and they got lost. We are afraid that we might somehow walk on the wrong path. The wrong path is the path of Shaitān. Allāh punished those who walked on the wrong path. Therefore, we pray to Allāh to guide us away from walking on the wrong path.

Words to know

Al-Fātiha: The Opening, the first sūrah in the Qur'an. *Fataha*: to open, to give victory. *Al-fath*: the Victory. *Fatha Mubīn*: Clear Victory.

Rahmān: most-Kind. *Rahima*: to love, to have mercy. *Rahīm*: most-Rewarding. *Rahmatun*: mercy. *Marhamah*: compassion.

Mālik: Master, Lord. *Malik*: king. *Malaka*: to own. *Malakat*: has owned. *Malakun*: angel. *Malāika*: angels.

Mustaqīm: straight, shortest, smooth, right. *Qāma*: to stand, to rise. *Aqīmū*: you follow, you do. *Maqāmun*: place where one stands. *Qiyaāmat*: rising up, resurrection.

An'amta: You have favored. *Na'ama*: to enjoy comfort. *In'ām*: favor. *Al-Ni'mat*: blessing.

Maghdūb: who earned anger or wrath. *Ghadhiba*: to be angry. *Ghadhab*: anger, wrath.

Sūrah Al-Fātihah
Word-by-word meaning

ٱلرَّحِيمِ ١ the Most-Rewarding	ٱلرَّحْمَـٰنِ the Most-Kind	ٱللَّهِ Allah	بِسْمِ In the name of
ٱلْعَـٰلَمِينَ ٢ the worlds.	رَبِّ the Rabb	لِلَّهِ for Allah	ٱلْحَمْدُ The Praise
يَوْمِ day	مَـٰلِكِ Master	ٱلرَّحِيمِ ٣ Most-Rewarding.	ٱلرَّحْمَـٰنِ Most-Kind
وَإِيَّاكَ and You alone	نَعْبُدُ we worship	إِيَّاكَ You alone	ٱلدِّينِ ٤ judgment, religion
ٱلْمُسْتَقِيمَ ٦ Right, straight.	ٱلصِّرَٰطَ the path	ٱهْدِنَا Guide us	نَسْتَعِينُ ٥ we seek for help.
عَلَيْهِمْ upon them.	أَنْعَمْتَ You have favored	ٱلَّذِينَ those who	صِرَٰطَ Path
وَلَا and not	عَلَيْهِمْ upon them	ٱلْمَغْضُوبِ those who earned wrath	غَيْرِ other than
			ٱلضَّآلِّينَ ٧ who are lost.

For additional reading, senior students may read "An-Analysis of Fātihah" and "Fātihah versus Lord's Payer" in Islamic Studies, Level 10 book from WeekendLearning Publishers.

Juz ‘Amma

Sūrah 114

Revealed in Makkah

An-Nās

The Mankind

Introduction

This is the ending sūrah of the Majestic Qur'ān. In this sūrah, we declare Allāh as the Lord and Master of Mankind. We state that the invisible creatures called Jinn and bad people whisper bad thoughts in our minds. Allāh teaches us to seek shelter and protection with Him from the evils arising from Jinn or from the bad people.

بِسۡمِ ٱللَّهِ ٱلرَّحۡمَـٰنِ ٱلرَّحِيمِ

Bismi-llāhi-r raḥmāni-r raḥīm
In the name of Allah, the Most-Kind, the Most-Rewarding.

قُلۡ أَعُوذُ بِرَبِّ ٱلنَّاسِ ﴿١﴾	Qul a'ūdhu bi-rabbi-n nās,	1. Say: "I take refuge with the Rabb of mankind,
مَلِكِ ٱلنَّاسِ ﴿٢﴾	maliki-n nās,	2. "the Master of mankind,
إِلَـٰهِ ٱلنَّاسِ ﴿٣﴾	ilāhi-n nās,	3. "the God of mankind,
مِن شَرِّ ٱلۡوَسۡوَاسِ ٱلۡخَنَّاسِ ﴿٤﴾	min sharri-l waswāsi-l khannās,—	4. "from the evil of the whisperings of the sneaking one,—
ٱلَّذِى يُوَسۡوِسُ فِى صُدُورِ ٱلنَّاسِ ﴿٥﴾	Alladhī yuwaswisu fī ṣudūri-n nās,	5. "who whispers into the hearts of mankind,
مِنَ ٱلۡجِنَّةِ وَٱلنَّاسِ ﴿٦﴾	mina-l jinnati wa-n nāss.	6. "from among the jinn and the mankind."

Explanation

1. The sūrah begins with the command *qul* which means "Say". Allāh is asking our Prophet (S) to say the message of the sūrah. As we read the sūrah, we seek refuge with Allāh, who is the *Rabb* of mankind. Seeking refuge means seeking protection, shelter and safety. We seek refuge with One who is called Rabb. The word Rabb means one who brings us up, feeds us, and takes care of us. He is our Guardian, Leader, Lord, and Chief—He is the one who has the power to do everything.
2. Allāh is not only the Rabb, but is also the *Malik* of mankind. The word *malik* means King or Ruler.
3. Allāh is not only Rabb and malik, but is also the *Ilah* of mankind. The word *ilah* means god. Allāh is the only God for mankind—therefore we should worship Him only.
4. We seek refuge with Allāh from evil (*sharr*). The evil often sneaks upon us, and we may not realize it. This evil is mentioned as *khannās*. The word means one who is sneaky, cunning or clever. He is called clever or sneaky because he brings evil thoughts into our hearts, and makes them look good. These thoughts come to our hearts in the form of whisperings (*waswas*).
5. The evil, sneaky thoughts appear in our hearts quietly, as in whispering.
6. Such evil whispering come to us from two sources: (i) from the bad people, and (ii) from jinn.

Words to know

A'ūdhu: I seek refuge, protection. *'Adha*: to seek refuge, to seek shelter.
An-Nās: mankind, people. *Insan*: human being, those who are familiar.
Khannas: one who hides, one who sneaks. *Khandaq*: a ditch (hidden from normal view). *Khanjar*: a dagger (usually kept hidden in a sheath)

Sūrah An-Nās
Word-by-word meaning

ٱلرَّحِيمِ	ٱلرَّحۡمَـٰنِ	ٱللَّهِ	بِسۡمِ
the Most-Rewarding	the Most-Kind	Allah	With the name
ٱلنَّاسِ ١	بِرَبِّ	أَعُوذُ	قُلۡ
of mankind.	in the Rabb	I take refuge	Say
ٱلنَّاسِ ٣	إِلَـٰهِ	ٱلنَّاسِ ٢	مَلِكِ
the mankind.	God	the mankind.	Master of

ٱلْخَنَّاسِ ﴿٤﴾	ٱلْوَسْوَاسِ	شَرِّ	مِن
the sneaking one	the whispers	evil	from
صُدُورِ	فِى	يُوَسْوِسُ	ٱلَّذِى
hearts	into	whispers	who
وَٱلنَّاسِ ﴿٦﴾	ٱلْجِنَّةِ	مِنَ	ٱلنَّاسِ ﴿٥﴾
and the mankind.	the jinn	from	the mankind

A few applications of the message:

Evil thoughts come to us from two sources—from bad people and from jinn. The evil thoughts come to us secretly and cleverly without making us realize these are evil. We tend to believe these are enjoyable, fun thoughts. We can lose our sense of good judgment and start to act upon these thoughts. Therefore, Allāh teaches us this sūrah, which is also a remarkable du'ā. Through this du'ā we seek protection with Allāh from the evil thoughts that come to our hearts.

We should remember that sometimes evil people appear as our friends. They tell us that they want good for us, but actually want us to lose in our lives. We need to be careful in selecting our friends.

With Allāh's help, we can minimize such thoughts by avoiding bad people and dismiss bad ideas passed by the invisible jinns. We should remember that as we recite this du'ā, we should also try to stay away from the evils. With Allāh's help and with our own efforts, we will be able to keep bad thoughts away.

Questions:

1. How do the evil thoughts usually appear in our minds?
2. What is the meaning of the Arabic word *khannas*?
3. What are the two sources from which evil thoughts appear to us?
4. What is the best way to avoid evil thoughts from appearing in our minds?

Sūrah 113

Revealed in Makkah

Al-falaq

The Daybreak

Introduction

Allāh created everything in this world for our benefit. If we do not use His creation properly, these could become evil. In this sūrah Allāh teaches us to seek protection with Him from evils that people create and the mischief of their black magic. The sūrah also teaches us to seek protection from those who are jealous of us and from those who want to harm us through their jealousy.

بِسۡمِ ٱللَّهِ ٱلرَّحۡمَٰنِ ٱلرَّحِيمِ

Bismi-llāhi-r raḥmāni-r raḥīm

In the name of Allah, the Most-Kind, the Most-Rewarding.

قُلۡ أَعُوذُ بِرَبِّ ٱلۡفَلَقِ ١	Qul a'ūdhu bi-rabbi-l falaq,	1 Say: "I seek refuge with the Rabb of Daybreak,—
مِن شَرِّ مَا خَلَقَ ٢	min sharri mā khalaq,	2. "from the evil of what He has created,
وَمِن شَرِّ غَاسِقٍ إِذَا وَقَبَ ٣	wa min sharri ghāsiqin idhā waqab,	3. "namely, from the evil of the darkness when it overspreads,
وَمِن شَرِّ ٱلنَّفَّٰثَٰتِ فِي ٱلۡعُقَدِ ٤	wa min sharri-n naffāthāti fil 'uqad,	4. "and from the evil of the blowers in knots,
وَمِن شَرِّ حَاسِدٍ إِذَا حَسَدَ ٥	wa min sharri ḥāsidin idhā ḥasad.	5. "and from the evil of the envier when he envies."

Explanation

1. In this verse Allāh says He is the *Rabb* of the Daybreak. In the previous sūrah we learned that *Rabb* means one who brings us up, feeds us, and takes care of us. He is our Guardian, Leader, Lord, Chief—He is the one who has the power to do everything. When daybreak happens, it breaks the darkness of

the night. Night is not bad—we sleep and rest during the night. But the darkness of ignorance and the evil of superstition are bad. The daybreak seems to bring us new promises as it breaks the darkness of people's evil activities. Allāh teaches us to seek refuge with Him, who is the Rabb of the Daybreak.

2. Allāh has created everything around us. Many things around us are good, but many things can be bad. Some times even the good things can be bad. Too much of good food can hurt us. We seek protection with Allāh from the evils (*sharr*) that are present in many things around us.
3. In this verse we are seeking protection from the darkness *(ghāshiq)* of anything bad—for example the darkness of poverty, the darkness of difficulty, ignorance, superstition, and bad influence. Such a darkness makes it difficult for us to see the right guidance. We recite this sūrah to seek Allāh's help in making everything easy for us.
4. Before Islam, people of Arabia used to practice witchcraft and black magic. Some of them used to tie knots on a string and blow magical charms on them, as if the knots and charms could cause harm to others. People who believed in these charms used to say their sicknesses were due to the magic.
5. Envy is another form of evil from which we seek Allāh's protection. Our own envy harms us because we become mean and unkind. Similarly, envy of other people can harm us as an envious person may make our lives difficult. We seek protection of Allāh from all these types of evils.

Words to know

Falaq: daybreak, dawn. *Falaqa*: To split, to separate. *Fāliqun*: who splits.
Khalaqa: He created. *Khāliqun*: Creator. *Khalaqnā*: We created.
Ghāsiqin: darkness. *Ghasaqa*: to become very dark.
Hāsidin: envious, jealous person. *Hasad*: he envied. *Hasada*: to envy.

Sūrah Al-Falaq
Word-by-word meaning

ٱلرَّحِيمِ	ٱلرَّحْمَٰنِ	ٱللَّهِ	بِسْمِ
the Most-Rewarding	the Most-Kind	Allāh	In the name
ٱلْفَلَقِ ١	بِرَبِّ	أَعُوذُ	قُلْ
the Daybreak.	with Rabb	I take refuge	Say
خَلَقَ ٢	مَا	شَرِّ	مِن
created.	what	evil of	from

إِذَا	غَاسِقٍ	شَرِّ	وَمِن
when	darkness	evil of	and from
ٱلنَّفَّٰثَٰتِ	شَرِّ	وَمِن	وَقَبَ ﴿٣﴾
the blowers	evil of	and from	it overspreads.
شَرِّ	وَمِن	ٱلْعُقَدِ ﴿٤﴾	فِى
evil of	and from	knots	in
	حَسَدَ ﴿٥﴾	إِذَا	حَاسِدٍ
	envies.	when	envier

A few applications of the message:

We live in a society with different types of people. Some of them are good and some are bad. Our activities in the world create good and bad results around us. In this sūrah, we are seeking refuge with Allāh from all forms of bad or evil that are around us. The purpose of seeking refuge is twofold: (i) seeking refuge from the evil *(sharr)* that has already taken place, and (ii) seeking refuge from the *sharr* that might take place in future. When we face difficulty in life and fear that someone or something might harm us, we should not lose hope. We should recite this sūrah regularly. This entire sūrah is an excellent *du'ā*. We use this *du'ā* to seek Allāh's help in making affairs easy for us and in overcoming the difficulties.

Questions:

1. How many types of mischief or evil (*sharr*) does Sūrah *al-Falaq* mention?
2. Before Islam, what type of black magic did some of the people practice? Write your answer based on the lesson on Sūrah *al-Falaq*.
3. Explain what is meant by darkness. Why can darkness be harmful to us?
4. Explain how envying others can harm us.

Sūrah 112

Revealed in Makkah

Al-Ikhlās

The Unity of Allāh

Introduction

This sūrah teaches us *tawhīd,* which means Oneness of Allāh. This sūrah also tells us about the main attributes of Allāh. If we understand who Allāh is and what some of His qualities are, it will help us set apart all other man-made false gods. This sūrah declares that Allāh is the One and Only, that He is eternal, that He does not give birth nor was He born, and that nothing is similar to Him.

بِسْمِ ٱللَّهِ ٱلرَّحْمَٰنِ ٱلرَّحِيمِ

Bismi-llāhi-r raḥmāni-r raḥīm

In the name of Allah, the Most-Kind, the Most-Rewarding.

قُلْ هُوَ ٱللَّهُ أَحَدٌ ﴿١﴾	Qul huwa-llāhu aḥad;	1. Say: "He is Allāh, the One;
ٱللَّهُ ٱلصَّمَدُ ﴿٢﴾	allāhu-ṣ ṣamad;	2. "Allāh, the Eternal Refuge.
لَمْ يَلِدْ وَلَمْ يُولَدْ ﴿٣﴾	lam yalid, wa lam yūlad,	3. "He does not beget, nor is He begotten;
وَلَمْ يَكُن لَّهُۥ كُفُوًا أَحَدٌۢ ﴿٤﴾	wa lam yakun lahū kufuwań aḥad.	4. "and no one can become equal to Him."

Explanation:

1. The title of the sūrah is *al-Ikhlās*, but the word is not used in the sūrah. The meaning of *ikhlās* is purification of our belief from the filth of worshipping other gods. The sūrah starts with the word *qul* which means to say or to declare. The verse tells us to declare Allāh as One *(ahad)*. One of Allāh's most beautiful names is *Al-Ahad* because He is the One. With this declaration, we confirm that Allāh is One, —there cannot be any other god.

2. After declaring Allāh as One, we now declare that He is *As-Samad.* The word means One who is eternal—who lives forever. This name is one of Allāh's most excellent names. The word also means

One who is independent, He does not need anyone or anything but everyone and everything needs Him. Since everything is in need of Him, everything and everyone returns to Him.

3. In this verse we declare another very important quality of Allāh. No one has created or given birth to Allāh. Therefore, He cannot be the son of another god. Moreover, Allāh does not give birth to anyone or anything. We have already declared that He is the One and the Only, therefore has no spouse, sons, or daughters. Allāh is the Creator. He creates everything. Creating is not the same as giving birth. Allāh is not in need of anyone or anything but everyone and everything has need of Him. Everything and everyone returns to Him for their every need

4. In this verse we declare that nothing is equal to Allāh. The word *kufu'* means something similar, equal or comparable. We declare that Allāh has nothing similar or equal to Him. How can anything or anyone ever be similar to Him?

Words to know

As-Samad: the Eternal, Absolute. This is one of the excellent names of Allāh. This word is mentioned in the Qur'ān only once.
Yalid: he begets. *Walada*: to beget, to give birth. *Yūlad*: he is begotten, born. *Aulād*: Children. *Wālidān*: parents.
Ahad: One, Alone. This word is used for Allāh alone. *Wāhid*: first.

Sūrah Al-Ikhlās
Word-by-word meaning

ٱلرَّحِيمِ	ٱلرَّحۡمَٰنِ	ٱللَّهِ	بِسۡمِ
the Most-Rewarding	the Most-Kind	Allāh	In the name
أَحَدٌ ١	ٱللَّهُ	هُوَ	قُلۡ
One.	Allāh	He	Say
يَلِدۡ	لَمۡ	ٱلصَّمَدُ ٢	ٱللَّهُ
begets	not	the Eternal Refuge	Allāh
يَكُن	وَلَمۡ	يُولَدۡ ٣	وَلَمۡ
be	and not	is born	and not
	أَحَدُۢ ٤	كُفُوًا	لَّهُۥ
	one	equal	to Him

A few applications of the message:

It is reported that our Prophet (S) said that Sūrah *al-Ikhlās* is equal to one third of the Qur'ān. This is because this sūrah declares some of the very important characteristics of Allāh. By knowing these, we can set Allāh apart from all other forms of man-made gods. This knowledge is so important that it makes us Muslims. If we do not believe in this message we become non-Muslim.

Once we declare this sūrah, we should make sure to never set any living or non-living thing equal to Allāh. Muslims never worship anything other than Allāh. But even a Muslim can sometimes mistakenly or unknowingly set something or someone as equal to Allāh. For example, we should never pray to any human being, any saints or any graves to fulfill our wishes. Allāh is the only Giver. To compare anything with Allāh is a sin. Believing in the power of gem stones, horoscopes, zodiac signs, astrology, black magic, etc. is equal to setting up something as equal to Allāh. Some people wear rubies, emeralds, sapphires or other stones thinking these can bring them good luck. Some people practice or believe in the power of black magic. All these practices are examples of setting others as equal to Allāh.

We should always remember that Allāh is One—He has no partners and no equals. Nothing is similar to Him. To make images of Allāh, to believe some idols are gods, to believe some human being is God's child or God himself appeared in human form are nothing but great sins. This sūrah teaches us the importance of recognizing the unique qualities and characteristics of Allāh.

Questions:

1. Which two beautiful names of Allāh did we learn from Sūrah *al-Ikhlās*? Write the two names in English.
2. Write five things we learned about Allāh from reading Sūrah *al-Ikhlās.*
3. Based on the message of Sūrah *al-Ikhlās,* write what you understand about the family of Allāh.
4. Why cannot 'Isa (A) be the son of Allāh? Explain your answer.

Sūrah 111

Revealed in Makkah

Al-Masad/Al-Lahab

The Palm Fiber/The Firebrand

Introduction

This sūrah is about the punishment of two of enemies of the Prophet (S). One enemy was Abu Lahab, an uncle of the Prophet (S); the other was Abu Lahab's wife. They were powerful and important people in Makkah. Both of them insulted, and ridiculed the Prophet (S), and wanted to harm him in many ways. This sūrah tells us that those who want to harm the Muslims or Islam actually harm themselves.

بِسْمِ ٱللَّهِ ٱلرَّحْمَـٰنِ ٱلرَّحِيمِ

Bismi-llāhi-r raḥmāni-r raḥīm

In the name of Allah, the Most-Kind, the Most-Rewarding.

تَبَّتْ يَدَآ أَبِى لَهَبٍ وَتَبَّ ﴿١﴾	Tabbat yadā abī lahabiw̃ wa tabb.	1. Let the two hands of Abu Lahab perish, and let him perish!
مَآ أَغْنَىٰ عَنْهُ مَالُهُۥ وَمَا كَسَبَ ﴿٢﴾	Mā aghnā 'anhu māluhū wa mā kasab.	2. His wealth and what he earns will not benefit him anything.
سَيَصْلَىٰ نَارًا ذَاتَ لَهَبٍ ﴿٣﴾	Sa-yaṣlā nāraṅ dẖāta lahab,—	3. He will soon undergo roasting in the fire full of flames—
وَٱمْرَأَتُهُۥ حَمَّالَةَ ٱلْحَطَبِ ﴿٤﴾	-wa-mra'atuhu. Ḥammālata-l ḥaṭab;	4. and his wife. The carrier of firewood;
فِى جِيدِهَا حَبْلٌ مِّن مَّسَدٍۭ ﴿٥﴾	fī jīdihā ḥablum̃ min masad.	5. around her neck will be a rope of twisted palm-fiber.

Explanation

1. This verse says two things will be destroyed—the two hands of Abu Lahab and Abu Lahab himself. This man's real name was *Abdul 'Uzzā* which meant servant of 'Uzzā. *Al-'Uzza* was an important idol

for the pagan Arabs. People called him Abu Lahab because of his reddish skin complexion. The hands of Abu Lahab means his power, wealth and strength.

2. Abu Lahab's power came from his wealth, which he earned by doing many trade activities. His wealth and power was of no use to him because he opposed the truth and the teachings of Allāh.
3. Because of his opposition to Islam, on the Day of Judgment Abu Lahab will be thrown in the flaming fire of Hell. He will burn in the fire as his punishment.
4. Abu Lahab's wife was *Umm Jamil bint Harb*. She was a sister of *Abū Sufyan*, who was also an enemy of the Prophet (S) for a long time. She used to lay thorny bushes on the path of our Prophet (S), speak bad words against him and make poems to ridicule him. As a partner in the evil activities of her husband, she will also suffer a similar punishment. During her life, she laid thorny bushes in the path of the Prophet (S), but in the Hereafter she will carry firewood for her own burning.
5. The wife of Abu Lahab used to carry the thorny bushes tied with a rope. The word *masad* means twisted ropes made of fibers from palm trees. She carried the ropes to harm the Prophet (S). In the Hereafter the ropes will wrap around her neck to suffocate her. In other words, her evil activities will come back to haunt her and cause her own suffering.

Words to know

Yadā: two hands. *Yadd*: might, power.
Nār: fire, burning flame. *Nūr*: light.
Kasaba: he earned. *Iktasaba*: he earned a sin. *Mā kasabat qulūbukum*: what your hearts have earned.
Habl: rope. *Habala*: tie with a rope. *Hibāl*: treaty, agreement, pact. *Habli-llāh*: pact with Allāh.

Sūrah Al-Masad/Al-Lahab
Word-by-word meaning

ٱلرَّحِيمِ	ٱلرَّحۡمَٰنِ	ٱللَّهِ	بِسۡمِ
the Most-Rewarding	the Most-Kind	Allāh	In the name of
وَتَبَّ ١	أَبِي لَهَبٖ	يَدَآ	تَبَّتۡ
and let him perish.	Abu Lahab	hands of	Perish
مَالُهُۥ	عَنۡهُ	أَغۡنَىٰ	مَآ
his wealth	to him	benefitted	not
نَارٗا	سَيَصۡلَىٰ	كَسَبَ ٢	وَمَا
fire	soon will enter	earned.	and what

ذَاتَ	of
لَهَبٍ ﴿٣﴾	flame.
وَٱمۡرَأَتُهُۥ	And his wife
حَمَّالَةَ	carrier
ٱلۡحَطَبِ ﴿٤﴾	the firewood
فِي	Around
جِيدِهَا	her neck
حَبۡلٌ	rope
مِّن	from
مَّسَدِۭ ﴿٥﴾	twisted palm-fiber.

A few applications of the message:

The message of this sūrah is much more than the fates of two eveil people. Allāh wants to let everybody understand the results of their actions. Those who do or support the evil deeds will face similar results. Their punishment will be similar to their bad deeds. Abu Lahab's temper was fiery towards the Prophet (S). People called him *"lahab"* because of his reddish skin and fiery nature, but in the Hereafter he will burn in fierce fire, also known as *lahab*.

When Abu Lahab' wife used to lay the thorny bushes in the path of the Prophet (S), he did not seek revenge or play dirty tricks on her. He used to remove the thorny bushes without complaining. He knew Allāh is the best Judge and that He would deal with the sinners. In the Hereafter, the thorny bushes and ropes will wrap around her neck and cause her to suffocate to death.

In this life, we may come across opposition, hatred, and enmity from many people. We should remember that as long as we remain righteous, Allāh will take the right course of action. If a person hates us, becomes jealous and an enemy, or spreads bad words about us, there is so much that we can do. Whatever way bad people want to harm us will come back to harm them in the Hereafter but with greater intensity.

Questions:

1. Who was Abu Lahab?
2. Why were Abu Lahab and his wife against Prophet Muhammad (S)?
3. What will happen to those who support the evil activities of others?
4. What did the Prophet (S) do when Abu Lahab's wife laid thorny bushes in his way?
5. How will our bad deeds affect us in the Hereafter?

Sūrah 110

Revealed in Makkah

An-Nasr

The Help

Introduction:

This sūrah was the last complete sūrah revealed to our Prophet (S). It was revealed shortly after his last Hajj in the 10th year of *Hijrah.* About one hundred thousand people attended Hajj in that year. Such a large gathering was unheard of at that time. Muslims had already achieved victory in the battles and almost all of Arabia had accepted Islam. Such a large gathering was truly an occasion to remind everybody about victory of Islam. The victory came with the help of Allāh. The Prophet (S) passed away within a few months of the revelation of this sūrah.

بِسۡمِ ٱللَّهِ ٱلرَّحۡمَٰنِ ٱلرَّحِيمِ

Bismi-llāhi-r raḥmāni-r raḥīm

In the name of Allah, the Most-Kind, the Most-Rewarding.

إِذَا جَآءَ نَصۡرُ ٱللَّهِ وَٱلۡفَتۡحُ ١	Idhā jā'a naṣru-llāhi wal fatḥ,	1. When the Help of Allah and the Victory comes,
وَرَأَيۡتَ ٱلنَّاسَ يَدۡخُلُونَ فِي دِينِ ٱللَّهِ أَفۡوَاجٗا ٢	wa ra'ayta-n nāsa yadkhulūna fī dīni-llāhi afwājā,	2. and you see people entering the Religion of Allāh in companies,—
فَسَبِّحۡ بِحَمۡدِ رَبِّكَ وَٱسۡتَغۡفِرۡهُۚ إِنَّهُۥ كَانَ تَوَّابَۢا ٣	fa-sabbiḥ bi-ḥamdi rabbika wa-staghfirhu. Innahū kāna tawwābā.	3. then glorify with praises of your Rabb, and ask His protection. Surely He is ever oft-Returning.

Explanation:

1. In many verses, Allāh repeated His promise of victory to the believers. In this sūrah also, Allāh reminds us that His help will always come and victory of Muslims will always happen. This sūrah also shows how Allāh's help benefited Muslims and Islam at the time of our Prophet (S).

2. Allāh's help and the Muslims' victory continued during the life of the Prophet (S). Towards the end of the Prophet's (S) life, such help and victory was clearly visible to all. Hundreds of thousands of people accepted Islam. Nearly all of Arabia became a Muslim nation. This was a major victory when we realize that in the early years of Prophet (S), only a few had accepted Islam.

3. Now that the Muslims had received victory, in return, Allāh is asking them to glorify Him and ask for His protection. The best way to praise or to glorify Allāh is to offer salāt and make du'ā. Along with praising Allāh, we are also required to seek forgiveness *(istighfār)* from Allāh. When we seek *istighfār,* we seek protection from any wrong doing in the future. When we are protected from sinful acts, we continue to enjoy victory. Allāh being oft-Returning means that He always turns with mercy and forgiveness to those who repent to Him and seek His forgiveness.

Words to know

Nasr: help. *Nasru-llāh*: help of Allāh. *Nasīrun*: helper. *Ansār*: helpers, plural of *nasīrun*, the people who helped the Prophet (S) and the Muslims in Madinah.
'Al-fath: the Victory. *Fataha*: to open, to give victory. *Al-Fātiha*: The Opening, the first sūrah in the Qur'an. *Fatha Mubīn*: Clear Victory.
Istighfār: asking for forgiveness. *Ghafara*: to forgive, cover, protect. *Ghaffār*: the most Forgiving, Protecting one (one of the most excellent names of Allāh).

Sūrah An-Nasr
Word-by-word meaning

ٱلرَّحِيمِ	ٱلرَّحْمَٰنِ	ٱللَّهِ	بِسْمِ
the Most-Rewarding	the Most-Kind	Allāh	In the name of
ٱللَّهِ	نَصْرُ	جَآءَ	إِذَا
Allah	help	comes	When
يَدْخُلُونَ	ٱلنَّاسَ	وَرَأَيْتَ	وَٱلْفَتْحُ ﴿١﴾
entering	the people	and you see	the Victory.
أَفْوَاجًا ﴿٢﴾	ٱللَّهِ	دِينِ	فِى
in companies	Allah	religion	in

وَٱسْتَغْفِرْهُ ج	رَبِّكَ	بِحَمْدِ	فَسَبِّحْ
and ask His protection	your Rabb	with praises	then glorify
	تَوَّابًۢا ﴿٣﴾	كَانَ	إِنَّهُۥ
	oft-Returning.	is	Surely He

A few applications of the message:

Whenever we get a gift or reward for some work, we feel very happy. When we are successful in any field, we want to celebrate. People celebrate their graduations, marriages, purchases of houses or promotions in jobs.

We should remember that without Allāh's help we could not have achieved any success. Therefore, we should always offer our thanks to Allāh. The best way to offer thanks is through salāt. When we offer thanks to Allāh, we realize that nothing on this earth is possible without Allāh's blessings. This realization makes us humble. Along with offering thanks to Allāh, we should also seek His forgiveness.

Every time we realize that something good happened to us, we should thank Allāh. It need not be a major event in our lives; even simple incidents can be a reason to celebrate. Simply ending the day or having a meal is enough to thank Allāh.

Questions:

1. What two things are we required to do when Allāh's help reaches us?
2. When Sūrah *an-Nasr* was revealed, why did Allāh ask the Muslims to celebrate the praises of Allāh?
3. What is the best way to say thanks to Allāh?
4. Why does Allāh want us to seek *istighfār*? Read verse 3 to explain.

Sūrah 109

Revealed in Makkah

Al-Kāfirùn

The Nonbelievers

Introduction:

Islam is a religion of tolerance. Islam teaches that in the matter of faith, nobody should force another person. Everybody has the right to follow their own religion. The idol-worshippers in Makkah wanted the Prophet (S) to give up some of his beliefs and follow their way of life. In return, this sūrah tells the Prophet (S) and all of us that we cannot compromise with truth.

بِسْمِ ٱللَّهِ ٱلرَّحْمَـٰنِ ٱلرَّحِيمِ

Bismi-llāhi-r raḥmāni-r raḥīm

In the name of Allah, the Most-Kind, the Most-Rewarding.

قُلْ يَـٰٓأَيُّهَا ٱلْكَـٰفِرُونَ ١	Qul yā ayyuha-l kāfirūn,	1. Say: "O you the disbelievers!
لَآ أَعْبُدُ مَا تَعْبُدُونَ ٢	lā a'budu mā ta'budūn;	2. "I do not serve what you serve,
وَلَآ أَنتُمْ عَـٰبِدُونَ مَآ أَعْبُدُ ٣	wa lā antum 'ābidūna mā a'bud;	3. "and you are not server of whom I serve.
وَلَآ أَنَا۠ عَابِدٌ مَّا عَبَدتُّمْ ٤	wa lā ana 'ābidum mā 'abadtum,	4. "Neither am I a server of what you serve,
وَلَآ أَنتُمْ عَـٰبِدُونَ مَآ أَعْبُدُ ٥	wa lā antum 'ābidūna mā a'bud.	5. "and you are not server of whom I serve.
لَكُمْ دِينُكُمْ وَلِىَ دِينِ ٦	Lakum dīnukum wa liya dīn.	6. "For you be your religion and for me my religion."

Explanation:

1. In the first verse of the sūrah, our beloved Prophet (S) calls the attention of those idol worshippers who wanted him to give up some of his beliefs.

2. Allāh asked our Prophet (S) to declare his position about religion. Prophet Muhammad (S) would not compromise on truth. He would not serve the false gods whom these idol worshippers worshipped.
3. Idol worshippers are greatly attached to their idols. They want to see their gods in a physical form, which is why they create the idols. For this reason they will not worship One Allāh, whom they cannot see. They cannot understand that these idols are useless objects. The Prophet (S) told them that even if they think that they were worshipping God through many idols, they were actually only worshipping idols.
4. The Prophet (S) again reminded the idol worshippers that he was not going to serve the idols, false beliefs and superstitions to which they were attached. By worshipping Allāh, our Prophet Muhammad (S) had not invented a new way to worship an idol. By making this point very clear to them, the Prophet (S) wanted them to understand that he would not compromise his beliefs in any manner.
5. This verse is identical to verse 3. By repeating it, the Prophet (S) reminded the idol worshippers that they could not see the truth as they were too involved with idol worshipping. Their worshipping is not the same as worshipping One and Only Allāh whom our Prophet (S) served.
6. Due to such serious differences in the matter of faith, no one was interested in following the other's faith. At this point Islam makes an important announcement—there would be no compulsion in religion and no compromise in teaching. Religion cannot be taught to others by force. Muslims would not give up their faith because Islam is their way of life. The path of the idol worshippers is different from the path of the Muslims. These two paths do not lead to the same place. Muslims are not to follow the path of the idol-worshippers.

Words to know

Kāfirun: those who refuse to believe. *Kafarū*: rejected Faith, disbelieved. *Kaffara*: he purged, he expiated.
A'budu: I serve, worship. *'Ibādat*: worship, prayer. *'Abdullāh*: servant of Allāh.
Dīn: religion, way of life.

Sūrah Al-Kāfirūn
Word-by-word meaning

ٱلرَّحِيمِ	ٱلرَّحْمَٰنِ	ٱللَّهِ	بِسْمِ
the Most-Rewarding	the Most-Kind	Allāh	In the name of
لَآ	ٱلْكَٰفِرُونَ ﴿١﴾	يَٰٓأَيُّهَا	قُلْ
not	the disbelievers.	O You	Say
وَلَآ	تَعْبُدُونَ ﴿٢﴾	مَا	أَعْبُدُ
and not	you serve.	what	I serve

أَعۡبُدُ ﴿٣﴾	مَآ	عَٰبِدُونَ	أَنتُمۡ
I serve.	what	server	you are
مَّا	عَابِدٞ	أَنَا۠	وَلَآ
what	server	I	and not
مَآ أَعۡبُدُ ﴿٥﴾	عَٰبِدُونَ	وَلَآ أَنتُمۡ	عَبَدتُّمۡ ﴿٤﴾
what I serve.	server	And you are not	you serve.
دِينِ ﴿٦﴾	وَلِيَ	دِينُكُمۡ	لَكُمۡ
my religion.	and for me	your religion	for you

A few applications of the message:

We know people in our communities come from different faiths and have different ideas. The question is how do we live and work with different groups of people? What does Islam teach us about dealing with people from different walks of life? This sūrah teaches us what our approach should be when we deal with people of different faiths and opinions. Islam is a religion of peace and it teaches us to live peacefully with people in our communities. One way to live peacefully is to tolerate other people's faiths and opinions.

Even among Muslims, people follow different Madhhabs, or schools of thought. People have different methods of solving problems, but they believe in the Oneness of Allāh and follow the Prophet (S).

Whenever we come across people with different opinions, we should remember the teachings of the Qur'ān and the Sunnah of our Prophet (S). They teach us tolerance in the matter of faith and opinion.

Questions:

1. What is the overall message of the Sūrah *al-Kāfirūn*? Write a short sentence in your own words.
2. What did the idol worshippers in Makkah want the Prophet (S) to do about his faith?
3. Which two verses in Sūrah *al-Kāfirūn* are repeated? Write the translation of the verse.

Sūrah 108

Revealed in Makkah

Al-Kawthar

The Abundance

Introduction:

This short sūrah tells us to be thankful to Allāh for His blessings upon us. The best way to show that we are thankful to Allāh is to make salāt and sacrifice. People who hate the Prophet (S) are at a loss.

بِسْمِ ٱللَّهِ ٱلرَّحْمَـٰنِ ٱلرَّحِيمِ

Bismi-llāhi-r raḥmāni-r raḥīm

In the name of Allah, the Most-Kind, the Most-Rewarding.

إِنَّآ أَعْطَيْنَـٰكَ ٱلْكَوْثَرَ ١	Innā a'ṭaynāka-l kawthar.	1. Surely We have given you the Kawthar.
فَصَلِّ لِرَبِّكَ وَٱنْحَرْ ٢	Fa-ṣalli li-rabbika wa-nḥar.	2. So perform Salāt for your Rabb, and do sacrifice.
إِنَّ شَانِئَكَ هُوَ ٱلْأَبْتَرُ ٣	Inna shāni'aka huwa-l abtar.	3. Surely your hater— he is cut off.

Explanation:

1. This short sūrah talks about *al-Kawthar*, a word that has several meanings. A special river in Paradise is named *al-Kawthar*. In this sūrah, *kawthar* means 'plenty of good things' that Allāh gave to the Prophet (S). These good things include divine revelation, knowledge, wisdom, leadership, success, victory and dignity in this life and in the Hereafter. The verse also reminds us that through the Prophet (S) all the believers will also receive plenty of good things. We should remember that these good things will happen to us in this life and more will happen in the Hereafter.
2. As the believers receive the good things in life, they are required to do two main duties: (a) perform salāt, and (b) sacrifice. The purpose is not just to sacrifice an animal, but to also sacrifice the good

things that we might have so that other people can benefit from our sacrifices. We should remember that salāt makes us good people and sacrificing the good things in our lives makes a better society and a better environment.

3. On seeing the good things given to the believers, many people might become jealous and start hating them. However, those who hate the believers will be left without the blessings of Allāh. They will be denied good in the Hereafter too. The term *abtar* means cutting off something entirely. Those who lead a life without salāt and sacrifice will find all good things are cut off from them in this life and in the Hereafter. A man used to insult the Prophet (S), as he had no sons who grew up to be an adult. This verse also refers to the this hater, who ultimatley was a loser.

Words to know

Kawthar: plenty of good things. *Takathur*: the act of increasing, multiplying.
Anhar: offer sacrifice. *Nahara*: to sacrifice, slaughter.
Abtar: childless, one from who all good is cut off. *Batara*: to cut off the tail.

Sūrah Al-Kawthar
Word-by-word meaning

ٱلرَّحِيمِ	ٱلرَّحْمَٰنِ	ٱللَّهِ	بِسْمِ
the Most-Rewarding	the Most-Kind	Allāh	In the name of
فَصَلِّ	ٱلْكَوْثَرَ ﴿١﴾	أَعْطَيْنَٰكَ	إِنَّآ
So perform salāt	the Kawthar.	We gave to you	Surely
شَانِئَكَ	إِنَّ	وَٱنْحَرْ ﴿٢﴾	لِرَبِّكَ
your enemy	Surely	and do sacrifice.	for your Rabb
		ٱلْأَبْتَرُ ﴿٣﴾	هُوَ
		cut off (the deprived).	(he) is

A few applications of the message:

This sūrah reminds us that Allāh sends plenty of good things to believers. Sometimes the good comes in the form of money, houses, and cars; sometimes good comes in the form of peace, family, name, fame, health, or knowledge. Sometimes we cannot see the good things or do not realize the good. We should remember that others may not have what we have. We should also remember that as long as we make salāt and sacrifice, good things will continue to come to us—in this life and more in the Hereafter. Regular performance of salāt will also help us become better Muslims. We should, therefore, remember to follow Allāh and hope to receive the endless blessings He has prepared for us.

Questions:

1. In Sūrah *al-Kawthar* Allāh tells us to do two duties. What are the two duties?
2. In Sūrah *al-Kawthar* Allāh tells that something will happen to those who hate us. What will happen to them?
3. What is the meaning of the word *Kawthar*?
4. Mention five blessings that our Prophet (S) received in his life.
5. Mention five blessings you have received in your life or in your family.

Sūrah 107

Revealed in Makkah

Al-Mā'ūn

The Acts of Kindness

Introduction:

This sūrah talks about a type of people who deny two things—(i) the teachings of the religion, and (ii) the duty to help the poor. These people think they are following religion, but they neglect the poor and orphans. They perform prayers but are careless about the prayers. They only pray for show and refuse to do smallest kindness to others. Therefore, Allāh does not like them.

بِسْمِ ٱللَّهِ ٱلرَّحْمَٰنِ ٱلرَّحِيمِ

Bismi-llāhi-r raḥmāni-r raḥīm

In the name of Allah, the Most-Kind, the Most-Rewarding.

أَرَءَيْتَ ٱلَّذِى يُكَذِّبُ بِٱلدِّينِ ﴿١﴾	A-ra'ayta-lladh̲ī yukadh̲dh̲ibu bid dīn.	1 Have you seen him who denies the Religion?
فَذَٰلِكَ ٱلَّذِى يَدُعُّ ٱلْيَتِيمَ ﴿٢﴾	Fa-dh̲ālika-lladh̲ī yadu'-'u-l yatīm,	2 That is the one who drives away the orphan,
وَلَا يَحُضُّ عَلَىٰ طَعَامِ ٱلْمِسْكِينِ ﴿٣﴾	wa lā yaḥuḍḍu 'alā ta'āmi-l miskīn.	3 and does not urge upon feeding the poor.
فَوَيْلٌ لِّلْمُصَلِّينَ ﴿٤﴾	Fa wayluḷ lil muṣallīn,—	4 So woe be to those performers of salāt,—
ٱلَّذِينَ هُمْ عَن صَلَاتِهِمْ سَاهُونَ ﴿٥﴾	Alladh̲īna hum 'an ṣalātihim sāhūn,—	5 those who are themselves unmindful of their salāt,—

ٱلَّذِينَ هُمْ يُرَآءُونَ ﴿٦﴾	Alladhīna hum yurā'ūn,	6 those who are themselves showy,
وَيَمْنَعُونَ ٱلْمَاعُونَ ﴿٧﴾	wa yamna'ūna-l mā'ūn.	7 and avoid the acts of kindness.

Explanation:

1. The sūrah begins by asking if we have seen a certain type of people. These people think they are following religion, but they do not follow the teachings of the religion. The word *dīn* means the Day of Judgment or the Hereafter. The word also means religion or way of life. If we use the second meaning, it seems these people deny the way of life a good Muslim should follow.

2. These people behave harshly with the orphans and drive them away. The orphans are those children who do not have one or both parents. If these orphans are without guardians, they are neglected even more. People who do not care about religion or the Hereafter do not bother with the orphans because they think they will not be judged by Allāh.

3. First we saw this type of people deny the religion. Then we saw them behave badly with the orphans. Now we see they do not care to feed the poor. They seem to be selfish, greedy or careless about others who need help.

4. The type of people mentioned above can be Muslims and perform salāt. The Qur'ān scolds these people who perform salāt, yet remain negligent with their responsibility towards the poor and the orphans.

5-6. These people think by making salāt they automatically become good Muslims. To them salāt is a causal process only to show others. In reality they are careless about their salāt. Making careless salāt does not make them better Muslims. Salāt should be a process to make them good Muslims and bring them closer to Allāh.

7. The word *mā'ūn* means small acts of kindness. These people are so bad that they do not care to show the smallest kindness towards anyone.

Words to know

A-ra'ayta: Have you seen? *Ra'a*: he saw. *A'lam tara*: Have you not seen? *Rū'yā*: vision. *Yurā'ūna*: showy.
Dīn: religion, way of life.
Yatīm: orphan. *Yatama*: to become an orphan.
Miskīn: Poor, weak, humble. *Sakinat*: peaceful, quiet, tranquil.
Musallīna: those who pray. *Musallā*: place of prayer. *Salāt*: prayer.
Mā'ūn: Acts of kindness. *Ma'īn*: pure and clean drink, clean running water.

Sūrah A-Mā'ūn
Word-by-word meaning

بِسْمِ	ٱللَّهِ	ٱلرَّحْمَٰنِ	ٱلرَّحِيمِ
In the name of	Allāh	the Most-Kind	the Most-Rewarding
أَرَءَيْتَ	ٱلَّذِى	يُكَذِّبُ	بِٱلدِّينِ ﴿١﴾
Have you seen	who	belies	the religion.
فَذَٰلِكَ	ٱلَّذِى	يَدُعُّ	ٱلْيَتِيمَ ﴿٢﴾
That is the (one)	who	drives away	the orphan.
وَلَا	يَحُضُّ	عَلَىٰ	طَعَامِ
and not	urge	upon	feeding
ٱلْمِسْكِينِ ﴿٣﴾	فَوَيْلٌ	لِّلْمُصَلِّينَ ﴿٤﴾	ٱلَّذِينَ
the poor.	So woe be	to those who do salāt.	those
هُمْ	عَن	صَلَاتِهِمْ	سَاهُونَ ﴿٥﴾
who	about	their salāt	unmindful.
ٱلَّذِينَ	هُمْ	يُرَآءُونَ ﴿٦﴾	وَيَمْنَعُونَ
those	they	showy	and refrain
ٱلْمَاعُونَ ﴿٧﴾			
acts of kindness.			

A few applications of the message:

The contents of this sūrah are aimed towards those Muslims who make salāt but are guilty of many bad conduct. The bad conduct is: (a) not following the religion properly, (b) driving away the orphans, (c) not feeding the poor, (d) being unmindful of salāt, (e) making salāt only to show off in front of others, and (f) not showing smallest act of kindness. Such people are Muslims but Allāh rejects them for not doing good acts.

In our daily lives we should not become like these people. We make salāt, but salāt alone will not help us. We need to show small acts of kindness whenever we can. In this sūrah many examples of small acts of kindness are given—e.g. caring for the orphans, feeding the poor, showing devotion in salāt, and avoiding all types of pride. Only if we do that, Allāh then will love us and He will not reject us.

Questions:

1. Mention three bad qualities of the type of person mentioned in Sūrah *al-Mā'ūn*.
2. What does the person in Sūrah *al-Mā'ūn* do during salāt?
3. Why do you think the person in Sūrah *al-Mā'ūn* does not want to feed the poor?
4. The type of person in Sūrah *al-Mā'ūn* is Muslim. Why does Allāh condemn him?
5. Based on the message in Sūrah *al-Mā'ūn*, what should we be doing for poor people?

Sūrah 106
Revealed in Makkah

Al-Quraish

The Quraish

Introduction:

This sūrah reminds the Quraish about the safety and security they enjoyed during their trade journey to Syria and Yemen. The Quraish were respected by tribes all over Arabia because they were the caretakers of the Ka'bah where all Arabs used to come for the annual pilgrimage. The Quraish became rich from their trade activities. Allāh reminds the Quraish that they should remember His blessings upon them and be grateful to Him.

بِسْمِ ٱللَّهِ ٱلرَّحْمَـٰنِ ٱلرَّحِيمِ

Bismi-llāhi-r raḥmāni-r raḥīm
In the name of Allah, the Most-Kind, the Most-Rewarding.

لِإِيلَـٰفِ قُرَيْشٍ ﴿١﴾	Li-īlāfi qurayshiṅ,	1. For the protection of the Quraish,—
إِۦلَـٰفِهِمْ رِحْلَةَ ٱلشِّتَآءِ وَٱلصَّيْفِ ﴿٢﴾	īlāfihim riḥlata-sh shitā'i waṣ ṣayf;	2. their protection during the journey in winter and in summer.
فَلْيَعْبُدُوا۟ رَبَّ هَـٰذَا ٱلْبَيْتِ ﴿٣﴾	fal ya'budū rabba hādha-l bayt,—	3. They should therefore worship the Rabb of this House,
ٱلَّذِىٓ أَطْعَمَهُم مِّن جُوعٍ وَءَامَنَهُم مِّنْ خَوْفٍۭ ﴿٤﴾	Alladhī aṭ'amahum min jū'iẇ, wa āmanahum min khawf.	4. Who feeds them against hunger, and gives them security against fear.

Explanation:

1. This sūrah continues from Sūrah *al Fīl*, where Allāh told us that He protected the Ka'bah by destroying the army of Abrahah. With a safe Ka'bah, the Quraish continued receiving Allāh's blessings. In this sūrah Allāh gave another example of how He blessed and protected the Quraish in the past.
2. The blessings upon the Quraish were many. This sūrah tells us only about some of the blessings. The Quraish used to go to Syria during the summer months and to Yemen during the winter months to do business. In Syria they used to trade goods brought from Mediterranean and Babylonian sources, and in Yemen they used to trade goods coming all the way from India and Africa. During these long trade journeys, Allāh always protected the Quraish from robbers, diseases and sudden attacks from foreign armies.
3. This verse asks the Quraish to know the actual Rabb of the House. The 'House' refers to the Ka'bah. The Rabb of the House is not the idols but Allāh. The Quraish should give up worshipping the idols and worship none but Allāh.
4. In addition to safe passage to Syria and Yemen, the Quraish were blessed with two other things. Makkah is a rocky terrain without any meaningful farming. During the Hajj season, people came to Makkah and did many types of business. This made the local people rich and they always had a food supply. All Arab tribes used to respect the Quraish because they were the caretakers of the Ka'bah. No one would dare attack the Quraish. Thus, they were safe from the danger of warfare.

Words to know

Rihlat: Journey. *Rahala*: to leave, travel, to put a saddle bag on a camel (for journey).
Shitā: winter. *Shata*: to pass the winter, to be cold.
Sayf: summer. *Sāfa*: to pass the summer.
Bayt: house. *Bayatan*: while sleeping at night. *Baytul-llāh*: House of Allāh, the Ka'bah.
Khawf: fear. *Khāfa*: to fear. *Lā takhaf*: do not fear.

Sūrah Al-Quraish
Word-by-word meaning

ٱلرَّحِيمِ	ٱلرَّحْمَٰنِ	ٱللَّهِ	بِسْمِ
the Most-Rewarding	the Most-Kind	Allāh	In the name of
رِحْلَةَ	إِۦلَٰفِهِمْ	قُرَيْشٍ ﴿١﴾	لِإِيلَٰفِ
journey	for protection	Quraish.	For protection
رَبَّ	فَلْيَعْبُدُوا۟	وَٱلصَّيْفِ ﴿٢﴾	ٱلشِّتَآءِ
Rabb	They should worship	and the summer.	the winter

أَطْعَمَهُم	ٱلَّذِىٓ	ٱلْبَيْتِ ٣	هَٰذَا
feeds them	who	the House.	this
مِّنْ	وَءَامَنَهُم	جُوعٍ	مِّن
from	and secures them	hunger,	from
			خَوْفٍۭ ٤
			fear.

A few applications of the message:

The sūrah reminds the Quraish to do two things: (a) to realize Allāh's blessings upon them, and (b) to worship Allāh as a way of saying thanks,.

When we apply this message in our lives, we can see hundreds of ways Allāh has blessed us. We enjoy the blessings but sometimes forget Allāh. Our life would be very difficult if Allāh stops sending a few blessings upon us. We should therefore remember to thank Allāh for His blessings. The best way to say thanks to Him is to worship Him.

Questions:

1. Which two places did the Quraish go for trade?
2. Why did Allāh remind the Quraish that they should obey Him?
3. Mention some of the blessings upon the Quraish.
4. Why would no tribes attack the Quraish during their trade journeys?
5. In return for hundreds of small and big blessings of Allāh upon us, what should we do?

Sūrah 105

Revealed in Makkah

Al-fil

The Elephant

Introduction:

This sūrah tells the story of how Allāh saved the Ka'bah from the evil plots of enemies. This incident happened in the year Prophet Muhammad (S) was born. A Christian ruler by the name of Abrahah attacked Makkah with large African elephants to destroy the Ka'bah. Before Abrahah could do anything to the Ka'bah, Allāh wiped out his army. Allāh sent a large number of birds to destroy the army. The army was knocked out with stones of baked clay and became like the chewed up dead crop from which grains had been eaten away.

بِسۡمِ ٱللَّهِ ٱلرَّحۡمَـٰنِ ٱلرَّحِيمِ

Bismi-llāhi-r raḥmāni-r raḥīm

In the name of Allah, the Most-Kind, the Most-Rewarding.

أَلَمۡ تَرَ كَيۡفَ فَعَلَ رَبُّكَ بِأَصۡحَـٰبِ ٱلۡفِيلِ ﴿١﴾	A-lam tara kayfa fa'ala rabbuka bi-aṣḥābi-l fīl.	1. Have you not seen how your Rabb dealt with the Fellows of the Elephant?
أَلَمۡ يَجۡعَلۡ كَيۡدَهُمۡ فِى تَضۡلِيلٍ ﴿٢﴾	A-lam yaj'al kaydahum fī taḍlīl,	2. Did He not turn their plan to confusion?
وَأَرۡسَلَ عَلَيۡهِمۡ طَيۡرًا أَبَابِيلَ ﴿٣﴾	-wa arsala 'alayhim ṭayran abābīl,	3. And He sent flocks of birds against them,
تَرۡمِيهِم بِحِجَارَةٍ مِّن سِجِّيلٍ ﴿٤﴾	tarmīhim bi-ḥijāratim min sijjīl,	4. pelting them with stones of baked clay;
فَجَعَلَهُمۡ كَعَصۡفٍ مَّأۡكُولِۭ ﴿٥﴾	fa-ja'alahum ka-'aṣfim ma'kūl.	5. so He made them like straw eaten up.

Explanation:

1. The incident of Abrahah took place about four decades before this sūrah was revealed. The Makkan people remembered the incident, but may not have realized that the Ka'bah and the local people were saved by a grand plan of Allāh. The verse reminds the people how Allāh dealt with the army of elephants. Abrahah, a king of Yemen, brought an army of elephants to destroy the Ka'bah. His intention was to stop the celebration of Hajj in Makkah, and to organize a gathering in his city in Yemen. The leader of the Quraish was Abdul Muttalib, who was the grandfather of our Prophet (S). The Quraish had no army to save the Ka'bah from the attack. They gave up and ran to the nearby mountains to hide.
2. The verse is asking the Quraish to remember that Allāh made the evil plan of Abrahah fail. Although the army had a big plan to destroy the Ka'bah, their plan ended up into confusion.
3. The army of elephants may look scary to people, but to Allāh it is a very petty affair. To counter such a large attack, a group of small birds was enough. The size of the creatures did not decide the fate of the battle. Allāh's plan to save the Ka'bah was indeed a better plan.
4. Due to the grand plan of Allāh, a large number of birds and baked rocks were the weapons that destroyed the mighty army. The army was helpless. They were trained, but not ready to fight birds.
5. The dead and dying army fell down on the ground. They were like chewed straw left by animals, or leftover bones after vultures had chewed up all their flesh. The soldiers who survived, left Makkah in a hurry and they, too, died of various diseases. Abrahah's army was totally destroyed. The Ka'bah was saved from the evil plots of enemies.

Words to know

Ashāb: fellows, people, group. *Sāhibun*: companion. *Sāhaba*: to bear companionship.
Kaida: Evil plan, plot. *Makīdun*: victim of their own plot.
Tāiran: birds, flying creatures. *Mustatīran*: wide-spread.
Hijarah: stone. *Mahjur*: strong barrier.
Sijjil: baked clay, a clay surface on which words can be written. *Sijil*: written scroll.

Sūrah Al-Fīl
Word-by-word meaning

ٱلرَّحِيمِ	ٱلرَّحْمَـٰنِ	ٱللَّهِ	بِسْمِ
the Most-Rewarding	the Most-Kind	Allāh	In the name of
فَعَلَ	كَيْفَ	تَرَ	أَلَمْ
dealt	how	seen	Have you not

أَلَمْ	ٱلْفِيلِ ﴿١﴾	بِأَصْحَٰبِ	رَبُّكَ
Did He not	the elephant.	with the fellows of	your Rabb
تَضْلِيلٍ ﴿٢﴾	فِى	كَيْدَهُمْ	يَجْعَلْ
confusion	in	their plan	turn
أَبَابِيلَ ﴿٣﴾	طَيْرًا	عَلَيْهِمْ	وَأَرْسَلَ
birds	flocks	upon them	And He sent
سِجِّيلٍ ﴿٤﴾	مِّن	بِحِجَارَةٍ	تَرْمِيهِم
baked clay	of	with stones	Pelting them
	مَّأْكُولٍۭ ﴿٥﴾	كَعَصْفٍ	فَجَعَلَهُمْ
	eaten up.	like straw	So He made them

A few applications of the message:

The sūrah tells us about a famous incident to remind that Allāh is in control of everything. Abrahah was powerful and his army was large. He brought mighty elephants to destroy the Ka'bah. The Quraish ran away from Makkah as they had no power to resist the army. Yet, Abrahah's evil plan to destroy the Ka'bah did not work. Think of the contrast of mighty elephants and small birds! Think of Allāh's ability to change the situation in a manner that no one could think of.

In our daily lives, we hear enemies of Islam are always trying to destroy Islam. In our personal lives we sometimes face hatred and conspiracies of bad people and our enemies. We should remember that as long as we remain on the right path, Allāh will help us. The dramatic destruction of an enemy and the saving of the Ka'bah shows our enemies can never harm us unless Allāh wills.

Questions:

1. What was the name of the Christian ruler who wanted to destory the Ka'bah?
2. Abrahah came with an army of elephants, but what type of army did Allāh send against them?
3. What other important event took place in the year the Ka'bah was attacked?
4. Who was the leader of the Quraish when the Ka'bah was attacked?
5. How did the Quraish respond when the Ka'bah was attacked?

Sūrah 104

Revealed in Makkah

Al-Humazah

The Slanderer

Introduction:

Many of the early Makkan people were greedy and stingy. They enjoyed talking about others. The sūrah criticizes them because of their bad conduct and cautions them about the severe punishment in the Hereafter. The sūrah also reminds us that if we show such bad behavior, then we are also going to face a severe punishment. Allāh dislikes people who save money but never spend wealth on a good cause. Allāh dislikes people who backbite, say terrible things, spread false rumors and call others bad names.

بِسۡمِ ٱللَّهِ ٱلرَّحۡمَٰنِ ٱلرَّحِيمِ

Bismi-llāhi-r raḥmāni-r raḥīm

In the name of Allah, the Most-Kind, the Most-Rewarding.

وَيۡلٌ لِّكُلِّ هُمَزَةٍ لُّمَزَةٍ ١	Wayluḷ li-kulli humazatiḷ lumazah,—	1. Woe be to every slanderer, defamer,
ٱلَّذِى جَمَعَ مَالًا وَعَدَّدَهُۥ ٢	Alladẖī jama'a mālaẇ wa 'addadah,	2. who hoards wealth and counts it,
يَحۡسَبُ أَنَّ مَالَهُۥٓ أَخۡلَدَهُۥ ٣	yaḥsabu anna mālahū akhladah,	3. he thinks that his wealth will make him live forever.
كَلَّاۖ لَيُنۢبَذَنَّ فِى ٱلۡحُطَمَةِ ٤	kallā la-yuṅbadẖanna fil ḥuṭamah,	4. No! he will surely be cast into the crushing disaster.
وَمَآ أَدۡرَىٰكَ مَا ٱلۡحُطَمَةُ ٥	wa mā adrāka mal ḥuṭamah.	5. And what will make you know what that crushing disaster is?
نَارُ ٱللَّهِ ٱلۡمُوقَدَةُ ٦	Nāru-llāhi-l mūqadah,—	6. The Fire of Allāh which has been kindled,—

ٱلَّتِى تَطَّلِعُ عَلَى ٱلْأَفْـِٔدَةِ ﴿٧﴾	-llatī taṭṭali'u 'ala-l af'idah.	7. which rises over the hearts.
إِنَّهَا عَلَيْهِم مُّؤْصَدَةٌ ﴿٨﴾	Innahā 'alayhim mu'ṣadah,	8. Surely it will close in on them,
فِى عَمَدٍ مُّمَدَّدَةٍۭ ﴿٩﴾	fī 'amadim mumaddadah.	9. in columns widely extended.

Explanation:

1. The title of the sūrah is based on the word *humazah* which means a slanderer or a backbiter. The word *lamazah* means a defamer. Slanderers and defamers ruin the good reputations of others by spreading lies about them. The verse begins by cursing every slanderer and defamer. The word "curse" means a prayer or a wish for harm or injury to happen upon someone. Any curse is bad; a Divine curse that comes from Allāh is very scary, because such a wish will become real. If we defame any person, we are included in the curse.

   Notice that the verse is not talking about only male or only female, but everybody. This is because both men and women can backbite or defame another person. Preserving the good name of a truthful person is very important in the sight of Allāh. The Qur'ān wants to make sure that no one falsely accuses any good person and brings a bad name to them.

2. The Divine curse mentioned in the previous verse continues in this verse. This verse talks about another category of person—the miserly person who hoards wealth and then carefully counts it. By hoarding wealth, this person is not helping others. Just as a slander or backbite hurts others, hoarding money also hurts others.

   Allāh's curse is not against the simple counting of money, such as before or after shopping. The curse is also not about a business person who counts money and tracks his or her expenses.

3. Hoarders are stingy because they believe their wealth will protect them in the future. They forget that only Allāh can protect us from difficulties. When we spend money on a good cause and help others, Allāh likes it. We should remember that Allāh does not condemn wealth, but condemns our fondness for collecting wealth and not spending it in a rightful manner.

   The selfish hoarder "thinks that his wealth will make him live forever." He fails to understand that the opposite will happen. His wealth will not make him live forever. This idea is expressed by the word *kalla* in the next verse.

4. In the Qur'ānic usage, the word *kalla* cancels the idea mentioned before it and supports the idea mentioned after it. The word *kalla* cancels the idea of the miser "that his wealth will make him live forever." Allāh is saying, no, it will not make him immortal. Instead, "he will surely be cast into the crushing disaster."

5. The previous verse creates a chilling suspense when it mentions "crushing disaster" or *al-hutamah*. Can we understand what the crushing disaster is? It is beyond our imaginations. The following three verses briefly explain the meaning of *al-hutamah*. The word *al-hutamah* is derived from root *hatama* (lit. he broke into small pieces) or *hutāma* (*lit.* that which crumbles due to dryness). *Al-hutamah* is

one of the names of Hell where the bad habits of the slandering, defaming and the stingy hoarding of money will be crushed.

6. This verse hints at the meaning of *al-hutamah*. It is a fire of Allāh, more intense than the fire that we know. The fire of *al-hutamah* has already been ignited. The crushing and intense heat give a scary view of the situation of the defamer and the hoarder.
7. The fire of *al-hutamah* rises over the sinners' hearts. The roasting fire starts from the core of the body, as the sinners go through a severe regret realizing their past sins.
8. The word *mu'sadah* is derived from *asada* (*lit.* cover up). It implies the fire will engulf them totally and there will be no escape from it.
9. The wide columns of fire bring to our mind the image of a prison. In this prison the sinners are detained and their hearts are burning in it. The fire has engulfed them totally. There is no escape from the prison since the columns of the prison originate from within their hearts.

Words to know

Humazah: slanderer. *Hamaza*: backbite, pinch.
Lumaza: defamer, faultfinder. *Lamaza*: to speak ill, to wink.
Akhlada: make him live forever. *Khālid*: one who lives forever.
Hutamah: crushing disaster, fire. *Hatama*: to break into small pieces. *Hatam ad-dunyā*: pride of this world.

Sūrah Al-Humazah
Word-by-word meaning

ٱلرَّحِيمِ	ٱلرَّحْمَٰنِ	ٱللَّهِ	بِسْمِ
the Most-Rewarding	the Most-Kind	Allāh	In the name of
لُّمَزَةٍ ﴿١﴾	هُمَزَةٍ	لِّكُلِّ	وَيْلٌ
defamer.	slanderer	to every	Woe
وَعَدَّدَهُۥ ﴿٢﴾	مَالًا	جَمَعَ	ٱلَّذِى
and counts it.	wealth	hoards	who

أَخْلَدَهُۥ ﴿٣﴾ will make him live forever	مَالَهُۥٓ his wealth	أَنَّ that	تَحْسَبُ he thinks
ٱلْحُطَمَةِ ﴿٤﴾ the Crushing Disaster.	فِى into	لَيُنۢبَذَنَّ he will surely be cast	كَلَّا ۖ No!
ٱلْحُطَمَةُ ﴿٥﴾ the crushing disaster is?	مَا what	أَدْرَىٰكَ will make you know	وَمَآ and what
ٱلَّتِى which	ٱلْمُوقَدَةُ ﴿٦﴾ been kindled	ٱللَّهِ Allah	نَارُ the Fire of
إِنَّهَا Surely	ٱلْأَفْـِٔدَةِ ﴿٧﴾ the hearts	عَلَى over	تَطَّلِعُ rises
مُّمَدَّدَةٍۭ ﴿٩﴾ widely extended.	فِى عَمَدٍ In columns	مُّؤْصَدَةٌ ﴿٨﴾ closes in.	عَلَيْهِم on them

Literary Notes

All early Makkan sūrahs have some kind of poetic rhymes. In this sūrah, the letter *'ha'* is repeated at the end of each verse. The letter *'ha'* is pronounced with a heavy breathing out—similar to the exhaustion from suffering that would affect the sinners. When the entire sūrah is recited, the pronouncing of the letter *'ha'* at the end of each verse also increases a sense of frustration which would be the condition of the sinners. Not only does the message of the sūrah bears a gloomy picture for the sinners, but even the recitation brings out the doom that cannot be escaped. Also notice in the last word of each verse, there is at least one heavy sounding letter that intensifies the climax and the unavoidable punishment. For example, ع in verse *wa'addadah*, خ in *akhladah*, ح in *hutamah*, ق in mūqadah, ص in *mūsadah*.

A few applications of the message:

This sūrah provides strict instructions to give up the evil habit of backbiting and defaming. We should not hurt others with our words; rather we should help others with kinds words and with our wealth. We should always avoid wasting money; but remember that charity is not a wasteful act. If we have millions and billions of dollars in savings, it cannot save us from death. A pauper and a king, both will face death. The worldly fortune of a king will not be of any help in the Hereafter, unless it is spent in the right way. If we defame others, hoard wealth and do not help others, we will face a severe punishment.

Questions:

1. What is the false hope of a hoarder who does not spend money to help others?
2. Explain the meaning of *al-hutamah* as we understand it from this sūrah.
3. How does backbiting and slandering hurt others?
4. Which body part will mainly be engulfed by the fire, as mentioned in Sūrah *al-Humazah*?

Sūrah 103

Revealed in Makkah

Al-'Asr

The Declining Day

Introduction:

This short sūrah gives four qualities needed for success. These are (a) believing in Allāh, (b) doing good deeds, (c) encouraging others to follow the truth, and (d) practicing perseverance.

بِسۡمِ ٱللَّهِ ٱلرَّحۡمَٰنِ ٱلرَّحِيمِ

Bismi-llāhi-r raḥmāni-r raḥīm

In the name of Allah, the Most-Kind, the Most-Rewarding.

وَٱلۡعَصۡرِ ﴿١﴾	Wal 'aṣr,	1. By the Declining day.
إِنَّ ٱلۡإِنسَٰنَ لَفِي خُسۡرٍ ﴿٢﴾	inna-l insāna la-fī khusr,—	2. Surely man is indeed in loss,
إِلَّا ٱلَّذِينَ ءَامَنُواْ وَعَمِلُواْ ٱلصَّٰلِحَٰتِ وَتَوَاصَوۡاْ بِٱلۡحَقِّ وَتَوَاصَوۡاْ بِٱلصَّبۡرِ ﴿٣﴾	illa-lladhīna āmanū wa 'amilu-ṣ ṣāliḥāti wa tawāṣaw bil ḥaqqi, wa tawāṣaw biṣ ṣabr.	3. except those who believe and do good, and encourage one another to Truth, and enjoin one another to perseverance.

Explanation:

1. The word *al-'Asr* means afternoon, or time. This sūrah reminds us that if we do not use time properly, we will suffer a heavy loss. When time is gone, it is gone forever, and it cannot be reversed. When time is over, each person will realize that they have not fulfilled their duties in life. When the verse mentions *Al-Asr*, it reminds us that the sun is going to set soon, and the day will be over.
2. The objectives in life are not about fulfilling our wishes, enjoying games, visiting beautiful places or leading a peaceful life. People will be at a loss because they did not do the good deeds that would make them successful in the Hereafter. They have neglected their duties towards Allāh.

3. Some of the people will not be at loss. These people do four types of activities, which will save them from the loss. The four activities are: (a) to believe, (b) to do good, (c) to seek truth and encourage others to seek truth, and (d) to practice perseverance. Seeking truth and practicing perseverance should happen on an individual and group level. Individually we should seek truth and practice perseverance and at the same time remind each other to do the same. Only if we can do all these four activities, will we avoid loss in the long run.

Words to know

Asr: Time, afternoon, passing of time.
Insān: Human being, mankind. *Anisa:* to be familiar, polite. *Musta'nisīn:* One who is familiar.
Khusr: loss, error. *Mukhsirīn*: one who causes others to lose.
Sālihāt: good work. *Muslihun:* One who is upright, reformer, peacemaker.

Sūrah Al-'Asr
Word-by-word meaning

ٱلرَّحِيمِ	ٱلرَّحْمَٰنِ	ٱللَّهِ	بِسْمِ
the Most-Rewarding	the Most-Kind	Allāh	In the name of
لَفِى	ٱلْإِنسَٰنَ	إِنَّ	وَٱلْعَصْرِ ﴿١﴾
indeed in	the man	Surely	And the Declining Day.
ءَامَنُوا۟	ٱلَّذِينَ	إِلَّا	خُسْرٍ ﴿٢﴾
believe	those (who)	Except	loss.
بِٱلْحَقِّ	وَتَوَاصَوْا۟	ٱلصَّٰلِحَٰتِ	وَعَمِلُوا۟
to truth	and encourage one another	good	and do
		بِٱلصَّبْرِ ﴿٣﴾	وَتَوَاصَوْا۟
		to perseverance.	and enjoin one another

A few applications of the message:

This sūrah gives us a formula for success. As with any formula, if you apply it correctly, you will get the best results. If you combine all the ingredients correctly, you will get the best product. This sūrah gives a recipe for success. The formula or recipe in sūrah *al-'Asr* has four parts or ingredients. The four parts are: (a) to believe in Allāh, (b) to do good, (c) to seek truth and (d) to practice perseverance.

We cannot expect to use one part of the formula or one ingredient of the recipe to get the best final product. If we think that belief in Allāh is enough, and fail to do anything else, then we will not get the good result. If we say we will only do the good work, but do not care about belief or truth or anything else, then we will not get a good result. Allāh says that unless we apply all four factors in the formula, in the long run we will be at a loss. We must therefore work in such a way so that we end up being winners. We should believe in Allāh and follow His teachings. We must turn our faith into action. We should constantly seek truth and exercise perseverance. We should encourage each other to do the same because we live in a society and we want the best for every one.

Questions:

1. As time goes by, why do people end up being at loss?
2. What four factors are mentioned in Sūrah *al-'Asr* as key to human success?
3. One or two of the key factors can still bring us success, but not the ultimate success. Based on Sūrah *al-'Asr* explain why all four factors are necessary for true success.

Sūrah 102

Revealed in Makkah

At-Takāthur

The Multiplication

Introduction

The desire to increase or pile up wealth is a bad habit that takes us away from the main goal of life. We start to see wealth in this world as the final success, while the true success lies in the Hereafter. If we ignore the success in the Hereafter and spend our efforts only for this world, we will face a disaster. Such a disaster will be crystal clear when it arrives.

بِسۡمِ ٱللَّهِ ٱلرَّحۡمَـٰنِ ٱلرَّحِيمِ

Bismi-llāhi-r raḥmāni-r raḥīm

In the name of Allah, the Most-Kind, the Most-Rewarding.

أَلۡهَىٰكُمُ ٱلتَّكَاثُرُ ۝١	Alhākumu-t takāthur,	1. The multiplication diverts you—
حَتَّىٰ زُرۡتُمُ ٱلۡمَقَابِرَ ۝٢	ḥattā jhurtumu-l maqābir.	2. until you visit the graves.
كَلَّا سَوۡفَ تَعۡلَمُونَ ۝٣	Kallā sawfa ta'lamūn,	3. No! you will soon know.
ثُمَّ كَلَّا سَوۡفَ تَعۡلَمُونَ ۝٤	thumma kallā sawfa ta'lamūn.	4. Again, by no means! you will soon know.
كَلَّا لَوۡ تَعۡلَمُونَ عِلۡمَ ٱلۡيَقِينِ ۝٥	Kallā law ta'lamūna 'ilma-l yaqīn.	5. No! if you knew with the Knowledge of Certainty!
لَتَرَوُنَّ ٱلۡجَحِيمَ ۝٦	La-tarawunna-l jaḥīm,	6. You will most certainly see the fierce Fire.
ثُمَّ لَتَرَوُنَّهَا عَيۡنَ ٱلۡيَقِينِ ۝٧	thumma la-tarawunnahā 'ayna-l yaqīn,	7. And then you will most certainly see it with the Certainty of Sight.

ثُمَّ لَتُسْـَٔلُنَّ يَوْمَئِذٍ عَنِ ٱلنَّعِيمِ ۝٨	thumma la-tus'alunna yawma'idhin 'ani-n na'īm.	8. And then, on that Day you will surely be questioned concerning the bounties.

Explanation:

1. The word *takāthur* is derived from *kathura,* which means multiplied or becoming abundant or numerous. The word is used to point out how people love to accumulate, increase and multiply worldly materials. The tendency to pile up wealth diverts a person from his good sense. The real objective of life should not be to pile up wealth, but to do good and worship Allāh.
2. People who selfishly accumulate wealth do not realize the real objective of life until they are about to die. At that time and after their death their souls realize the piled up wealth has no value in the Hereafter. When they are in their graves, their souls will realize they missed the real opportunities in this life. Then they will see the punishment that lies ahead of them.
3. The verse begins by *kalla* which means 'no.' The verse is saying by no means should people run after material gains by leaving aside the spiritual duties of life. If people do not listen, then soon they will come to know the sad reality.
4. This verse stresses the importance of the message in the previous three verses. There is no doubt that the truth will become crystal clear when the person dies and is put in his grave.
5. People who do not pay attention to these warnings will surely recognize the consequences. Only then will they believe. The word *'ilm al-yaqin* means knowledge of certainty. After their death, while in their graves, they will become very sure about their punishment. Earlier they ignored the warning, but then they will realize it was mistake to run after wealth.
6. In the graves, the souls of these people will see the fierce fire. On seeing the intense fire, they will be convinced of the punishment. They will realize that the warnings in the Qur'ān were true.
7. When they see the fierce fire, it will be with their *'ain al-yaqin*, or sight of certainty. Along with the knowledge of certainty, the sight of certainty will convince them that the rush for wealth was a bad choice.
8. After spending time in their graves, on the Day of Awakening people will be questioned about their wealth. Allāh does not give wealth to every one, but He chooses to give some people wealth during their earthly lives. Whoever gets wealth should spend it on good causes. The type of person mentioned in this sūrah did not spend his wealth, but kept on piling up wealth upon wealth, selfishly.

Words to know

Takāthur: Multiplying, competition to increase worldly matters. *Kawthar:* a lot of good things, a river in Paradise.
Yaqīn: Certainty. *Mūqinīn:* One who is certain. *Yūqinūna:* they are certain.
Na'īm: blessings, bounties. *An 'amta:* You have bestowed your blessings. *Al-Ni'mat:* Abundance, plentiful, enormous, intense comfort.

Sūrah Al-Takathur
Word-by-word meaning

ٱلرَّحِيمِ	ٱلرَّحۡمَـٰنِ	ٱللَّهِ	بِسۡمِ
the Most-Rewarding	the Most-Kind	Allāh	In the name of
زُرۡتُمُ	حَتَّىٰ	ٱلتَّكَاثُرُ ﴿١﴾	أَلۡهَىٰكُمُ
you visit	until	the multiplication	diverts you
تَعۡلَمُونَ ﴿٣﴾	سَوۡفَ	كَلَّا	ٱلۡمَقَابِرَ ﴿٢﴾
you know	soon	No!	the graves.
تَعۡلَمُونَ ﴿٤﴾	سَوۡفَ	كَلَّا	ثُمَّ
you will know	soon	no	Again,
عِلۡمَ	تَعۡلَمُونَ	لَوۡ	كَلَّا
Knowledge	you knew	if	no
ثُمَّ	ٱلۡجَحِيمَ ﴿٦﴾	لَتَرَوُنَّ	ٱلۡيَقِينِ ﴿٥﴾
then	the Fire	most certainly see	Certainty.
ثُمَّ	ٱلۡيَقِينِ ﴿٧﴾	عَيۡنَ	لَتَرَوُنَّهَا
then	the Certainty	of Sight	most certainly see
ٱلنَّعِيمِ ﴿٨﴾	عَنِ	يَوۡمَئِذٍ	لَتُسۡـَٔلُنَّ
the bounties	concerning	that Day	surely be questioned

A few applications of the message:

We should remember that Allāh has not discouraged wealth. Prophets Dāwūd (A) and Sulaimān (A) were wealthy. Prophet Sulaimān (A) prayed for a vast country and Allāh gave him one. Other prophets such as Ayyūb (A) and Yūsuf (A) were wealthy too. Abu Bakr (R) and Uthman (R) were wealthy. All of them treated wealth as gift from Allāh. They spent wealth to benefit others. They did not pile up wealth selfishly.

In our daily lives we should remember the message of the sūrah. It may so happen that Allāh will give someone more money than others. We should not let wealth divert us from the remembrance of Allāh. No matter how much wealth we get in life, we should remember wealth will not go with us in the Hereafter. Only our good deeds will go with us.

Questions:

1. Explain how competing to accumulate wealth turns us away from remembering Allāh.
2. At what stage will a person realize that accumulating wealth was not a good idea?
3. On the Day of Judgment what will people have to answer about their wealth?
4. The sūrah repeats "you will soon come to know." What will people come to know?
5. When people will come know, what will they see clearly?

Sūrah 101

Revealed in Makkah

Al-Qāri'ah

The Disaster

Introduction:

This sūrah, again, reminds us to prepare for the Day of Awakening. The world and its strong supports will not be able to rescue us unless we do good deeds. Wealth or worldly prestige will not matter on that Day. Whoever does more good deeds now in this world, will have the most blessings and satisfaction on the Day of Awakening.

بِسۡمِ ٱللَّهِ ٱلرَّحۡمَٰنِ ٱلرَّحِيمِ

Bismi-llāhi-r raḥmāni-r raḥīm

In the name of Allah, the Most-Kind, the Most-Rewarding.

ٱلۡقَارِعَةُ ﴿١﴾	Al qāri'ah,	1. The Great Calamity!
مَا ٱلۡقَارِعَةُ ﴿٢﴾	mal qāri'ah;	2. What is the Great Calamity?
وَمَآ أَدۡرَىٰكَ مَا ٱلۡقَارِعَةُ ﴿٣﴾	wa mā adrāka mal qāri'ah.	3. and what will make you know the Great Calamity!
يَوۡمَ يَكُونُ ٱلنَّاسُ كَٱلۡفَرَاشِ ٱلۡمَبۡثُوثِ ﴿٤﴾	Yawma yakūnu-n nāsu kal farāshi-l mabthūth,	4. On that Day mankind will be like moths scattered,
وَتَكُونُ ٱلۡجِبَالُ كَٱلۡعِهۡنِ ٱلۡمَنفُوشِ ﴿٥﴾	wa takūnu-l jibālu kal 'ihni-l manfūsh.	5. and the mountains will become like wool fluffed up.

فَأَمَّا مَن ثَقُلَتْ مَوَٰزِينُهُۥ ٦	Fa-ammā man thaqulat mawāzīnuhū,	6. Then as to him whose balances are heavy,
فَهُوَ فِي عِيشَةٍ رَّاضِيَةٍ ٧	fa-huwa fī ‘īshatir rāḍiyah.	7. he will then be in a life of satisfaction.
وَأَمَّا مَنْ خَفَّتْ مَوَٰزِينُهُۥ ٨	Wa ammā man khaffat mawāzīnuhū,	8. But as to him whose balances are light,
فَأُمُّهُۥ هَاوِيَةٌ ٩	fa-ummuhū hāwiyah.	9. the abyss will then be his mother.
وَمَآ أَدْرَىٰكَ مَا هِيَهْ ١٠	Wa mā adrāka mā hiyah.	10. And what will make you know what that is?
نَارٌ حَامِيَةٌۢ ١١	Nāruṅ ḥāmiyah.	11. A blazing Fire.

Explanation:

1-3. The theme of the sūrah deals with some of the events that will take place during the Awakening and in the Hereafter. The verse creates a sense of suspense with the word *qari‘ah* which means severe striking, disaster, or adversity. With the definitive article ‘*al-*’ in the beginning of the word, *al-qari‘ah* now signifies the Great Calamity during the Last Hour. The Arab audience at the time of the Prophet (S) was aware of the word *al-qari‘ah*. However, they did not truly realize the severity of *al-qari‘ah*. Therefore, the Qur’ān asked them if they really understood the meaning of *al-qari‘ah*. If they knew its meaning, they would not have rejected its truth.

3. The opening particle ‘*wa*’ is a conjunction but sometimes it implies an exclamation to add suspense. In this case, ‘*wa*’ adds to the suspense, pain and intensity connected with the calamity on the Final Hour. As humans, we cannot fully understand the events at the time of the Awakening. Therefore, the Qur’ān describes it using earthly experiences in easy to understand terms.

4. On that day human beings will be like confused moths (*farāsh*). The comparison seems to bring out the close similarity of miserable human beings with flimsy moths that get attracted towards a fire, swarm around it and die in the fire. Man’s final return towards his God will be in groups, much like a swarm of moths. They will be confused and reluctant to return. However, they will be brought to their final accounting. They cannot avoid it, just as the moths cannot but get attracted to the fire.

5. The lofty mountains, as we see now, are solid and enormous structures. When the calamity and tremor begins, these rock-solid structures will melt away as if they are soft fluffs of wool floating in the air.

6-7. When everyone will be assembled on the Day of Awakening, they will face the most important affair—to realize their deeds. Their worldly actions will be weighed in order to reward or punish them accordingly. Those who did enough good deeds will tip their balances to the state of satisfaction. They will live a pleasant life in Paradise.

8-9. Those whose balances are light with only a few good deeds, they will be in a deep pit of suffering. The word *hāwiya* represents a deep hole, normally used to denote the lowest pit of Hell. This abyss is symbolically termed as a mother (*umm*). Just like a mother carries her child on her lap or in the cradle with due care, the bottom of Hell will hug the sinners with 'due care'—through its blazing fire. A mother hugs her child and never parts with him or her under any circumstance until nursing and bringing up is complete. Similarly Hell will hug the sinners and 'nurse' them with punishments until the spiritual filth is wiped away.

10-11. The deepest pit of Hell is not an empty hole, but full of blazing fire.

Words to know

Yawm: day, time. *Yawma'idhin:* then on that day.
Mawāzīnuhū: his balances, his weight (of deeds), *Wazan:* weighing. *Mizān:* weight, balance.
Rādiyat: satisfaction, pleasant. *Ridwan:* good pleasure.
Nār: fire, burning flame. *Nūr*: light.

Sūrah Al-Qari'ah
Word-by-word meaning

ٱلرَّحِيمِ	ٱلرَّحۡمَٰنِ	ٱللَّهِ	بِسۡمِ
the Most-Rewarding	the Most-Kind	Allāh	In the name of
وَمَآ	ٱلۡقَارِعَةُ ٢	مَا	ٱلۡقَارِعَةُ ١
and what	the Great Calamity?	what	the Great Calamity!
يَوۡمَ	ٱلۡقَارِعَةُ ٣	مَا	أَدۡرَىٰكَ
the Day	Great Calamity.	what	do you know
ٱلۡمَبۡثُوثِ ٤	كَٱلۡفَرَاشِ	ٱلنَّاسُ	يَكُونُ
scattered	like moths	mankind	be like
ٱلۡمَنفُوشِ ٥	كَٱلۡعِهۡنِ	ٱلۡجِبَالُ	وَتَكُونُ
fluffed up	like wool	the mountains	and become

فَأَمَّا	مَن	ثَقُلَتْ	مَوَٰزِينُهُۥ ٦
Then as to him	whose	heavy	balances
فَهُوَ	فِى	عِيشَةٍ	رَّاضِيَةٍ ٧
he will then	in	life	pleasant
وَأَمَّا	مَنْ	خَفَّتْ	مَوَٰزِينُهُۥ ٨
and as for	whose	are light	balances
فَأُمُّهُۥ	هَاوِيَةٌ ٩	وَمَآ	أَدْرَىٰكَ
then his mother	abyss	And what	will make you know
مَا	هِيَهْ ١٠	نَارٌ	حَامِيَةٌۢ ١١
what	that is?	fire	blazing

A few applications of the message:

Allāh does not want us to go the Hereafter without knowing what to expect. There should not be any surprises when we reach there. In the Qur'ān, Allāh has repeatedly mentioned how He will judge and what we should look for.

The message of this sūrah is to make our scale heavy with plenty of good deeds. With a heavy load of good deeds, we will enjoy a pleasant life in Jannah. If our scale is light, with little good work compared to the big load of bad deeds, we will enter the deepest pit of blazing fire. We should use every opportunity to make our scales heavy. In addition to making salāt, paying zakāt and observing sawm (fasting), we can do an endless number of good deeds. Sometimes we need to do a good deed to make the balance heavy, sometimes we need to stay away from bad things to make the balance heavy, because staying away from bad things is a good deed too. For example, not gossiping, not lying, not stealing, not spreading rumors, and not insulting others are all good deeds.

We do not know how much a good deed or a bad deed weighs. We should not take chances with bad deeds that may seem small sins. We should minimize the bad deeds and sins as much as possible. We should continue to increase the amount of good deeds we do every day for the rest of our lives.

Questions:

1. What is the meaning of the word *al-Qāri'ah*?
2. What will happen to mankind on the Day of *al-Qāri'ah*?
3. What will happen to the mountains on the Day of *al-Qāri'ah*?
4. Explain what will happen to people who will have different types of scales?
5. What type of scales should all Muslims want to have?
6. What is the significance of Hell being a deep abyss?

Sūrah 100

Revealed in Makkah

Al-'Ādiyāt

The Attackers

Introduction:

This sūrah continues with the reminder that people should prepare for the Day of Awakening. We may spend our time carelessly, but the Day of Awakening will surely arrive. It will be sudden, but we now have a warning of its arrival. If we do not pay attention to the teachings of the Qur'ān, we will be caught unprepared as a sleepy, drowsy group of people unable to save ourselves.

بِسْمِ ٱللَّهِ ٱلرَّحْمَـٰنِ ٱلرَّحِيمِ

Bismi-llāhi-r raḥmāni-r raḥīm

In the name of Allah, the Most-Kind, the Most-Rewarding.

وَٱلْعَـٰدِيَـٰتِ ضَبْحًا ﴿١﴾	Wal 'ādiyāti ḍabḥā,	1. And the snorting assaulters,
فَٱلْمُورِيَـٰتِ قَدْحًا ﴿٢﴾	fal mūriyāti qadḥā,	2. those dashing, striking fire,
فَٱلْمُغِيرَٰتِ صُبْحًا ﴿٣﴾	fal mughīrāti subḥā,	3. and those making raids at dawn,
فَأَثَرْنَ بِهِۦ نَقْعًا ﴿٤﴾	fa atharna bihī naq'ā,	4. then raising up with a cloud of dust,
فَوَسَطْنَ بِهِۦ جَمْعًا ﴿٥﴾	fa-wasaṭna bihī jam'ā,	5. then penetrating by it through the troops.
إِنَّ ٱلْإِنسَـٰنَ لِرَبِّهِۦ لَكَنُودٌ ﴿٦﴾	inna-l insāna li-rabbihī la-kanūd;	6. Surely man is ungrateful to his Rabb.
وَإِنَّهُۥ عَلَىٰ ذَٰلِكَ لَشَهِيدٌ ﴿٧﴾	wa innahū 'alā dhālika la-shahīd;	7. And surely he is indeed a witness to that.

وَإِنَّهُۥ لِحُبِّ ٱلْخَيْرِ لَشَدِيدٌ ٨	wa innahū li-ḥubbi-l khayri la-shadīd.	8. And surely due to the love of wealth he is indeed rigid.
أَفَلَا يَعْلَمُ إِذَا بُعْثِرَ مَا فِى ٱلْقُبُورِ ٩	A-fa-lā ya'lamu idhā bu'thira mā fil qubūr,	9. Ha! does he not know that when what is in the graves will be raised up;—
وَحُصِّلَ مَا فِى ٱلصُّدُورِ ١٠	wa ḥuṣṣila mā fiṣ ṣudūr,	10. and what is in the hearts will be made manifest?
إِنَّ رَبَّهُم بِهِمْ يَوْمَئِذٍ لَّخَبِيرٌۢ ١١	inna rabbahum bihim yawma'idhiḷ la-khabīr.	11. Surely their Rabb this Day is Aware of them.

Explanation:

1. This sūrah reminds us about the Awakening through a series of images during a battle. The word *al-'Ādiyāt* denotes camels employed during the time of Hajj, or war-horses employed by the nomadic Arabs at the time of battle.

2. The striking of the hooves of the horses on rocky terrain creates sparks. These sparks created by a large number of horses, quickly galloping through a sleepy town, add a sense of mayhem and panic.

3. The attackers begin their surprise assault in the early morning, when the residents in the town are in deep sleep and are least prepared to defend themselves. The tiny sparks from the hooves are too bright in the darkness of the early dawn. When the sleepy residents wake up, they are faced with the sounds and lights of the looming assault.

4-5. The attack by the charging horses creates a cloud of dust that almost blinds the sleepy town. The sounds of the hooves, lights from the sparks, and the confusion of the dust creates images of a sudden attack, similar to the Day of Awakening. The chaos and the dust will engulf everyone on the Day of Awakening, when the people of the earth will be least expecting it.

The first five verses of the sūrah paint a scene of utter destruction. The remaining verses of the sūrah point out the people who will be caught unprepared.

6-8. All three verses begin with *innahū*— indicating a certainty of the environment mentioned in each verse. Verse 6 reminds us that man is ungrateful towards his Rabb. Man loves to receive blessings from his Rabb, but, in return, he does not fulfill his duties towards his Rabb. Verse 7 tells us that surely man knows that he is being ungrateful towards his Rabb. Verse 8 explains that man is ungrateful because he becomes greedy with his wealth. His wealth makes him detached from his duties towards Allāh. Man becomes reluctant to do good deeds.

9-11. In verse 9, the greedy, ungrateful man is reminded about his final journey. After he is dead and buried in his grave, a day will come when he will be ejected from it. The word *bu'thira* gives a sense of a violent volcanic eruption, where the 'ingredients' are overthrown suddenly and violently. During the Awakening, man will be awakened to the grim reality amid utter helplessness. On that day, all the secrets of his heart will be revealed and Allāh will remain well aware of everything that man did.

Words to know

Subha: morning. *Sabaha*: to visit or greet in the morning. *Misbāh:* lamp.
Shadīd: rigid, strong. *Ashudd:* age of full strength. *Ushdud:* strengthen.
Qubūr: graves, *Maqābir:* place of graves, cemetery.
Sudūr: Heart, chest, important place.
Khabīr: Knowing, One who knows. *Akhbar:* news, reports.

Sūrah Al-'Adiyat
Word-by-word meaning

ٱلرَّحِيمِ	ٱلرَّحْمَٰنِ	ٱللَّهِ	بِسْمِ
the Most-Rewarding	the Most-Kind	Allāh	In the name of
قَدْحًا ٢	فَٱلْمُورِيَٰتِ	ضَبْحًا ١	وَٱلْعَٰدِيَٰتِ
striking fire	dashing	snorting	And the assaulters
بِهِۦ	فَأَثَرْنَ	صُبْحًا ٣	فَٱلْمُغِيرَٰتِ
up with that	raising	at dawn	raids
جَمْعًا ٥	بِهِۦ	فَوَسَطْنَ	نَقْعًا ٤
troops	through	penetrating	dust
لَكَنُودٌ ٦	لِرَبِّهِۦ	ٱلْإِنسَٰنَ	إِنَّ
ungrateful	to his Rabb	man	surely
لَشَهِيدٌ ٧	ذَٰلِكَ	عَلَىٰ	وَإِنَّهُۥ
indeed witness	to	that	and surely
لَشَدِيدٌ ٨	ٱلْخَيْرِ	لِحُبِّ	وَإِنَّهُۥ
rigid	wealth	love of	and surely

بُعۡثِرَ	إِذَا	يَعۡلَمُ	أَفَلَا
raised up	when	know	does he not
مَا فِي	وَحُصِّلَ	ٱلۡقُبُورِ ﴿٩﴾	مَا فِي
what is in	and manifest	the graves	what is in
بِهِمۡ	رَبَّهُم	إِنَّ	ٱلصُّدُورِ ﴿١٠﴾
with them	their Rabb	surely	the hearts
		لَّخَبِيرُۢ ﴿١١﴾	يَوۡمَئِذٖ
		Aware	this Day

A few applications of the message:

In this sūrah we get a vivid image of the disarray and commotion on a battlefield. The image is used to remind us about our final journey in the Hereafter. The sūrah reflects on human character. We often become ungrateful towards Allāh and show a detachment from Him with our sinful activities. Allāh gives us blessings; but after receiving them, we break the ties with Allāh. Our love of wealth makes our hearts rigid towards the duties Allāh wants us to do.

A day will come when we will be raised from our graves to account for our deeds. Allāh knows very well what we do and what we do not do. On that day, we will not be able to hide anything. Everything will become exposed and all hidden, unknown, and forgotten deeds will become vivid in front of us. Keeping this in mind, we should do as much good work as we can and eliminate all bad deeds so that we are not humiliated on the Day of Judgment.

Questions

1. What are some of the images mentioned in the beginning of Sūrah *al-'Adiyāt*?
2. Verse 6 of Sūrah *al-'Adiyāt* reminds us about certain behavior of mankind. What is the behavior?
3. What are some of the reasons people are ungrateful to their Lord?
4. After everyone dies and is buried in the grave, what will happen to them on the Day of Awakening?
5. After people are raised, what will become clear to them?

Sūrah 99

Revealed in Makkah

Az-Zalzalah

The Quake

Introduction:

This sūrah also briefly, but vividly, describes a picture of the Day of Awakening. Surah *al-Ādiyāt, al-Qāri'ah* and *at-Takāthur* carried a similar message of preparing for the Final Day. Every material thing will be destroyed, but the records of our good or bad deeds will remain. Even the smallest of the small deeds will be carefully recorded and presented to us for a clear understanding of our fates in the Hereafter.

بِسْمِ ٱللَّهِ ٱلرَّحْمَـٰنِ ٱلرَّحِيمِ

Bismi-llāhi-r raḥmāni-r raḥīm

In the name of Allah, the Most-Kind, the Most-Rewarding.

إِذَا زُلْزِلَتِ ٱلْأَرْضُ زِلْزَالَهَا ﴿١﴾	Idẖā zulzilati-l arḍu zilzālahā,	1. When the earth quakes with her quaking,
وَأَخْرَجَتِ ٱلْأَرْضُ أَثْقَالَهَا ﴿٢﴾	wa akhrajati-l arḍu atẖqālahā,	2. and the earth brings out her burdens,
وَقَالَ ٱلْإِنسَـٰنُ مَا لَهَا ﴿٣﴾	wa qāla-l insānu mā lahā;	3. and man says: "What is with her?"
يَوْمَئِذٍ تُحَدِّثُ أَخْبَارَهَا ﴿٤﴾	yawma'idẖiṅ tuḥadditẖu akhbāraha.	4. That Day she will relate her news,
بِأَنَّ رَبَّكَ أَوْحَىٰ لَهَا ﴿٥﴾	Bi-anna rabbaka awḥā laha.	5. as if your Rabb had revealed to her.
يَوْمَئِذٍ يَصْدُرُ ٱلنَّاسُ أَشْتَاتًا لِّيُرَوْا۟ أَعْمَـٰلَهُمْ ﴿٦﴾	Yawma'idẖiẏ yaṣduru-n nāsu ashtātaḷ, li-yuraw a'mālahum.	6. On that Day, people will come forth in separate groups that they might be shown their deeds.

فَمَن يَعْمَلْ مِثْقَالَ ذَرَّةٍ خَيْرًا يَرَهُۥ ۝٧	Fa maṅ ya'mal mith̲qāla dh̲arratiṅ khayraẏ yarah.	7. So whoever does an atom's weight of good will see it.
وَمَن يَعْمَلْ مِثْقَالَ ذَرَّةٍ شَرًّا يَرَهُۥ ۝٨	Wa maṅ ya'mal mith̲qāla dh̲arratiṅ sharraẏ yarah.	8. And whoever does an atom's weight of evil will see it.

Explanation:

1-2. The sūrah derives its name from the word *zalzalah* mentioned in this verse. The meaning of the word is earthquake or some kind of terrible shake-up. A sudden, terrible shake-up of the earth will happen at the time of the Awakening. The details of Awakening and its fierce extents are beyond our imagination. On that terrible day of shaking, the ground will be turned upside down, and the earth will bring out all that is buried deep inside it.

3. As the violent shaking begins, people will be gripped with terror and panicked at the extraordinary happenings. They will scream out wondering what is the matter with the earth!

4-5. The shaking will be on the Day of Awakening. On that day, the earth will inform every human deed that it has witnessed. Allāh will inspire the earth to reveal the information and act as a witness to every human action.

6. Islam teaches that each person will be judged based on his or her actual deeds. The righteous people will be together and the sinners will be together. There will be no mistake in the groupings, as every deed is carefully and completely recorded.

7-8. It is not possible for us to remember accurately each and every deed, good or bad, big or small. If we cannot remember everything done knowingly, there is no way we can remember everything done unknowingly. If a person forgets a deed, it does not mean the deed will not be recorded. Every person will see all of his or her deeds even if a deed is as small as the weight of an atom (*dharrat*, lit. a grain, particle, tiny ant, atom). Everyone will receive his or her due reward or punishment.

Words to know

Mithqāla: weight. *Thaqulat:* became heavy. *Thaqīl:* heavy, weighty.
Dh̲arrat: atom, small ant, smallest seed. *Dh̲uriyyatun:* Offspring, children.
Khayr: good. *Khayrāt*: good things, good deeds.
Sharra: to do evil, to be wicked. *Ashrār*: evil, bad.

Sūrah Az-Zalzalah
Word-by-word meaning

ٱلرَّحِيمِ	ٱلرَّحْمَـٰنِ	ٱللَّهِ	بِسْمِ
the Most-Rewarding	the Most-Kind	Allāh	In the name of

إِذَا	زُلْزِلَتِ	ٱلْأَرْضُ	زِلْزَالَهَا (١)
when	quakes	the earth	its quaking
وَأَخْرَجَتِ	ٱلْأَرْضُ	أَثْقَالَهَا (٢)	وَقَالَ
and brings out	the earth	its burdens	and says
ٱلْإِنسَٰنُ	مَا لَهَا (٣)	يَوْمَئِذٍ	تُحَدِّثُ
man	what is it?	that Day	relate
أَخْبَارَهَا (٤)	بِأَنَّ	رَبَّكَ	أَوْحَىٰ
its news	as if	your Rabb	revealed
لَهَا (٥)	يَوْمَئِذٍ	يَصْدُرُ	ٱلنَّاسُ
to it.	that Day	come forth	the people
أَشْتَاتًا	لِّيُرَوْا	أَعْمَٰلَهُمْ (٦)	فَمَن
separate groups	to be shown	their deeds	whoever
يَعْمَلْ	مِثْقَالَ	ذَرَّةٍ	خَيْرًا
does	weight	atom	of good
يَرَهُۥ (٧)	وَمَن	يَعْمَلْ	مِثْقَالَ
will see it	and whoever	does	weight
ذَرَّةٍ	شَرًّا	يَرَهُۥ (٨)	
atom	evil	will see it	

A few applications of the message:

This sūrah is about human accountability. On the terrible day of Awakening we will be held accountable for each and every action that we did, and did not do, but were required to do. For example, we are required to make salāt and fast (sawm). If we did not do them, then they will still be accounted for. Even if an action is as small as an atom or dust, it will be brought forth and measured.

Think of this: if we are inside a room with our parents, we will not do any thing that our parents do not like us to do. If we are in a room where there are many closed circuit cameras watching our every action, we will not do anything that will embarrass us. In this world we are, as if, under a closed circuit camera. Allāh is watching us. Our every action, small or big, is getting recorded. Not only that, these recordings will be used against us on the Day of Judgment. Therefore, why do any bad deed that Allāh has prohibited? Why do any small bad deed knowing that nothing escapes Allāh and He knows the tiniest of our deeds? Why embarrass ourselves on the Day of Judgment? Let this sūrah be a reminder to us to stay away from all bad things and follow the true teachings of Islam.

Questions:

1. What is the meaning of the word *zilzāl*?
2. On the Day of Quaking what will the earth do?
3. On the Day of Awakening why will people assemble in separate groups?
4. On the Day of Awakening what will both the groups see?
5. On the Day of Awakening what will you want to see in large quantities?

Sūrah 98

Revealed in Makkah

Al-Bayyinah

The Clear Proof

Introduction:

This late Makkan sūrah (possibly early Madīnan) refers to the clear proof (*al-bayyinah*) that came to the People of the Book. Even though they received the proof, they later deviated. In their books they were advised to worship One Allāh, establish the prayer and pay zakāt. The sūrah tells People of the Book and the idol worshippers that they cannot be freed from their deviated faith until a new clear proof in the form of the Qur'ān comes to them. Those who reject faith after receiving the clear proof in the Qur'ān will be in fire of Hell. Those who believe and do good deeds will receive their reward from Allāh. They will be in the Garden and Allāh will be pleased with them just as they will be pleased with Allāh.

بِسۡمِ ٱللَّهِ ٱلرَّحۡمَٰنِ ٱلرَّحِيمِ

Bismi-llāhi-r raḥmāni-r raḥīm

In the name of Allah, the Most-Kind, the Most-Rewarding.

لَمۡ يَكُنِ ٱلَّذِينَ كَفَرُواْ مِنۡ أَهۡلِ ٱلۡكِتَٰبِ وَٱلۡمُشۡرِكِينَ مُنفَكِّينَ حَتَّىٰ تَأۡتِيَهُمُ ٱلۡبَيِّنَةُ ١	Lam yakuni-lladhīna kafarū min ahli-l kitābi wal mushrikīna munfakkīna ḥattā ta'tiyahumu-l bayyinah,	1. Those disbelievers from among the People of the Book, and the polytheists, could not be freed until the Clear Proof came to them,—
رَسُولٌ مِّنَ ٱللَّهِ يَتۡلُواْ صُحُفًا مُّطَهَّرَةً ٢	rasūlum mina-llāhi yatlū ṣuḥufam muṭahharah,	2. a Rasūl from Allāh who recites purified pages,
فِيهَا كُتُبٌ قَيِّمَةٌ ٣	fīhā kutubuṅ qayyimah.	3. in it are straight scriptures.

وَمَا تَفَرَّقَ ٱلَّذِينَ أُوتُوا۟ ٱلْكِتَـٰبَ
إِلَّا مِنۢ بَعْدِ مَا جَآءَتْهُمُ ٱلْبَيِّنَةُ ٤

Wa mā tafarraqa-lladh̲īna ūtu-l kitāba illā miṅ ba‘di mā jā’athumu-l bayyinah.

4. And those who were given the Scripture did not divide except after the Clear Proof had come to them.

وَمَآ أُمِرُوٓا۟ إِلَّا لِيَعْبُدُوا۟ ٱللَّهَ مُخْلِصِينَ
لَهُ ٱلدِّينَ حُنَفَآءَ وَيُقِيمُوا۟ ٱلصَّلَوٰةَ
وَيُؤْتُوا۟ ٱلزَّكَوٰةَ ۚ وَذَٰلِكَ دِينُ
ٱلْقَيِّمَةِ ٥

Wa mā umirū illā li-ya‘budu-llāha mukhliṣīna lahu-d dīna, ḥunafā’a wa yuqīmuṣ ṣalāta wa yu’tu-jhjhakāta wa dh̲ālika dīnu-l qayyimah.

5. And they were not commanded but to worship Allāh, be sincere to Him in religion,— be upright, and establish the Salāt and pay the Zakat. And that is the Right Religion.

إِنَّ ٱلَّذِينَ كَفَرُوا۟ مِنْ أَهْلِ ٱلْكِتَـٰبِ
وَٱلْمُشْرِكِينَ فِى نَارِ جَهَنَّمَ خَـٰلِدِينَ
فِيهَآ ۚ أُو۟لَـٰٓئِكَ هُمْ شَرُّ ٱلْبَرِيَّةِ ٦

Inna-lladh̲īna kafarū min ahli-l kitābi wal mushrikīna fī nāri jahan-nama khālidīna fīha. Ulā’ika hum sharru-l bariyyah.

6. Surely those who reject Faith from among the People of the Book, and the polytheists, will be in the Fire of Hell, abiding in it. These— they are the worst creatures.

إِنَّ ٱلَّذِينَ ءَامَنُوا۟ وَعَمِلُوا۟
ٱلصَّـٰلِحَـٰتِ أُو۟لَـٰٓئِكَ هُمْ خَيْرُ
ٱلْبَرِيَّةِ ٧

Inna-lladh̲īna āmanū wa ‘amiluṣ ṣāliḥāti, ulā’ika hum khayru-l bariyyah.

7. Surely those who believe and do good!— These— they are the best of creatures.

جَزَآؤُهُمْ عِندَ رَبِّهِمْ جَنَّـٰتُ عَدْنٍ
تَجْرِى مِن تَحْتِهَا ٱلْأَنْهَـٰرُ خَـٰلِدِينَ
فِيهَآ أَبَدًا ۖ رَّضِىَ ٱللَّهُ عَنْهُمْ وَرَضُوا۟
عَنْهُ ۚ ذَٰلِكَ لِمَنْ خَشِىَ رَبَّهُۥ ٨

Jajhā’uhum ‘inda rab-bihim jannātu ‘adniṅ tajrī min taḥtiha-l anhāru khālidīna fīhā abadā. Raḍiya-llāhu ‘anhum wa raḍū ‘anhu. Dh̲ālika liman khashiya rabbah.

8. Their reward in the Presence of their Rabb will be Gardens of Eden, beneath which flow the rivers, abiding in them forever. Allāh is well-pleased with them, and they are well-pleased with Him. That is for him who fears his Rabb.

Explanation:

1. The People of the Book—the Jews and the Christians—once received Divine guidance to worship One God and to follow the Divine rules. Later on, they changed many of the rules and deviated from the original teachings. This verse states that it is possible to free the People of the Book and the idol worshippers from their wrong form of beliefs and practices by following the Clear Proof. This clear proof is contained in the Qur'ān.
2. A messenger from Allāh, that is our Prophet Muhammad (S), would recite to them the purified pages. The purified pages refer to the pages of the Qur'ān. The Qur'ān is considered purified since, from the very beginning of its revelation, the text was kept pure and protected—free from any changes and corruption.
3. This messenger, Prophet Muhammad (S) would recite to the People of the Book and the idol worshippers the Qur'ān that contains correct and the right teachings
4. Prior to Prophet Muhammad (S), the People of the Book also received Divine books. Those books also contained the clear proof of the Oneness of Allāh and the core teachings of Islam. All the past prophets taught their people the same core teachings. However, after the clear proof was sent to them, these people either understood or misunderstood the message. As a result, they were divided into either believers or disbelievers.
5. One of the core teachings of all past prophets was worshipping Allāh without associating anything or anyone with Him. These past prophets also taught their people to remain sincere to Allāh, remain upright (*hanif*) in religion, perform salāt and pay zakāt.
6. Whether or not the People of the Book believe in the Qur'ān, they have no excuse because the core teachings were taught to them. Now, if the People of the Book read the Qur'ān, they will find the same core teachings are also present in the Qur'ān. If, after this, they as well as the idol worshippers reject the truth, their punishment will be in the fire of Hell. Due to their rejection of truth they are called the "worst of the creatures."
7. Those who believe and do good deeds are considered to the "best of the creatures." This is because they follow the Divine teachings and worship one Allāh.
8. Those who have faith in the Islamic teachings and demonstrate their faith through righteous deeds are the ultimate inheritors of the Garden, to live there forever. Allāh will be well pleased with them because they followed His command. They will be well pleased with Allāh because they will have received the promised reward.

Words to know

Kafarū: rejected faith, disbelieved. *Kāfirun*: one who refuses to believe. *Kaffara*: he purged, he expiated.
Mutahharah: purified one. *Tahara*: to be pure, clean, chaste.
Qayyimah: straight, upright. *Qum*: you stand up. *Maqām*: place to stand. *Qiyāmat*: resurrect.
Mukhlis: one who is truly sincere. *Khalasa*: to be pure.
Hunafā: (plural of *Hanīf*) being upright, lean to the right side. *Hanīf*: one who inclines to the right deeds and away from sin, upright person.

Sūrah Al-Bayyinah
Word-by-word meaning

ٱلرَّحِيمِ	ٱلرَّحۡمَٰنِ	ٱللَّهِ	بِسۡمِ
the Most-Rewarding	the Most-Kind	Allāh	In the name of
كَفَرُواْ	ٱلَّذِينَ	يَكُنِ	لَمۡ
reject faith	those	were	not
وَٱلۡمُشۡرِكِينَ	ٱلۡكِتَٰبِ	أَهۡلِ	مِنۡ
and the polytheists	the Book	people	from
ٱلۡبَيِّنَةُ ﴿١﴾	تَأۡتِيَهُمُ	حَتَّىٰ	مُنفَكِّينَ
the Clear Proof	came to them	until	could be freed, parted
يَتۡلُواْ	ٱللَّهِ	مِّنَ	رَسُولٞ
recites	Allah	from	A Rasul
كُتُبٞ	فِيهَا	مُّطَهَّرَةٗ ﴿٢﴾	صُحُفٗا
scriptures	in it	purified	pages
ٱلَّذِينَ	تَفَرَّقَ	وَمَا	قَيِّمَةٞ ﴿٣﴾
those	become divided	and not	straight, upright
مِنۢ بَعۡدِ	إِلَّا	ٱلۡكِتَٰبَ	أُوتُواْ
after	except	the Scriptures	were given
أُمِرُوٓاْ	وَمَآ	ٱلۡبَيِّنَةُ ﴿٤﴾	مَا جَآءَتۡهُمُ
commanded	and not	the Clear Proof	what came to them

إِلَّا except	لِيَعْبُدُوا۟ to worship	ٱللَّهَ Allah	مُخْلِصِينَ sincerely
لَهُ for him	ٱلدِّينَ the religion	حُنَفَآءَ being upright	وَيُقِيمُوا۟ and establish
ٱلصَّلَوٰةَ the salāt	وَيُؤْتُوا۟ and give	ٱلزَّكَوٰةَ ۚ zakāt	وَذَٰلِكَ and that
دِينُ religion	ٱلْقَيِّمَةِ ۝٥ Right	إِنَّ Surely	ٱلَّذِينَ those
كَفَرُوا۟ reject faith	مِنْ among	أَهْلِ people	ٱلْكِتَٰبِ the Book
وَٱلْمُشْرِكِينَ and polytheists	فِى نَارِ in fire	جَهَنَّمَ hell	خَٰلِدِينَ abiding
فِيهَآ ۚ in it	أُو۟لَٰٓئِكَ these	هُمْ they	شَرُّ worst
ٱلْبَرِيَّةِ ۝٦ creatures	إِنَّ Surely	ٱلَّذِينَ those	ءَامَنُوا۟ believe
وَعَمِلُوا۟ and do	ٱلصَّٰلِحَٰتِ good deeds	أُو۟لَٰٓئِكَ these	هُمْ they

عِندَ	جَزَآؤُهُمْ	ٱلْبَرِيَّةِ ۝٧	خَيْرُ
with	their reward	creatures	best
تَجْرِى	عَدْنٍ	جَنَّٰتُ	رَبِّهِمْ
flow	Eden	Garden	their Rabb
خَٰلِدِينَ	ٱلْأَنْهَٰرُ	تَحْتِهَا	مِن
abiding	the rivers	underneath it	from
ٱللَّهُ	رَّضِىَ	أَبَدًا ۖ	فِيهَآ
Allah	pleased	forever	in it
ذَٰلِكَ	عَنْهُ ۚ	وَرَضُوا۟	عَنْهُمْ
that	with Him	and they are pleased	with them
	رَبَّهُۥ ۝٨	خَشِىَ	لِمَنْ
	his Rabb	fears	for who

A few applications of the message:

As we read the sūrah, let us think for a while as to why the People of the Book deviated after receiving clear proof about the Oneness of God and divine teachings. One reason is that they took the teachings lightly and ignored some of the teachings. As a result, even after receiving the clear proof, they moved far away from the original teachings. The consequence of deviating from the true teachings is severe, as mentioned in verse 6.

We should, therefore, remain very alert not to deviate from the teachings of the Qur'ān. In order for us not to deviate from the Qur'ān, we must first clearly understand the message of the Qur'ān and then follow its teachings carefully.

We must remain alert not to adopt innovations and un-Islamic practices and beliefs. Only when we believe and practice the core Islamic teachings, will our reward be in the Garden. Allāh will be pleased with us and we will be pleased with Him when we receive our reward.

Questions:

1. The People of the Book were required to do certain duties. What duties were they required to do?
2. According to Sūrah *al-Bayyinah*, at what point did the forefathers of the People of the Book move away from the true teaching?
3. What type of creatures are those who disbelieve in the clear proof of the Qur'ān?
4. What type of creatures are those who believe and do good deeds?
5. According to Sūrah *al-Bayyinah*, what is needed for the People of the Book to give up their false way of life?
6. Who will be well pleased with whom? Explain the reason for being well pleased.

Sūrah 97

Revealed in Makkah

Al-Qadr

The Majesty

Introduction:

This sūrah, revealed in Makkah, is about the initial revelation or sending down of the Qur'an. The revelation began on a night, appropriately called *Lailat-ul Qadr* or the Night of Majesty. The events of this night changed the course of humanity forever. This sūrah reminds us to seek blessings and forgiveness on this night that lasts until dawn. This peaceful night is surely better than a thousand months combined.

بِسۡمِ ٱللَّهِ ٱلرَّحۡمَٰنِ ٱلرَّحِيمِ

Bismi-llāhi-r raḥmāni-r raḥīm

In the name of Allah, the Most-Kind, the Most-Rewarding.

إِنَّآ أَنزَلۡنَٰهُ فِي لَيۡلَةِ ٱلۡقَدۡرِ ١	Innā anjhalnāhu fī layla-ti-l qadr;	1. Surely We have revealed it during the Night of Majesty.
وَمَآ أَدۡرَىٰكَ مَا لَيۡلَةُ ٱلۡقَدۡرِ ٢	wa mā adrāka mā laylatu-l qadr.	2. And what will make you know what the Night of Majesty is?
لَيۡلَةُ ٱلۡقَدۡرِ خَيۡرٞ مِّنۡ أَلۡفِ شَهۡرٖ ٣	Laylatu-l qadri, khayrum min alfi shahr.	3. The Night of Majesty is better than a thousand months.
تَنَزَّلُ ٱلۡمَلَٰٓئِكَةُ وَٱلرُّوحُ فِيهَا بِإِذۡنِ رَبِّهِم مِّن كُلِّ أَمۡرٖ ٤	Tanajhjhalu-l malā'ikatu war rūḥu fīhā bi-idhni rabbihim; min kulli amr,—	4. The angels and the Spirit descend in it by the permission of their Rabb concerning every affair.
سَلَٰمٌ هِيَ حَتَّىٰ مَطۡلَعِ ٱلۡفَجۡرِ ٥	salāmun,— hiya ḥattā maṭla'i-l fajr.	5. Peace. It is until the rising of the dawn.

Explanation:

1. The verse begins by reminding us that Allāh surely sent the Qur'ān during the Night of *al-Qadr.* The Night of *al-Qadr* falls in the month of Ramadan, particularly in the last ten days of the month. More specifically, it falls on one of the odd number of nights (21st, 23rd, 25th, 27th or 29th). However, we do not know for sure which night is the exact Night of *al-Qadr*. On the Night of *al-Qadr* the revelation of the first five verses of the Qur'ān started. It happened when the Prophet (S) was meditating in cave Hira on a mountain known as *Jabal an-Nūr*. Later, the first five verses were placed at the beginning of sūrah *al-Alaq*, the 96th sūrah.

2-3. The importance of the Night of *al-Qadr* is enormous. It is better than a thousand months. The term 'thousand months' indicates a substantial amount of time. In the history of mankind, this is the night that witnessed the beginning of the revelation of the Qur'an. This revelation soon changed the condition of the entire population in Arabia, and later that of billions of people all over the world. Mankind will never be the same after the events of that Night of *Al-Qadr*.

4. On this blessed night, angels and the *rūh* come down on earth with the permission from Allāh. The word *rūh,* in this case, refers to angel Jibrīl (A). The angels come down with blessings and mercy of Allāh, to inspire the people for devotion and to make them righteous.

5. When we realize that the night is so blessed, we devote more time doing prayer and remembrance of Allāh. This night of peace lasts until dawn.

Words to know

Qadr: Majesty, Power. *Qadīr*: One who has Power (one of the excellent names of Allah). *Taqdīr*: decree, disposition. *Muqtadir*: All powerful.
Rūh: Spirit, soul, inspiration, Jibril. *Raihan*: Fragrant flowery plants.
Salāmun: peace. *Islam*: peace with Allāh, obedience to Allāh. *Muslimūn*: one who submits and has peace with Allāh.

Sūrah Al-Qadr
Word-by-word meaning

ٱلرَّحِيمِ	ٱلرَّحْمَـٰنِ	ٱللَّهِ	بِسْمِ
the Most-Rewarding	the Most-Kind	Allāh	In the name of
لَيْلَةِ	فِى	أَنزَلْنَـٰهُ	إِنَّآ
night	in	We have revealed	Surely

مَا	أَدْرَىٰكَ	وَمَآ	ٱلْقَدْرِ ﴿١﴾
what	do you know	and what	Majesty
خَيْرٌ	لَيْلَةُ ٱلْقَدْرِ	ٱلْقَدْرِ ﴿٢﴾	لَيْلَةُ
better	Night of Majesty	Majesty	night
تَنَزَّلُ	شَهْرٍ ﴿٣﴾	أَلْفِ	مِّنْ
descend	months	thousand	than
بِإِذْنِ	فِيهَا	وَٱلرُّوحُ	ٱلْمَلَٰٓئِكَةُ
with permission	in it	and the Spirit	angels
أَمْرٍ ﴿٤﴾	كُلِّ	مِّن	رَبِّهِم
affair	every	for	their Rabb
مَطْلَعِ	حَتَّىٰ	هِىَ	سَلَٰمٌ
rising	until	it is	Peace
			ٱلْفَجْرِ ﴿٥﴾
			dawn

A few applications of the message:

We do not know exactly which night is *Lailat-ul-Qadr*. But we know that it is one of the odd nights of the last ten nights of Ramadan. Allāh wants us to search for the night. To search means to pray more and remember Allāh more on that night. When the blessed month of Ramadan arrives, we should remember that, in one of its night, Allāh began sending the Qur'ān to Prophet Muhammad (S). We should remember that the night of *al-Qadr* is better than a thousands months. A thousand months is equal to about 83 years! Worshipping on that night will give us blessing equal to 83 years of worshipping! On that night, we should spend as much time as possible to worship Allāh. We should not miss the opportunity of getting blessings on that Majestic Night.

Questions:

1. In which month does *Lailatul Qadr* fall?
2. On which night should we search for *Lailatul Qadr*?
3. Which verses were revealed in the Night of *al-Qadr*?
4. The night of *Lailatul Qadr* is better than how many months?
5. What three things happen on the Night of *al-Qadr*?

Sūrah 96

Revealed in Makkah

Al-'Alaq

The Clot

Introduction:

With the first five verses of this sūrah, the revelation of the Qur'ān began. Prophet Muhammad (S) was meditating in a cave named Hira, on a mountain named *Jabal an-Nūr*, located slightly outside Makkah. These verses were sent in Ramadan of 610 C.E. The rest of the verses of this sūrah were sent a few years later.

بِسْمِ ٱللَّهِ ٱلرَّحْمَٰنِ ٱلرَّحِيمِ

Bismi-llāhi-r raḥmāni-r raḥīm

In the name of Allah, the Most-Kind, the Most-Rewarding.

ٱقْرَأْ بِٱسْمِ رَبِّكَ ٱلَّذِى خَلَقَ ﴿١﴾	Iqra' bi-smi rabbika-lladhī khalaq;	1. Read in the name of your Rabb Who created.
خَلَقَ ٱلْإِنسَٰنَ مِنْ عَلَقٍ ﴿٢﴾	khalaqa-l insāna min 'alaq;	2. He created man from a clot.
ٱقْرَأْ وَرَبُّكَ ٱلْأَكْرَمُ ﴿٣﴾	iqra' wa rabbuka-l akram,—	3. Read! and your Rabb is the most Honorable
ٱلَّذِى عَلَّمَ بِٱلْقَلَمِ ﴿٤﴾	Alladhī 'allama bil qalam,	4. Who has taught by the pen,—
عَلَّمَ ٱلْإِنسَٰنَ مَا لَمْ يَعْلَمْ ﴿٥﴾	'allama-l insāna mā lam ya'lam.	5. has taught man what he did not know.
كَلَّآ إِنَّ ٱلْإِنسَٰنَ لَيَطْغَىٰٓ ﴿٦﴾	Kallā inna-l insāna la-yaṭghā,	6. No, surely man does transgress,
أَن رَّءَاهُ ٱسْتَغْنَىٰٓ ﴿٧﴾	an ra'āhu-s taghna.	7. because he sees himself as self sufficient.

إِنَّ إِلَىٰ رَبِّكَ ٱلرُّجْعَىٰٓ ﴿٨﴾	Inna ilā rabbika-r ruj‘a.	8. Surely to your Rabb is the return.
أَرَءَيْتَ ٱلَّذِى يَنْهَىٰ ﴿٩﴾	A-ra’ayta-lladh̲ī yanhā,	9. Have you seen him who forbids—
عَبْدًا إِذَا صَلَّىٰٓ ﴿١٠﴾	‘abdaṅ idh̲ā ṣalla.	10. a servant when he performs Salāt ?
أَرَءَيْتَ إِن كَانَ عَلَى ٱلْهُدَىٰٓ ﴿١١﴾	A-ra’ayta in kāna ‘ala-l hudā,	11. Do you see if he is upon the guidance,
أَوْ أَمَرَ بِٱلتَّقْوَىٰٓ ﴿١٢﴾	aw amara bi-t taqwa.	12. or he enjoins reverence?
أَرَءَيْتَ إِن كَذَّبَ وَتَوَلَّىٰٓ ﴿١٣﴾	A-ra’ayta in kadh̲dh̲aba wa tawalla.	13. Do you see if he rejects and turns back?
أَلَمْ يَعْلَم بِأَنَّ ٱللَّهَ يَرَىٰ ﴿١٤﴾	A-lam ya‘lam bi-anna-llāha yara.	14. Does he not know that Allah surely sees?
كَلَّا لَئِن لَّمْ يَنتَهِ لَنَسْفَعًۢا بِٱلنَّاصِيَةِ ﴿١٥﴾	Kallā lai’ṅ lam yantahi, la-nasfa‘aṅ bin nāṣiyah,	15. No, if he does not desist, We shall surely drag him by the forelock,—
نَاصِيَةٍ كَـٰذِبَةٍ خَاطِئَةٍ ﴿١٦﴾	nāṣiyatiṅ kādh̲ibatiṅ khāṭi’ah;	16. a forelock— lying, sinful!
فَلْيَدْعُ نَادِيَهُۥ ﴿١٧﴾	fal yad‘u nādiyah,	17. Then let him call his council,
سَنَدْعُ ٱلزَّبَانِيَةَ ﴿١٨﴾	sa-nad‘u-jh jhabāniyah,	18. We shall also summon the guards.
كَلَّا لَا تُطِعْهُ وَٱسْجُدْ وَٱقْتَرِب ۩ ﴿١٩﴾	kalla. Lā tuṭi‘hu wa-sjud wa-qtarib. (Sajdah)	19. No, do not obey him, and perform SAJDAH, and draw near.

Explanation:

1. The sending down of the Qur’ān was started with the first five verses of this sūrah. When Angel Jibril (A) first brought these verses, he asked the Prophet (S): *Iqra’* which means to read or recite. The verse tells us one very important quality of Rabb—He creates (*khalaqa*). Creation out of nothing is a quality exclusive to the Rabb. No false gods or idols can create or make anything. We can make many things, but we cannot create something out of nothing.

2. Allāh created everything when there was nothing. He created human being (*insān*) from a type of clot or tiny lump of flesh.

3-4. Our Rabb created everything, including human beings because He is kind. One of His greatest blessings to us is our special ability to acquire knowledge. Knowledge cannot be acquired if there were no tool with which to write. Our ability to use the pen gave us the power to acquire and then transmit knowledge from person to person, community to community, nation to nation, and generation to generation.

5. All our knowledge comes from Allāh. In our minds, He put a nature to be curious. The more we try to find out about things, the more we learn. Our nature to explore and learn is a gift from Allāh.

6-8. Human beings learned many things, but many people are not thankful. They have moved away from Allāh. They do not feel that the knowledge is a gift from Him. These people feel that they are smart and powerful, as if they can do everything on their own. They do not understand that one day they will return to Allāh to answer for their actions.

9-10. These verses are about Abū Jahl, an enemy of Islam. He used to insult the Prophet (S) and try to stop him from praying. Prophet Muhammad (S) and the Muslims are servants of Allāh. We should listen to Allāh only.

11-14. This set of verses is charging Abū Jahl and his supporters. Why did they oppose Prophet Muhammad (S)? Did they not see that Prophet Muhammad (S) was truly guided? Was Prophet Muhammad (S) not a righteous person? Would Prophet Muhammad (S) reject the divine message and turn back from the truth? Did they not know that Allāh watches whatever they do?

15-16. If the bad people, like Abū Jahl, do not stop their evil acts, Allāh will drag them by their forelocks. A forelock is a part of hair right above the forehead, and is often a sign of respect. To be dragged by the forelock is a big insult.

17-18. Abū Jahl and his group may appear to be powerful, and they may be successful for a short time, but in the long run, they will suffer. They may gather many supporters, but they cannot stand in front of the angels who can bring punishment upon the evil people.

19. Allāh guides the Prophet (S) and all the righteous people. He tells us not to follow the evil people. A true believer should come closer to Allāh by showing humility in prayer. The word *wasjud* means to bow down in sajdah (prostration). When we do sajdah we completely surrender to Allāh. Now that we have read the verse, we should make an actual ***sajdah*** as a sign of our surrender to Him.

Words to know

Iqra': Read, recite! *Qur'ān*: Reading. *Qara'a*: he read, he recited. *Quri'a*: it is recited.
Qalam: pen. *Aqlām*: plural of pen, quill.
Hudā: guidance. *Hidāyat*: guidance. *Hādi*: leader, guide.
Taqwā: reverence, protection, warding off evil. *Muttaqī*: reverent, who protects against evil.
wa-sjud: and perform Sajdah (prostration). *Sujūd*: prostration. *Masjidun*: place of prostration. *Masājid*: plural of masjid.

Sūrah Al-'Alaq
Word-by-word meaning

ٱلرَّحِيمِ	ٱلرَّحْمَٰنِ	ٱللَّهِ	بِسْمِ
the Most-Rewarding	the Most-Kind	Allāh	In the name of
ٱلَّذِى	رَبِّكَ	بِٱسْمِ	ٱقْرَأْ
Who	your Rabb	in the name	Read
مِنْ	ٱلْإِنسَٰنَ	خَلَقَ	خَلَقَ ﴿١﴾
from	the man	created	created
ٱلْأَكْرَمُ ﴿٣﴾	وَرَبُّكَ	ٱقْرَأْ	عَلَقٍ ﴿٢﴾
most Honorable	and your Rabb	read	clot
عَلَّمَ	بِٱلْقَلَمِ ﴿٤﴾	عَلَّمَ	ٱلَّذِى
taught	with pen	taught	Who
يَعْلَمْ ﴿٥﴾	لَمْ	مَا	ٱلْإِنسَٰنَ
he knew	not	what	the man
لَيَطْغَىٰٓ ﴿٦﴾	ٱلْإِنسَٰنَ	إِنَّ	كَلَّآ
transgresses	the man	surely	no
إِنَّ	ٱسْتَغْنَىٰٓ ﴿٧﴾	رَّءَاهُ	أَن
surely	self-sufficient	looks upon himself	that
أَرَءَيْتَ	ٱلرُّجْعَىٰٓ ﴿٨﴾	رَبِّكَ	إِلَىٰ
have you seen	the return	your Rabb	to

إِذَا	عَبۡدًا	يَنۡهَىٰ ٩	ٱلَّذِى
when	a servant	forbids	who
كَانَ	إِن	أَرَءَيۡتَ	صَلَّىٰٓ ١٠
is	if	do you see	performs salāt
أَمَرَ	أَوۡ	ٱلۡهُدَىٰٓ ١١	عَلَى
enjoins	or	guidance	upon
كَذَّبَ	إِن	أَرَءَيۡتَ	بِٱلتَّقۡوَىٰٓ ١٢
rejects	if	do you see	reverence
بِأَنَّ	يَعۡلَم	أَلَمۡ	وَتَوَلَّىٰٓ ١٣
that	know	does he not	and turns back
لَئِن	كَلَّا	يَرَىٰ ١٤	ٱللَّهَ
if	no	sees	Allāh
بِٱلنَّاصِيَةِ ١٥	لَنَسۡفَعَۢا	يَنتَهِ	لَّمۡ
by the forelock	surely drag him	desist	not
فَلۡيَدۡعُ	خَاطِئَةٖ ١٦	كَٰذِبَةٍ	نَاصِيَةٖ
let him call	sinful	lying	a forelock
كَلَّا	ٱلزَّبَانِيَةَ ١٨	سَنَدۡعُ	نَادِيَهُۥ ١٧
no	the guards	We shall summon	his council
وَٱقۡتَرِب ۩ ١٩	وَٱسۡجُدۡ	تُطِعۡهُ	لَا
and draw near	and perform SAJDAH	obey him	do not

A few applications of the message:

This sūrah reminds us about Allāh's blessings. He created us and gave us knowledge. We should not become proud and think that are we do not need Him. If we think we do not heed Allāh, we are ungrateful to Him. We should remember that Allāh is the source of everything we have. Our health, wealth, power, talent, and technology—are all gifts from Allāh. We should realize Allāh's gifts in our lives and be thankful to Him. One way of saying thanks is by making a humble *sajdah* in our prayer. We come closer to Allāh by following His teachings.

Some people may make fun of or stop others from worshipping Allāh. They may think that they are powerful, but they are not. Allāh can easily ruin their status and bring big insults to them.

Questions:

1. Where were the first five verses of Sūrah *al-'Alaq* revealed?
2. Why do you think the first verse says "read" instead of "tell," "listen" or " have you seen"?
3. Sūrah *al-'Alaq* says that human being is rebellious for a reason. What is the reason?
4. If the sinner does not stop from his evil acts, Allāh will catch him in a certain way. How will he be caught, as mentioned in Sūrah *al-'Alaq*?
5. In Sūrah *al-'Alaq* a person is said to have prevented Prophet Muhammad (S) from performing prayer in the Ka'bah. Who was that person?
6. What do you understand by the word forelock? Explain what is meant if a person is dragged by the forelock.

Sūrah 95

Revealed in Makkah

At-Tīn

The Fig

Introduction:

This sūrah connects the teachings of Islam with Judaism and Christianity by using the symbols of the fig and the olive. Allah blessed the people with Divine messages, as human are the best of creations. Yet, many people ignore the messages and become the lowest of the low. This sūrah reminds us of the rewards of good deeds, and the punishment for bad deeds.

بِسْمِ ٱللَّهِ ٱلرَّحْمَٰنِ ٱلرَّحِيمِ

Bismi-llāhi-r raḥmāni-r raḥīm

In the name of Allah, the Most-Kind, the Most-Rewarding.

وَٱلتِّينِ وَٱلزَّيْتُونِ ﴿١﴾	Wa-ttīni waz zaytūn,	1. By the fig, and the olive;
وَطُورِ سِينِينَ ﴿٢﴾	wa ṭūri sīnīn,	2. and Mount Sinai,
وَهَٰذَا ٱلْبَلَدِ ٱلْأَمِينِ ﴿٣﴾	wa hādha-l baladi-l amīn,	3. and this Secure City!
لَقَدْ خَلَقْنَا ٱلْإِنسَٰنَ فِىٓ أَحْسَنِ تَقْوِيمٍ ﴿٤﴾	la-qad khalaqna-l insāna fī aḥsani taqwīm;	4. Certainly We have created Man in the finest form.
ثُمَّ رَدَدْنَٰهُ أَسْفَلَ سَٰفِلِينَ ﴿٥﴾	thumma radadnāhu asfala sāfilīn,	5. Then We revert him to the lowest of the low,
إِلَّا ٱلَّذِينَ ءَامَنُوا۟ وَعَمِلُوا۟ ٱلصَّٰلِحَٰتِ فَلَهُمْ أَجْرٌ غَيْرُ مَمْنُونٍ ﴿٦﴾	illa-l ladhīna āmanū wa 'amilu-ṣ ṣāliḥāti fa-lahum ajrun ghayru mamnūn.	6. except those who believe and do good; for them is then a reward without interruption.

فَمَا يُكَذِّبُكَ بَعْدُ بِالدِّينِ ﴿٧﴾	Fa-mā yukadhdhibuka ba'du bid dīn.	7. What then causes you afterwards to deny the Judgment?
أَلَيْسَ اللَّهُ بِأَحْكَمِ الْحَاكِمِينَ ﴿٨﴾	A-laysa-llāhu bi-aḥkami-l ḥākimīn.	8. Is not Allāh the Wisest of the judges?

Explanation:

1. The sūrah begins with a reminder of fig and olive trees or fruits. This reminder connects the teachings of Islam with Judaism and Christianity. The original teachings of all these religions support the idea that whoever believes and does good deeds will receive a reward without any interruption.

   Fig and olive trees are native to the Mediterranean and Middle Eastern countries and their fruits have been a major food for the people living in the area for thousands of years. Both trees symbolize the continuation of the teachings preached by many past prophets. For example, the fig is used to designate the teachings of Ibrāhīm (A). The teachings continued through his son Ishāq (A), and later through other Jewish prophets.

2. The sūrah also reminds us about Mount Sinai. This mountain symbolizes the teachings of Mūsā (A) since he devoted much of time in and around the region.

3. The secured city (*balad al-amīn*) refers to Makkah. The city became known from the time of Ibrāhīm (A) when he established one of his sons in this land and later rebuilt the Ka'bah. The reference of Makkah along with Mount Sinai and the fig provides a link with the fundamental teachings of all religions originated in the region.

4. Allāh has created mankind in the finest form—by giving them the perfect shape, intelligent brain and skillful fingers. As a result of which, mankind was elevated to a level higher than that of the angels.

5. In spite of mankind having such a high position, they, from time to time, engage in corrupt actions. For such actions, Allāh makes them suffer the consequences. They go down to the status of the lowest of the low.

6. Not every human being goes down to the lowest position. The exceptions are people who believe and do good deeds. For such people Allāh sends endless rewards in this life and in the Hereafter.

7-8. In every period in time, people who believed and did good deeds received Allāh's reward. Others went down to the lowest of the low levels. This is Allāh's judgment. It happens on this earth and it will happen in the Hereafter. After witnessing the examples of the past, how can we, human beings, deny the Day of Judgment? We know Allāh is the Best Judge of every action of human beings and will pay us according to the merits of our actions. So, why do men not take up the right path as shown by Islam?

Words to know

Ahsan: best, finest. *Hasanāt*: good deeds. *Muhsin*: Well-doer. *Ihsān*: kindness.
'Āmanū: they believed. *Imān*: faith, belief. *Mū'min*: believer.
Al-hākimīn: the judges. *Hukmun*: judgment, wisdom. *Hakīm*: Wise, full of wisdom. *Muhkamāt*: definite, without any doubt, unambiguous.

Sūrah At-Tīn
Word-by-word meaning

بِسۡمِ In the name of	ٱللَّهِ Allāh	ٱلرَّحۡمَٰنِ the Most-Kind	ٱلرَّحِيمِ the Most-Rewarding
وَٱلتِّينِ And the fig	وَٱلزَّيۡتُونِ ﴿١﴾ and the olive.	وَطُورِ and Mount	سِينِينَ ﴿٢﴾ Sinai.
وَهَٰذَا and this	ٱلۡبَلَدِ the city	ٱلۡأَمِينِ ﴿٣﴾ the secure	لَقَدۡ Certainly
خَلَقۡنَا We created	ٱلۡإِنسَٰنَ the man	فِيٓ in	أَحۡسَنِ finest
تَقۡوِيمٖ ﴿٤﴾ form	ثُمَّ Then	رَدَدۡنَٰهُ We revert him	أَسۡفَلَ lowest
سَٰفِلِينَ ﴿٥﴾ of the low	إِلَّا except	ٱلَّذِينَ those	ءَامَنُواْ believe
وَعَمِلُواْ and do	ٱلصَّٰلِحَٰتِ good deeds	فَلَهُمۡ for them	أَجۡرٌ reward
غَيۡرُ without	مَمۡنُونٖ ﴿٦﴾ interruption	فَمَا what then	يُكَذِّبُكَ causes you to deny
بَعۡدُ afterwards	بِٱلدِّينِ ﴿٧﴾ Judgment	أَلَيۡسَ Is not	ٱللَّهُ Allāh

بِأَحْكَمِ	ٱلْحَٰكِمِينَ ﴿٨﴾
Wisest	of the judges

A few applications of the message:

We, human beings, are the best of the creation. Allāh made us in the finest form. But now and then we let ourselves come down from our high rank. Many people do not believe and do not do good deeds. Some people only believe but they do not do any good deeds, some people do many good deeds but do not believe. In order to get Allāh's endless reward, we must believe *and* do good deeds. If we fail to do both, we cannot expect to get the reward. This is Allāh's judgment.

Questions:

1. Explain the significance of the fig and the olive in the beginning of Sūrah *at-Tīn*.
2. What are some of the measures that made human beings superior over all other creations?
3. What makes the status of some people become lower than others?
4. The status of some people does not go lower because they do something. Why doesn't it go lower?
5. What do the believers who do good deeds receive from Allāh? Write your answer based on Sūrah *at-Tīn*.

Sūrah 94

Revealed in Makkah

Al-Inshirāh

The Expansion

Introduction:

This sūrah was revealed to encourage the Prophet (S) when he was going through a tough time in Makkah. The sūrah reminded the Prophet (S) of Allāh's favor upon him at various times. It assured him that although he was facing many challenges, his difficulties would soon be over. The future would be easier for him. He should, therefore, continue his duties as usual.

بِسۡمِ ٱللَّهِ ٱلرَّحۡمَٰنِ ٱلرَّحِيمِ

Bismi-llāhi-r raḥmāni-r raḥīm
In the name of Allah, the Most-Kind, the Most-Rewarding.

أَلَمۡ نَشۡرَحۡ لَكَ صَدۡرَكَ ﴿١﴾	A-lam nashraḥ laka ṣadrak,	1. Have We not expanded for you your heart,
وَوَضَعۡنَا عَنكَ وِزۡرَكَ ﴿٢﴾	wa waḍaʻnā ʻanka wizrak,—	2. and We have removed from you your burden,
ٱلَّذِىٓ أَنقَضَ ظَهۡرَكَ ﴿٣﴾	'Alladẖī anqaḍa zahrak,	3. which weighed down your back,
وَرَفَعۡنَا لَكَ ذِكۡرَكَ ﴿٤﴾	wa rafaʻnā laka dẖikrak.	4. and We have elevated for you your mention?
فَإِنَّ مَعَ ٱلۡعُسۡرِ يُسۡرًا ﴿٥﴾	Fa-inna maʻal ʻusri yusrā.	5. Then truly with hardship there is ease;
إِنَّ مَعَ ٱلۡعُسۡرِ يُسۡرًا ﴿٦﴾	Inna maʻal ʻusri yusrā.	6. surely with hardship there will be ease.

فَإِذَا فَرَغْتَ فَٱنصَبْ ۝٧	Fa idhā faraghta fa-nṣab,	7. So when you are free, then work hard,
وَإِلَىٰ رَبِّكَ فَٱرْغَب ۝٨	wa ilā rabbika fa-rghab.	8. and towards your Rabb attend then whole-heartedly.

Explanation:

1. A person's heart is symbolically the seat of knowledge. The verse reminds the Prophet (S) that Allāh has expanded and illuminated his heart so that he can receive Divine revelation. The meaning of expanding the heart *(sharaha)* indicates the heart becomes worthy of receiving truth from God. Narrowness and rigid thinking is removed so that a person can see the truth. In verse 20:25 Mūsā (A) prayed to Allāh to expand his heart. In 6:125 Allāh expands (*sharaha*) the hearts of all believers who wish to be guided. In all these examples, expansion of heart means making it suitable and worthy to receive guidance.

2-3. It was an enormous job for a person to carry the responsibility of communicating the Divine message. Almost everyone in Makkah was opposed to the truth. During the early part of his prophethood, Prophet Muhammad (S) used to worry about the success of his mission. The duty of receiving and communicating the Divine message appeared a heavy burden. Yet the Prophet (S) continued to achieve success and make inroads into the hearts of the people. Allāh eased the burden for him.

4. The sūrah was revealed during the early Makkan period when the name and fame of Prophet Muhammad (S) was not yet established. Yet, the verse makes a prophecy that the mention of his name and deeds would be recognized with dignity and honor by future generations. Even at the time of all the opposition in Makkah, the enemies still recognized him as *al-Amin,* or truthful.

5-6. The repetition of verse gives extra emphasis. Whenever people face difficulties or hardships, Allāh always provides relief and solution. Such relief, or ease, comes along with the difficulty, not always after the difficulty. In the example of the Prophet (S), along with the difficulties, he continued to feel ease and relief in the way the problems continued to be resolved.

7-8. When the Prophet (S) was free from anxiety, he was advised to continue his efforts to spread Islam. These two verses teach us how we should properly use our time. Whatever may be our current circumstance, we should never feel unhappy or unsatisfied. Our effort should always be to bring about changes in our personal and social circles. To turn our attention to our Rabb or to strive to please Him means to engage in the remembrance of Allāh. Such remembrance can be done through the performance of salāt, and acceptance of His teachings in our daily lives.

Words to know

Nashrah: We expand. *Sharahah*: expand, spread. *Ishrih*: Enlighten.
Wizra: burden. *Wazara*: to carry a burden. *Wazīr*: one who carries the burden (usually of a country, minister).
Dhikra: mention. reminder. *Dhakara*: to remember. *Mudhakkir*: person who reminds, admonisher.
'*Usra*: hardship. *'Asura*: to be difficult.
Yusra: Ease, relief. *Yasara*: to become gentle, easy. *Yasīran*: simple, easy, light.

Sūrah Al-Inshirah
Word-by-word meaning

ٱلرَّحِيمِ the Most-Rewarding	ٱلرَّحۡمَـٰنِ the Most-Kind	ٱللَّهِ Allāh	بِسۡمِ In the name of
صَدۡرَكَ ١ your heart	لَكَ for you	نَشۡرَحۡ expanded	أَلَمۡ Did We not
ٱلَّذِىٓ which	وِزۡرَكَ ٢ your burden	عَنكَ from you	وَوَضَعۡنَا and we removed
لَكَ for you	وَرَفَعۡنَا and elevated	ظَهۡرَكَ ٣ your back	أَنقَضَ weighed down
ٱلۡعُسۡرِ hardship	مَعَ with	فَإِنَّ the truly	ذِكۡرَكَ ٤ your mention
ٱلۡعُسۡرِ hardship	مَعَ with	إِنَّ surely	يُسۡرًا ٥ ease
فَٱنصَبۡ ٧ then work hard	فَرَغۡتَ you are free	فَإِذَا so when	يُسۡرًا ٦ ease
	فَٱرۡغَب ٨ attend fully	رَبِّكَ your Rabb	وَإِلَىٰ and towards

A few applications of the message:

In our lives we will often face difficulties, challenges or hardships. This sūrah reminds us that even our dear Prophet (S) suffered hardships in his life. The sūrah reminds us of a noble principle of Allāh. The principle is "with hardship there is ease." We should remember that ease, or relief, does not necessarily come only after hardship—it comes along with hardship. In English writing, it is often mentioned that there is a light at the end of the tunnel. This sūrah teaches us that there is light while we are already inside the tunnel. As Muslims we should never feel hopeless during any type of hardship; rather we should turn to Allāh and seek His help and mercy.

The sūrah also reminds us that our difficulties will not last forever. They will end. At that time we should not feel relaxed and do nothing. Whenever we feel that the hardship is over, we should continue to work. We should always do work that pleases Allāh.

Questions:

1. In Sūrah *al-Inshirāh*, Allāh reminded the Prophet (S) about three special blessings that were given to him. What were the three blessings?
2. Sūrah *al-Inshirāh* mentions a special principle that applies to everyone who is having difficulty. What is that special principle?
3. In Sūrah *al-Inshirāh* what did Allāh ask the Prophet (S) to do after his anxiety was over?
4. As a Muslim, when you have free time or when you are not busy with other things, what should you be doing?

Sūrah 93

Revealed in Makkah

Ad-Duhā

The Forenoon

Introduction:

This sūrah was revealed after a long break in receiving revelations. Our Prophet (S) became worried at the long gap thinking Allāh became unhappy with him. The Makkan idol worshippers took this opportunity to laugh at and taunt him. At that time, Allāh sent this sūrah to console him and remind him of His favors. Allāh told him that He had not forsaken him. The sūrah asks the Prophet (S) to help the needy and orphans.

بِسْمِ ٱللَّهِ ٱلرَّحْمَـٰنِ ٱلرَّحِيمِ

Bismi-llāhi-r raḥmāni-r raḥīm

In the name of Allah, the Most-Kind, the Most-Rewarding.

وَٱلضُّحَىٰ ﴿١﴾	waḍ ḍuḥā,	1. By the Forenoon Brightness;
وَٱلَّيْلِ إِذَا سَجَىٰ ﴿٢﴾	wal layli idhā sajā,	2. and the Night when it darkens.
مَا وَدَّعَكَ رَبُّكَ وَمَا قَلَىٰ ﴿٣﴾	mā wadda'aka rabbuka wa mā qalā.	3. Your Rabb has not forsaken you, nor is He displeased.
وَلَلْأَخِرَةُ خَيْرٌ لَّكَ مِنَ ٱلْأُولَىٰ ﴿٤﴾	Wa lal ākhiratu khayruḷ laka mina-l ūlā.	4. And surely the Latter will be better for you than the Former;
وَلَسَوْفَ يُعْطِيكَ رَبُّكَ فَتَرْضَىٰٓ ﴿٥﴾	Wa la-sawfa y'ṭīka rabbuka fa-tarḍā.	5. and in time your Rabb will give you that you will be fully satisfied.
أَلَمْ يَجِدْكَ يَتِيمًا فَـَٔاوَىٰ ﴿٦﴾	A-lam yajidka yatīmaṅ fa-āwā,	6. Did He not find you an orphan, so He gave you shelter?

وَوَجَدَكَ ضَآلًّا فَهَدَىٰ ﴿٧﴾	wa wajadaka ḍāllaṅ fa-hadā,	7. And He found you unaware, so He guided;
وَوَجَدَكَ عَآئِلًا فَأَغْنَىٰ ﴿٨﴾	wa wajadaka 'ā'ilaṅ fa-aghnā.	8. and He found you in need, so He enriched?
فَأَمَّا ٱلْيَتِيمَ فَلَا تَقْهَرْ ﴿٩﴾	Fa-amma-l yatīma fa-lā taqhar.	9. So as to the orphan,—do not then oppress.
وَأَمَّا ٱلسَّآئِلَ فَلَا تَنْهَرْ ﴿١٠﴾	Wa amma-s sāi'la fa-lā tanhar.	10. And as to the seeker, do not then drive away.
وَأَمَّا بِنِعْمَةِ رَبِّكَ فَحَدِّثْ ﴿١١﴾	Wa ammā bi-ni'mati rabbika fa-ḥaddith.	11. And as to the blessing of your Rabb, then go on declaring.

Explanation:

1-2. The sūrah begins with a Divine oath in the name of the forenoon *(ad-duha)* and night *(layl)*. Both forenoon and night are symbols of Allāh's infinite power. The forenoon also symbolizes Allāh's mercy and help, which always appear after the darkness of night that symbolizes hardship. Difficult periods may seem long, but are never permanent.

3. A long time had passed when no new revelation was sent to the Prophet (S). This made the Prophet (S) wondering if he did something wrong, or was Allāh unhappy with him. The Makkan idol worshippers began taunting the Prophet (S) by saying that Allāh had forsaken him and became angry with him. After a long break, this sūrah was revealed to assure the Prophet (S) that Allāh was not displeased with him and did not abandoned him.

4-5. Although the Prophet (S) was facing difficulties at the time, these verses assured him that the future would be better. The life of the Prophet (S) in Makkah and Madīnah proved that this promise was fulfilled. The Prophet's (S) mission continued to gain ground and momentum. The verses are not only about life in this world, but also about when the promise will fulfill in the Hereafter.

6-8. These verses remind the Prophet (S) that compared to his childhood and earlier life, the present was indeed much better. Before his birth, his father had passed away. His mother passed away when he was six years old. His grandfather, who then became his guardian, also passed away within two years. Later, when he married Khadījah, she supported him financially. During the pre-Islamic period, Prophet Muhammad (S) used to feel disturbed at the spiritual and social conditions of the people. These people used to do many bad things and worship idols that did not benefit them. He wanted to find a solution for them. He used to often go to a cave to meditate about how these people could be benefited. This is referred to as wandering in darkness until Allāh guided him through revelation.

9-10. Allāh instructed Rasulullah (S) to be kind to orphans. Because he, himself, was an orphan, he understood their feelings and suffering. His kind treatment of orphans and others caused many helpless people to come to him for help. A *sā'il* is a person who seeks help. He could be a beggar seeking help for food, an ignorant person seeking knowledge, or a harassed person seeking comfort and support. The rich Makkan people used to drive these people away. Allāh asked the Prophet (S) not to drive them away but to treat them well.

11. Blessings of Allāh are endless. We can never name all our blessings. In this sūrah, only a few blessings upon the Prophet (S) are mentioned to give us examples. The greatest blessing in the life of the Prophet (S) was Divine revelation. The Prophet (S) was asked to go on preaching the blessings throughout his life. We can proclaim the same blessings by first adopting the Divine teachings in our lives and then sharing the teachings with others.

Words to know

Da'aka: forsaken you, pushed you away. *Yadu'u*: he drives away (107:2)
Wajada: to find what was lost. *Wajad*: found. *Tajidū:* you will find.
Yatīman: : orphan. *Yatīmain*: two orphans. *Yatāmā*: orphans.
Lā Taqhar: do not oppress. *Qahara*: to oppress. *Qāhir*: supreme. *Al-Qāhir*: The Supreme, one of the most Excellent names of Allāh.
Lā Tanhar: do not drive away, do not chide, do not repel. *Nahara*: make a stream to flow. *Nahrun*: river. *Anhār*: rivers, streams.

Sūrah Ad-Duhā
Word-by-word meaning

ٱلرَّحِيمِ	ٱلرَّحۡمَٰنِ	ٱللَّهِ	بِسۡمِ
the Most-Rewarding	the Most-Kind	Allāh	In the name of
سَجَىٰ ٢	إِذَا	وَٱلَّيۡلِ	وَٱلضُّحَىٰ ١
it darkens	when	and the night	By the Forenoon Brightness
وَمَا	رَبُّكَ	وَدَّعَكَ	مَا
and not	your Rabb	forsaken you	not
لَّكَ	خَيۡرٞ	وَلَلۡأٓخِرَةُ	قَلَىٰ ٣
for you	better	and surely the Latter	displeased
يُعۡطِيكَ	وَلَسَوۡفَ	ٱلۡأُولَىٰ ٤	مِنَ
will give you	and in time	the Former	than

يَجِدْكَ	أَلَمْ	فَتَرْضَىٰ ٥	رَبُّكَ
find you	did He not	you be satisfied	your Rabb
ضَآلًّا	وَوَجَدَكَ	فَـَٔاوَىٰ ٦	يَتِيمًا
unaware	and found you	gave you shelter	an orphan
فَأَغْنَىٰ ٨	عَآئِلًا	وَوَجَدَكَ	فَهَدَىٰ ٧
enriched you.	in need	and found you	guided you
تَقْهَرْ ٩	فَلَا	ٱلْيَتِيمَ	فَأَمَّا
oppress	do not	the orphan	so as to
تَنْهَرْ ١٠	فَلَا	ٱلسَّآئِلَ	وَأَمَّا
drive away	do not	the seeker	and as to
فَحَدِّثْ ١١	رَبِّكَ	بِنِعْمَةِ	وَأَمَّا
declare, report.	your Rabb	blessings	and as to

A few applications of the message:

We often want things that we don't have and forget that we already have so many things that others do not. If we look at ourselves we can find many blessings of Allāh in our lives. No person can say Allāh has not blessed him or her. Allāh also promises us that our future will be better than our past. He will give us more than what we have. However, if we are ungrateful and not religious, we will never realize the blessings. We will forever remain dissatisfied and restless.

The examples of the Prophet's (S) past prove that the future is always better than the past. We should trust Allāh, follow His guidance and do good deeds. Allāh's promise will be fulfilled in our lives.

Questions:

1. Why did the Prophet (S) think that Allāh had forsaken him?
2. Sūrah *Ad-Duhā* states that something would be better. What would be better? Better from what?
3. What three things are mentioned in Sūrah *Ad-Duhā* that Allāh had given the Prophet (S) when he was a child or a young man?
4. In Sūrah *Ad-Duhā,* which two things were the Prophet (S) asked not to do?

Sūrah 92

Revealed in Makkah

Al-Lail

The Night

Introduction:

Similar to sūrahs 89 and 93, thus sūrah also employs day and night to symbolize Allāh's infinite Power. The sūrah then speaks about the actions of a person and the results. Some people may follow the truth, while others may follow falsehood. Those who follow falsehood will be punished in a flaming Fire. Whereas, those who are righteous will be rewarded.

بِسۡمِ ٱللَّهِ ٱلرَّحۡمَٰنِ ٱلرَّحِيمِ

Bismi-llāhi-r raḥmāni-r raḥīm
In the name of Allah, the Most-Kind, the Most-Rewarding.

وَٱلَّيۡلِ إِذَا يَغۡشَىٰ ١	Wal layli idẖā yaghshā,	1. By the Night when it draws a covering,
وَٱلنَّهَارِ إِذَا تَجَلَّىٰ ٢	wan nahāri idẖā tajallā,	2. and the day when it shines in brilliance;
وَمَا خَلَقَ ٱلذَّكَرَ وَٱلۡأُنثَىٰٓ ٣	wa mā khalaqa-dẖ dẖakara wal untẖā,	3. and what He created—the male and the female!
إِنَّ سَعۡيَكُمۡ لَشَتَّىٰ ٤	inna sa'yakum lashattā.	4. surely your effort is diverse.
فَأَمَّا مَنۡ أَعۡطَىٰ وَٱتَّقَىٰ ٥	Fa-ammā man a'ṭā wa-t taqā,	5. Then as to him who gives and practices reverence,
وَصَدَّقَ بِٱلۡحُسۡنَىٰ ٦	wa ṣaddaqa bil ḥusnā,	6. and testifies to what is the best,
فَسَنُيَسِّرُهُۥ لِلۡيُسۡرَىٰ ٧	fa-sa-nuyassiruhū lil yusrā.	7. so We shall soon ease for him every ease.

وَأَمَّا مَنۢ بَخِلَ وَٱسۡتَغۡنَىٰ ﴿٨﴾	Wa ammā maṅ bakhila was taghnā,	8. And as for him who acts miserly, and considers himself self-sufficient,
وَكَذَّبَ بِٱلۡحُسۡنَىٰ ﴿٩﴾	wa kadh̲dh̲aba bil ḥusnā,	9. and denies the best,
فَسَنُيَسِّرُهُۥ لِلۡعُسۡرَىٰ ﴿١٠﴾	fa-sa-nuyassiruhū lil ‘usrā.	10. We shall then soon ease him to hardship.
وَمَا يُغۡنِي عَنۡهُ مَالُهُۥٓ إِذَا تَرَدَّىٰٓ ﴿١١﴾	Wa mā yughnī ‘anhu māluhū idh̲ā taraddā.	11. And his wealth will not avail him anything when he is thrown.
إِنَّ عَلَيۡنَا لَلۡهُدَىٰ ﴿١٢﴾	Inna ‘alaynā lal hudā,	12. Surely it is upon Us to show the guidance;
وَإِنَّ لَنَا لَلۡأٓخِرَةَ وَٱلۡأُولَىٰ ﴿١٣﴾	wa inna lanā lal ākhirata wal ūlā.	13. and surely unto Us belong the Hereafter and the Former.
فَأَنذَرۡتُكُمۡ نَارٗا تَلَظَّىٰ ﴿١٤﴾	Fa andh̲artukum naraṅ talazzā;	14. Therefore I have warned you of a flaming Fire.
لَا يَصۡلَىٰهَآ إِلَّا ٱلۡأَشۡقَى ﴿١٥﴾	lā yaṣlāhā illa-l ashqā,—	15. No one will roast in it except the most wretched,
ٱلَّذِي كَذَّبَ وَتَوَلَّىٰ ﴿١٦﴾	Alladh̲ī kadh̲dh̲aba wa tawalla.	16. who denies and turns away.
وَسَيُجَنَّبُهَا ٱلۡأَتۡقَى ﴿١٧﴾	Wa sa-yujannabuha-l atqa,—	17. And the most reverent will be kept far away from it,—
ٱلَّذِي يُؤۡتِي مَالَهُۥ يَتَزَكَّىٰ ﴿١٨﴾	Alladh̲ī yu’tī mālahū yatajhakkā,	18. who gives his wealth purifying himself,
وَمَا لِأَحَدٍ عِندَهُۥ مِن نِّعۡمَةٖ تُجۡزَىٰٓ ﴿١٩﴾	wa mā li-aḥadiṅ ‘indahū min ni‘matiṅ tujjhā,	19. and no one has with him any favor that has to be rewarded,—
إِلَّا ٱبۡتِغَآءَ وَجۡهِ رَبِّهِ ٱلۡأَعۡلَىٰ ﴿٢٠﴾	illa-btighā’a waj-hi rabbihi-l a‘lā;	20. except the seeking of the pleasure of his Rabb, the Most High.
وَلَسَوۡفَ يَرۡضَىٰ ﴿٢١﴾	wa la-sawfa yarḍa.	21. And soon he will be well-satisfied.

Explanation:

1-2. The cycle of day and night automatically affects our lives. Allāh's infinite power controls these natural events. We can appreciate Allāh's absolute Power if we think about the many things in nature, such as day and night.

3. While day and night are inanimate—they are not living or moving—Allah also created all the living creatures. For each type of creature, He also created males and females so that they can give birth and continue their species. The creation of male and female also shows Allāh's absolute Power.

4. In addition to giving life, Allāh also gave Man a mind to think and the liberty to act on his own desires. Human nature aims for different objectives in life. Some people follow the path of righteousness and some follow the wrong path. Their ultimate result will be based on which path they follow.

5-7. Some people give generously, fear Allāh, do their duty and support what is best. As a result, Allāh makes everything easy for them. Their lives in this world are satisfying, successful and peaceful. Their lives in the Hereafter will be even more satisfying, successful and peaceful.

8-11. Some people are stingy *(bakhil)*; they think they are rich *(ghani)*, self-sufficient and independent of Allāh's help. They do not care for the good deeds. As an end result, Allāh will make their lives difficult (*'usrah*, difficulty, distress) in this world and in the Hereafter. On this earth, their wealth and property will not give them comfort, peace of mind or benefit. In the Hereafter, their wealth will be of no help at all, and they will be punished.

12-13. Allāh provides clear guidance towards the Right Path. Allāh also warned as to which path would lead people to their destruction. The warning is a type of guidance—since it helps people realize the mistake and turn them to the Right Path. Ultimately, everything belongs to Allāh. He is the Master of the Hereafter and the former life—i.e. the present life.

14-16. Allāh warns people about a flaming Fire that awaits the most wretched or horrible people. The wretched people is the one who denies the truth and also turns away from it. In other words, he does not respond to Allāh's message. He, instead, turns away from it.

17-18. This set of verses speaks of the righteous people. A righteous person is one who gives his wealth for the cause of Allāh. Such giving purifies him from evils.

19-21. No one has the right to get any favor from Allāh except the righteous people. The righteous people seek the approval of Allāh. The best reward is Allāh's pleasure, as it will take a person to Heaven. A person who gets such a reward will experience peace, pleasure and satisfaction from every corner.

Words to know

Al-Akhirat: Hereafter, next life. *Akhara*: to put back. *Ākhiru*: last, final. *Mustākhirīna*: who are left behind.

Ūlā: former. *Awwal:* first. *Āla:* to return, to be back. *Awwalūn*: of the former days, of ancient days.

Yaslā: he will enter a fire, will roast. *Salā*: to warm at a fire, endure the heat, roast. *Yaslauna*: they shall burn.

Sūrah Al-Lail
Word-by-word meaning

ٱلرَّحِيمِ the Most-Rewarding	ٱلرَّحْمَٰنِ the Most-Kind	ٱللَّهِ Allāh	بِسْمِ In the name of
وَٱلنَّهَارِ and the day	يَغْشَىٰ ١ draws a covering	إِذَا when	وَٱلَّيْلِ By the night
خَلَقَ created	وَمَا and what	تَجَلَّىٰ ٢ shines in brilliance	إِذَا when
سَعْيَكُمْ your effort	إِنَّ surely	وَٱلْأُنثَىٰٓ ٣ and the female	ٱلذَّكَرَ the male
أَعْطَىٰ gives	مَنْ who	فَأَمَّا then as to	لَشَتَّىٰ ٤ diverse
فَسَنُيَسِّرُهُۥ We will ease him	بِٱلْحُسْنَىٰ ٦ what is the best	وَصَدَّقَ and testifies	وَٱتَّقَىٰ ٥ and reveres
بَخِلَ acts miserly	مَنۢ who	وَأَمَّا And as to	لِلْيُسْرَىٰ ٧ to ease
فَسَنُيَسِّرُهُۥ We will ease him	بِٱلْحُسْنَىٰ ٩ what is the best	وَكَذَّبَ and denies	وَٱسْتَغْنَىٰ ٨ and considers himself self-sufficient
عَنْهُ him	يُغْنِى avail	وَمَا and not	لِلْعُسْرَىٰ ١٠ to hardship

مَالُهُۥ his wealth	إِذَا when	تَرَدَّىٰٓ ﴿١١﴾ he is thrown	إِنَّ Surely
عَلَيْنَا upon Us	لَلْهُدَىٰ ﴿١٢﴾ to guide	وَإِنَّ and surely	لَنَا to Us
لَلْءَاخِرَةَ the Hereafter	وَٱلْأُولَىٰ ﴿١٣﴾ and the former	فَأَنذَرْتُكُمْ So I warned you	نَارًا fire
تَلَظَّىٰ ﴿١٤﴾ flaming	لَا no	يَصْلَىٰهَآ roast in it	إِلَّا except
ٱلْأَشْقَى ﴿١٥﴾ the most wretched	ٱلَّذِى who	كَذَّبَ denies	وَتَوَلَّىٰ ﴿١٦﴾ and turns away
وَسَيُجَنَّبُهَا and will be kept away	ٱلْأَتْقَى ﴿١٧﴾ the reverent	ٱلَّذِى who	يُؤْتِى gives
مَالَهُۥ his wealth	يَتَزَكَّىٰ ﴿١٨﴾ purifies	وَمَا and no	لِأَحَدٍ one
عِندَهُۥ to him	مِن any	نِّعْمَةٍ favor	تُجْزَىٰٓ ﴿١٩﴾ rewarded
إِلَّا except	ٱبْتِغَآءَ seeking	وَجْهِ pleasure	رَبِّهِ his Rabb
ٱلْأَعْلَىٰ ﴿٢٠﴾ the Most high	وَلَسَوْفَ and soon	يَرْضَىٰ ﴿٢١﴾ well-satisfied	

A few applications of the message:

This sūrah reminds us of the importance of doing good and the risks of doing bad. If we remember to spend in the cause of Allāh, remain dutiful to Him and believe in doing good, our every affair will become easy. This is the promise of Allāh, and His promise is always true. Giving wealth does not make us poor, but it increases even though we may not realize. Giving wealth also purifies our souls.

On the other hand, if we hoard money and never spend it in the cause of Allāh, we may feel content, but the money will not benefit us. Our lives will become miserable. This is also Allāh's promise. We see many people who have wealth but they are not happy. If we dig further, we may find that they never spend money on good causes, as such, Allāh made their lives miserable. They have more suffering in store in the Hereafter.

Questions:

1. In Sūrah *al-Lail* Allāh says He will make life easy for some people. What do these people need to do so that Allāh will make their lives easy?
2. In Sūrah *al-Lail* Allāh says He will make the lives of some people difficult. What three things do these people do that make their lives difficult?
3. In Sūrah *al-Lail* the character of the most wretched is given. What two things does he do?
4. In Sūrah *al-Lail* the nature of the righteous person is given. Mention two things that he does.
5. In Sūrah *al-Lail* what do the righteous people seek?

Revealed in Makkah

Sūrah 91 Ash-Shams

The Sun

Introduction:

This sūrah draws attention to six creations of Allāh. They are placed into three pairs of opposite functions. These are the sun and the moon, the night and the day, and the earth and the heavens. The sūrah then reminds us that human soul has opposite natures—it has the ability to choose between right and wrong. Those who choose the right course purify their souls, and those who choose the wrong path harm themselves. The example of the Thamūd shows that they chose the wrong course and perished with a severe punishment.

بِسۡمِ ٱللَّهِ ٱلرَّحۡمَٰنِ ٱلرَّحِيمِ

Bismi-llāhi-r raḥmāni-r raḥīm
In the name of Allah, the Most-Kind, the Most-Rewarding.

وَٱلشَّمۡسِ وَضُحَىٰهَا ١	Wash shamsi wa ḍuḥāhā,	1. By the Sun, and its advancing brightness,
وَٱلۡقَمَرِ إِذَا تَلَىٰهَا ٢	wal qamari idha̱ talāhā,	2. and the Moon when she follows it,
وَٱلنَّهَارِ إِذَا جَلَّىٰهَا ٣	wan nahāri idha̱ jallāhā,	3. and the Day when it reveals its brilliance,
وَٱلَّيۡلِ إِذَا يَغۡشَىٰهَا ٤	wal layli idha̱ yaghshāhā,	4. and the Night when it draws a covering on it.
وَٱلسَّمَآءِ وَمَا بَنَىٰهَا ٥	was samā'i wa mā banāhā,	5. And the sky and Who made it;
وَٱلۡأَرۡضِ وَمَا طَحَىٰهَا ٦	wal arḍi wa mā ṭaḥāhā,	6. and the earth and Who spread it out;
وَنَفۡسٍ وَمَا سَوَّىٰهَا ٧	wa nafsiw wa mā sawwāhā,	7. and the Soul and Who perfected it;

فَأَلْهَمَهَا فُجُورَهَا وَتَقْوَىٰهَا ٨	fa-alhamahā fujūrahā wa taqwāhā,	8. and He inspired into it its wickedness and its piety.
قَدْ أَفْلَحَ مَن زَكَّىٰهَا ٩	qad aflaḥa man jhakkāhā,	9. He indeed prospers who purifies it;
وَقَدْ خَابَ مَن دَسَّىٰهَا ١٠	wa qad khāba man dassāhā.	10. and he certainly fails who corrupts it.
كَذَّبَتْ ثَمُودُ بِطَغْوَىٰهَآ ١١	Kadh̲dh̲abat th̲amūdu bi-taghwāhā,	11. Thamud denied in their violation,
إِذِ ٱنۢبَعَثَ أَشْقَىٰهَا ١٢	idh̲i-ṅba'ath̲a ashqāhā,	12. when the most wicked of them rose up,
فَقَالَ لَهُمْ رَسُولُ ٱللَّهِ نَاقَةَ ٱللَّهِ وَسُقْيَٰهَا ١٣	fa-qāla lahum rasūlu-llāhi nāqata-llāhi wa suqyāhā.	13. then the rasul of Allāh told them: "A she-camel of Allāh, and let her drink."
فَكَذَّبُوهُ فَعَقَرُوهَا فَدَمْدَمَ عَلَيْهِمْ رَبُّهُم بِذَنۢبِهِمْ فَسَوَّىٰهَا ١٤	Fa-kadh̲dh̲abūhu fa-'aqarūhā, fa-damdama 'alayhim rabbuhum bi-dh̲aṅbihim fa-sawwāhā,	14. But they rejected him, and hamstrung her; so their Rabb crushed them because of their sin, and He leveled them.
وَلَا يَخَافُ عُقْبَٰهَا ١٥	wa lā yakhāfu 'uqbāhā.	15. And He did not fear of its consequences.

Explanation:

1-4. The four verses contrast four creations of Allāh—the sun and the moon, the day and the night. The bright sun makes everything visible on the earth, while the moon follows the sun—by borrowing light from the sun and by rotating on a path along with the earth. They are opposites, yet they are related to each other. Similarly, the day shows the glory of the sun, and the night draws a cover over the daylight. They have two different functions.

5-6. The two verses ask us to think about the universe and who created it. The verses are also asking us to think about the earth as to who created it and spread it out. Spreading or expanding the earth means Allāh made it suitable for living things to inhabit it and survive.

7-8. The verses remind us of our souls. Allāh created the soul and perfected and proportioned it over the course of time. During the process, Allāh gave human beings knowledge, intelligence and freedom to choose between right and wrong. The divine inspiration helped human beings understand the consequence of *fujur* (i.e. deviation from truth) and *taqwā* (i.e. reverence, loving and fearing Allāh at the same time).

9-10. Based on the Divine inspiration about the consequences of following a good or bad path, we will get our results. A person purifies his soul by practicing goodness and avoiding wickedness. Such a person indeed prospers in this life and in the Hereafter. A person corrupts his soul by adopting wickedness in life. Such a person fails in this life and in the Hereafter.

11-12. The example of the tribe of Thamūd is given here. Their example shows how an entire nation sometimes fails to follow the Divine teachings to purify the souls of each member. The tribe refused the truth and engaged in wicked activities. Their most wicked person came forward to oppose their prophet.

13. Sālih (A) was the prophet for the tribe of Thamūd. He brought an ownerless she-camel as a sign for the tribe. He asked them to let the she-camel graze and drink and not to harm her in any manner. The tribe refused to obey Sālih (A). Their activities corrupted their souls. They did not want to be inspired by Sālih (A).

14. The tribe hamstrung the she-camel. It means they cut the back side of the animal's ankle. When an animal is hamstrung, it cannot stand up or walk. The she-camel could not walk, find food or drink. She died from starvation. As a result of this cruel action, Allāh sent destruction upon the tribe of Thamūd. The tribe was crushed and destroyed as they and their dwellings were leveled to the ground.

15. The massive scale of destruction might appear terrifying or painful to think about. But Allāh did not care for the evil tribe. Such is Allāh's justice and punishment for wrongdoing.

Words to know

Jallaha: reveals its brilliance, shows its glory. *Jalla*: to be glorious. *Jalāl*: Majesty, Glory.
Sawwaha: perfected it. *Sawwa*: make perfect, make balanced, proportioned. *Sawāun*: similar, alike.
Aflaha: to be successful. *Falāh*: prosperity, success. *Muflihūna*: successful ones. *Hayya 'ala-l falāh*: hurry to success.
Zakkaha: purifies it. *Zakā*: purify, to grow, be pure and clean. *Zakāt*: purity, purifying alms, poor-due.
Kadhdhabat: He denied. *Kadhaba*: to lie. *Mukadhdhibun*: One who falsely denies, rejects.

Sūrah As-Shams
Word-by-word meaning

ٱلرَّحِيمِ	ٱلرَّحۡمَـٰنِ	ٱللَّهِ	بِسۡمِ
the Most-Rewarding	the Most-Kind	Allāh	In the name of
إِذَا	وَٱلۡقَمَرِ	وَضُحَىٰهَا ١	وَٱلشَّمۡسِ
when	and the moon	and its advancing brightness	By the sun

جَلَّىٰهَا ٣	إِذَا	وَٱلنَّهَارِ	تَلَىٰهَا ٢
reveals its brilliance	when	and the day	follows it
وَٱلسَّمَآءِ	يَغۡشَىٰهَا ٤	إِذَا	وَٱلَّيۡلِ
and the sky	draws a covering on it	when	and the night
وَمَا	وَٱلۡأَرۡضِ	بَنَىٰهَا ٥	وَمَا
and who	and the earth	made it	and who
سَوَّىٰهَا ٧	وَمَا	وَنَفۡسٖ	طَحَىٰهَا ٦
perfected it	and who	and the soul	spread it out
قَدۡ	وَتَقۡوَىٰهَا ٨	فُجُورَهَا	فَأَلۡهَمَهَا
indeed	its piety	its wickedness	inspired it
وَقَدۡ	زَكَّىٰهَا ٩	مَن	أَفۡلَحَ
and indeed	purifies it	who	prospers
كَذَّبَتۡ	دَسَّىٰهَا ١٠	مَن	خَابَ
denied	corrupts it	who	fails
ٱنۢبَعَثَ	إِذِ	بِطَغۡوَىٰهَآ ١١	ثَمُودُ
rose up	when	their violation	Thamud
رَسُولُ	لَهُمۡ	فَقَالَ	أَشۡقَىٰهَا ١٢
Rasul	to them	said	most wicked of them

وَسُقْيَٰهَا ١٣	ٱللَّهِ	نَاقَةَ	ٱللَّهِ
and let her drink	Allāh	she-camel	Allāh
عَلَيْهِمْ	فَدَمْدَمَ	فَعَقَرُوهَا	فَكَذَّبُوهُ
them	crushed	hamstrung her	rejected him
وَلَا	فَسَوَّىٰهَا ١٤	بِذَنۢبِهِمْ	رَبُّهُم
and not	He leveled it	for their sin	their Rabb
		عُقْبَٰهَا ١٥	تَخَافُ
		its consequence	fear

A few applications of the message:

The sūrah *ash-Shams* reminds us about entire tribe of Thamūd was destroyed for their refusal to follow the truth. Their destruction was terrifying and painful. When we think deeply about it we realize Allāh inspired every soul with the sense of right and wrong. The people of Thamūd followed the wrong course. Their punishment was based on the severity of their conduct.

We must learn a lesson from the fate of Thamūd. Even though they lived thousands of years ago, the message from their story is still valid. Our mind will constantly battle to choose between the right and the wrong. The sūrah teaches us those who want to purify their soul by doing the right deeds ultimately become successful. We should seek help from Allāh so that we get the courage to adopt the right course.

Questions:

1. What six creations of Allāh are mentioned in Sūrah *ash-Shams* in 3 pairs? Mention them in pairs.
2. With what two things did Allāh inspire our soul?
3. According to Sūrah *ash-Shams* what is the criteria for success?
4. Explain how the people of Thamūd hamstrung the she-camel?
5. Explain why Allāh sent severe punishment for the people of Thamūd.

Sūrah 90

Revealed in Makkah

Al-Balad

The Territory

Introduction:

The sūrah begins with an oath in the name of a territory or city. The city is Makkah. The sūrah then reminds us about various facts that are important in our lives. Everyone is created to bear difficulties in life. But no one can overcome the difficulty or achieve goal in life without hard work. We cannot do everything on our own unless Allāh helps us. The sūrah reminds us of two paths—the path of righteousness and the path of wrong. The path of righteousness is difficult but its reward is plentiful. The wrong path may have lots of fun on it, but it will lead to our destruction.

بِسۡمِ ٱللَّهِ ٱلرَّحۡمَـٰنِ ٱلرَّحِيمِ

Bismi-llāhi-r raḥmāni-r raḥīm

In the name of Allah, the Most-Kind, the Most-Rewarding.

لَآ أُقۡسِمُ بِهَـٰذَا ٱلۡبَلَدِ ١	Lā uqsimu bi hādha-l balad,	1. No! I swear by this Territory!—
وَأَنتَ حِلُّۢ بِهَـٰذَا ٱلۡبَلَدِ ٢	wa anta ḥillum bi-hādha-l balad,	2. and you have lawful rights in this Territory,
وَوَالِدٖ وَمَا وَلَدَ ٣	wa wālidiw wa mā walad,	3. and the begetter, and whom he has begotten.
لَقَدۡ خَلَقۡنَا ٱلۡإِنسَـٰنَ فِي كَبَدٍ ٤	la-qad khalaqna-l insāna fī kabad.	4. We have certainly created man into hardship.
أَيَحۡسَبُ أَن لَّن يَقۡدِرَ عَلَيۡهِ أَحَدٌ ٥	A-yaḥsabu an lan yaqdira 'alayhi aḥad.	5. Does he think that no one has power over him?

يَقُولُ أَهْلَكْتُ مَالًا لُّبَدًا ﴿٦﴾	Yaqūlu ahlaktu mālaḷ lubada.	6. He says: "I have spent heaps of wealth."
أَيَحْسَبُ أَن لَّمْ يَرَهُۥٓ أَحَدٌ ﴿٧﴾	A yaḥsabu aṅ lam yarahū aḥad.	7. Does he think that no one sees him?
أَلَمْ نَجْعَل لَّهُۥ عَيْنَيْنِ ﴿٨﴾	A-lam naj'al lahū 'aynayn,	8. Have We not made for him two eyes,
وَلِسَانًا وَشَفَتَيْنِ ﴿٩﴾	wa lisānaẇ wa shafatayn,	9. and a tongue and two lips,
وَهَدَيْنَٰهُ ٱلنَّجْدَيْنِ ﴿١٠﴾	wa hadaynāhu-n najdayn;	10. and pointed out to him the two highways?
فَلَا ٱقْتَحَمَ ٱلْعَقَبَةَ ﴿١١﴾	fa-la-qtaḥama-l 'aqabah,	11. But he does not rush ahead to the uphill road;
وَمَآ أَدْرَىٰكَ مَا ٱلْعَقَبَةُ ﴿١٢﴾	wa mā adrāka ma-l 'aqabah.	12. and what will make you know what the uphill road is?
فَكُّ رَقَبَةٍ ﴿١٣﴾	Fakku raqabah,	13. The freeing of a captive,
أَوْ إِطْعَٰمٌ فِى يَوْمٍ ذِى مَسْغَبَةٍ ﴿١٤﴾	aw iṭ'āmuṅ fī yawmiṅ dẖī masghabah,	14. or the feeding in the days of famine—
يَتِيمًا ذَا مَقْرَبَةٍ ﴿١٥﴾	yatīmaṅ dẖā maqrabah,	15. an orphan of near relation,
أَوْ مِسْكِينًا ذَا مَتْرَبَةٍ ﴿١٦﴾	aw miskīnaṅ dẖā maqrabah.	16. or the poor lying in dust.
ثُمَّ كَانَ مِنَ ٱلَّذِينَ ءَامَنُوا۟ وَتَوَاصَوْا۟ بِٱلصَّبْرِ وَتَوَاصَوْا۟ بِٱلْمَرْحَمَةِ ﴿١٧﴾	Tẖumma kāna mina-l ladẖīna āmanū wa tawāṣaw bi-ṣ ṣabri wa tawāṣaw bil marḥamah.	17. Then he is of those who believe, and enjoin one another to perseverance and enjoin one another to mercy.
أُو۟لَٰٓئِكَ أَصْحَٰبُ ٱلْمَيْمَنَةِ ﴿١٨﴾	Ulā'ika aṣḥābul maymanah.	18. These are the companions of the Right-hand.

وَٱلَّذِينَ كَفَرُواْ بِـَٔايَـٰتِنَا هُمْ أَصْحَـٰبُ ٱلْمَشْـَٔمَةِ ﴿١٩﴾	Wal ladhīna kafarū bi-āyātinā hum aṣḥābu-l mash'amah.	19. But as to those who disbelieve in Our Messages, they are the companions of the Left-hand.
عَلَيْهِمْ نَارٌ مُّؤْصَدَةٌۢ ﴿٢٠﴾	'Alayhim nārum mu'ṣadah.	20. On them will be a Fire vaulted over.

Explanation:

1. The sūrah derives its title from the mention of *balad* (*lit.* territory, place) in the first verse. The term *balad* signifies the city of Makkah, where the Prophet (S) was born and received his early revelations. By virtue of his birth in the land, the Prophet (S) had lawful rights to the land.

2. In the second verse, the pronoun "you" refers to Prophet Muhammad (S). Although in future he would migrate to Madīnah, he would have lawful rights in the city.

3. How is the Prophet's (S) right to the city established? In this verse the bond between parent and son and through them the bond with the land is established. The word "begetter" shows the link—with Ibrāhīm (A) who is the forefather of Arabs, and begotten is his son Ismā'īl (A) who settled in Makkah. Both Ibrāhīm and Ismā'īl (A) rebuilt the Ka'bah as the center of worshipping Allāh. With Prophet Muhammad (S) being the offspring of Ibrāhīm (A), how can he not have the lawful rights on the city of Makkah? The word "begetter" can also mean prophet Adam (A) and begotten are his children.

4. Whether it was Prophet Muhammad (S) or any other human being, everyone is created to bear difficulties in life. Everyone must strive hard to overcome the difficulties and achieve the objective in life. Facing difficulties in life is under the plan of Allāh.

5-7. Since human beings are made to suffer and overcome difficulties, sometimes they think they are self-sufficient and do not need the Creator—as if they can do everything on their own. We human beings earn wealth and spend it thinking we are in control of everything. We often think no one sees us, not even Allāh.

8-9. Because human beings are arrogant, they fail to realize that the Creator gave them the power to use their judgment. The two eyes stand for the faculties to see and sort out right from wrong. The tongue and lips stand for speaking out the right thing for him and urging others to follow the right path.

10. The two highways refer to paths of right and wrong—the two major paths—one leads human beings to Heaven and the other to destruction.

11-12. Out of the two paths mentioned in verse 10, the path of righteousness, is not always easy to follow. It may seem as difficult as climbing a hill. On the other hand, the wrong path is full of fun. Therefore, most human beings do not follow the right path.

13-16. Similar to climbing an uphill road, walking on the Right path needs hard actions. It requires a person to free a slave, to help the needy during the time of scarcity, to feed the orphans and near relatives and the poor who are lying in the dust—i.e. poor who are extremely hungry and penniless.

17-18. Only the righteous people who help the poor and needy are qualified to become the "People of the Right Hand." The People of the Right Hand are qualified to enter Heaven.

19-20. Those who disbelieve in the message of Allāh are the "People of the Left Hand." They are the people who will suffer in the Fire.

Words to know

Uqsimu: I swear, I call to witness. *Qasamun*: oath. *Qasama*: to divide, distribute. *Qismatun*: partition, division.
Malā: riches, wealth. *Māla:* to be rich. *Amwal*: my wealth.
Raqabah: slave. *Raqaba*: to guard, tie by the neck. *Riqāb:* neck, slave, captives of war.
Masghabatun: famine, starvation, hunger. *Saghaba:* to be hungry, starve.
Maqrabatun: near relation. *Qariba*: near. *Qurbān*: sacrifice, means of coming close to God.
Marhamah: mercy, compassion. *Rahima*: to love, have mercy. *Rahmān*: Most-Kind, Most-Merciful. *Rahīm*: Most-Rewarding.

Sūrah Al-Balad
Word-by-word meaning

ٱلرَّحِيمِ	ٱلرَّحۡمَٰنِ	ٱللَّهِ	بِسۡمِ
the Most-Rewarding	the Most-Kind	Allāh	In the name of
ٱلۡبَلَدِ ١	بِهَٰذَا	أُقۡسِمُ	لَآ
territory	this	I call to witness	No
ٱلۡبَلَدِ ٢	بِهَٰذَا	حِلُّۢ	وَأَنتَ
territory	in this	lawful rights	and you
لَقَدۡ	وَلَدَ ٣	وَمَا	وَوَالِدٖ
surely	begotten	and what	and the begetter
كَبَدٍ ٤	فِي	ٱلۡإِنسَٰنَ	خَلَقۡنَا
hardship	into	the man	we have created

يَقْدِرَ	لَّن	أَن	أَيَحْسَبُ
power	no	that	does he think
أَهْلَكْتُ	يَقُولُ	أَحَدٌ ﴿٥﴾	عَلَيْهِ
I spent	he says	any one	upon him
أَن	أَيَحْسَبُ	لُّبَدًا ﴿٦﴾	مَالًا
that	does he think	heaps	wealth
أَلَمْ	أَحَدٌ ﴿٧﴾	يَرَهُۥٓ	لَّمْ
have not	any one	sees him	no
وَلِسَانًا	عَيْنَيْنِ ﴿٨﴾	لَّهُۥ	نَجْعَل
and a tongue	two eyes	for him	We made
فَلَا	ٱلنَّجْدَيْنِ ﴿١٠﴾	وَهَدَيْنَٰهُ	وَشَفَتَيْنِ ﴿٩﴾
so not	the two highways	and pointed out to him	and two lips
أَدْرَىٰكَ	وَمَآ	ٱلْعَقَبَةَ ﴿١١﴾	ٱقْتَحَمَ
will make you know	and what	the uphill road	rush ahead
رَقَبَةٍ ﴿١٣﴾	فَكُّ	ٱلْعَقَبَةُ ﴿١٢﴾	مَا
a slave	freeing	the uphill road	what is
يَوْمٍ	فِي	إِطْعَٰمٌ	أَوْ
days	in	feeding	or

ذَا	يَتِيمًا	مَسْغَبَةٍ ﴿١٤﴾	ذِى
of	orphan	famine	of
ذَا	مِسْكِينًا	أَوْ	مَقْرَبَةٍ ﴿١٥﴾
in	poor	or	near relation
مِنَ	كَانَ	ثُمَّ	مَتْرَبَةٍ ﴿١٦﴾
of	is	then	the dust
بِٱلصَّبْرِ	وَتَوَاصَوْا۟	ءَامَنُوا۟	ٱلَّذِينَ
to perseverance	and enjoin	who believe	those
أَصْحَٰبُ	أُو۟لَٰٓئِكَ	بِٱلْمَرْحَمَةِ ﴿١٧﴾	وَتَوَاصَوْا۟
companions	those	to mercy	and enjoin
بِـَٔايَٰتِنَا	كَفَرُوا۟	وَٱلَّذِينَ	ٱلْمَيْمَنَةِ ﴿١٨﴾
in our Messages	disbelieve	but those who	the right hand
عَلَيْهِمْ	ٱلْمَشْـَٔمَةِ ﴿١٩﴾	أَصْحَٰبُ	هُمْ
on them	the left hand.	companions	they are
		مُّؤْصَدَةٌۢ ﴿٢٠﴾	نَارٌ
		vaulted over	fire

A few applications of the message:

This sūrah reminds us that we all have to face difficulties—even the prophets faced difficulties in their lives. In order to overcome the difficulties in life, we must work hard and have faith in Allāh. Our difficulties in life will not disappear automatically. We should remember that facing difficulties in life is under the plan of Allāh. We should not lose hope under any circumstance. At the same time, we should also remember we are not self sufficient to do everything on our own. We do need the help and blessings of the Creator.

Allāh's help and blessings will reach us if we follow the right path. In fact, the world has two types of paths—the path of righteousness and the path of wrong. One path leads us to the rewarding life in Heaven and the other to sufferings in Hell.

Allāh also reminds us that the path of righteousness is not an easy path. It is tough and requires lots of hard work. However, the end is rewarding. On the other hand, the wrong path is full of fun and excitement. It is an easy path. We may not realize that walking on the easy path is actually full of problems. The wrong path will destroy us. As we read the sūrah, let us think for a while—which path will ultimately lead us to achieve success and reward in the Hereafter. If we know the correct path, let us follow it. Allāh will make our efforts easy for us.

Questions:

1. In the beginning of Sūrah *Balad*, why did Allāh say the Prophet (S) has rights to the city?
2. How were the rights of the Prophet (S) rooted in the city of Makkah?
3. Why do you think people tend to believe no one has power over them?
4. What are the two roads mentioned in Sūrah *Balad*?
5. What are some of the reasons people do not want to follow the uphill or the difficult path?
6. What are some of the duties required for those who would follow the uphill path?
7. In order to be a Companion of the Right-hand, what should a person do?

Sūrah 89

Revealed in Makkah

Al-Fajr

The Dawn

Introduction:

This sūrah groups together some of the variations and diversities in nature to draw attention to human character. Human beings have both a good and bad nature. Examples of past communities show that painful punishment fell upon those who followed their bad nature and rejected Allāh's message. The sūrah then shows how Allāh tests people and how they fail or qualify in the test. Next, the sūrah tells some of the basic human nature that causes them to suffer in this world and in the Hereafter. Finally, the sūrah points out the tragedy of the sinners in the Hereafter and the triumph of the righteous people.

بِسۡمِ ٱللَّهِ ٱلرَّحۡمَـٰنِ ٱلرَّحِيمِ

Bismi-llāhi-r raḥmāni-r raḥīm
In the name of Allah, the Most-Kind, the Most-Rewarding.

وَٱلۡفَجۡرِ ﴿١﴾	Wal fajr,	1. By the Dawn,
وَلَيَالٍ عَشۡرٍ ﴿٢﴾	wa layālin 'ashr,—	2. and the ten nights,
وَٱلشَّفۡعِ وَٱلۡوَتۡرِ ﴿٣﴾	-wash shaf'i wal watr,	3. and the Even, and the Odd,
وَٱلَّيۡلِ إِذَا يَسۡرِ ﴿٤﴾	wa-llayli idhā yasr;	4. and the night when it departs.
هَلۡ فِي ذَٰلِكَ قَسَمٌ لِّذِي حِجۡرٍ ﴿٥﴾	hal fī dhālika qasamuṇ li-dhī ḥijr.	5. Is there not in these things an oath for one who has understanding?
أَلَمۡ تَرَ كَيۡفَ فَعَلَ رَبُّكَ بِعَادٍ ﴿٦﴾	A-lam tara kayfa fa'ala rabbuka bi-'ād,	6. Have you not seen how your Rabb dealt with 'Ad,

إِرَمَ ذَاتِ ٱلْعِمَادِ ٧	irama dẖāti-l ‘imād,—	7. Iram, having lofty structures,
ٱلَّتِى لَمْ يُخْلَقْ مِثْلُهَا فِى ٱلْبِلَٰدِ ٨	-llatī lam yukhlaq mitẖluhā fil bilād,	8. these— the like of which had not been created in cities;
وَثَمُودَ ٱلَّذِينَ جَابُوا۟ ٱلصَّخْرَ بِٱلْوَادِ ٩	wa tẖamūda-l ladẖīna jābu-ṣ ṣakhra bil wād,	9. and Thamud who carved out rocks in the valley;
وَفِرْعَوْنَ ذِى ٱلْأَوْتَادِ ١٠	wa fir‘awna dẖil awtād,—	10. and Fir‘awn the lord of hosts,—
ٱلَّذِينَ طَغَوْا۟ فِى ٱلْبِلَٰدِ ١١	Alladẖīna ṭaghaw fil bilād,	11. who had rebelled in the cities,
فَأَكْثَرُوا۟ فِيهَا ٱلْفَسَادَ ١٢	fa-aktẖarū fīha-l fasād,	12. so they increasingly made mischief therein?
فَصَبَّ عَلَيْهِمْ رَبُّكَ سَوْطَ عَذَابٍ ١٣	fa ṣabba ‘alayhim rabbuka ṣawṭa ‘adẖāb,	13. So, Your Rabb poured upon them diverse punishment.
إِنَّ رَبَّكَ لَبِٱلْمِرْصَادِ ١٤	inna rabbaka la-bil mirṣād.	14. Surely, your Rabb is on watch.
فَأَمَّا ٱلْإِنسَٰنُ إِذَا مَا ٱبْتَلَىٰهُ رَبُّهُۥ فَأَكْرَمَهُۥ وَنَعَّمَهُۥ فَيَقُولُ رَبِّىٓ أَكْرَمَنِ ١٥	Fa-amma-l insānu idẖā ma-btalāhu rabbuhū fa-akramahū wa na‘-‘amahū, fa-yaqūlu rabbī akraman.	15. Then as for man, when his Rabb disciplines him and honors him and favors him, then he says: “My Rabb has honored me.”
وَأَمَّآ إِذَا مَا ٱبْتَلَىٰهُ فَقَدَرَ عَلَيْهِ رِزْقَهُۥ فَيَقُولُ رَبِّىٓ أَهَٰنَنِ ١٦	Wa ammā idẖā ma-btalāhu fa-qadara ‘alayhi rijhqahū, fa-yaqūlu rabbī ahānan;	16. But when He disciplines him and measures out to him his provision, then he says: “My Rabb has disgraced me.”
كَلَّا ۖ بَل لَّا تُكْرِمُونَ ٱلْيَتِيمَ ١٧	kallā bal lā tukrimūna-l yatīm,	17. No, but you do not honor the orphan,

وَلَا تَحَٰٓضُّونَ عَلَىٰ طَعَامِ ٱلْمِسْكِينِ ﴿١٨﴾	wa lā taḥāḍḍūna ‘alā ṭa‘āmi-l miskīn,	18. nor do you urge on feeding the poor;
وَتَأْكُلُونَ ٱلتُّرَاثَ أَكْلًا لَّمًّا ﴿١٩﴾	wa ta’kulūna-t turātha aklaḷ lamma,—	19. and you devour the inheritance an entire devouring;
وَتُحِبُّونَ ٱلْمَالَ حُبًّا جَمًّا ﴿٢٠﴾	-wa tuḥibbūna-l māla ḥubbaṅ jammā.	20. and you love wealth with an exceeding love.
كَلَّآ إِذَا دُكَّتِ ٱلْأَرْضُ دَكًّا دَكًّا ﴿٢١﴾	Kallā idhā dukkati-l arḍu dakkaṅ dakka,—	21. By no means! when the earth is crushed with a crushing after crushing,
وَجَآءَ رَبُّكَ وَٱلْمَلَكُ صَفًّا صَفًّا ﴿٢٢﴾	-wa jā’a rabbuka wal malaku ṣaffaṅ ṣaffā;	22. and your Rabb comes, and the angles, row after row;
وَجِاْىٓءَ يَوْمَئِذٍۭ بِجَهَنَّمَ ۚ يَوْمَئِذٍ يَتَذَكَّرُ ٱلْإِنسَٰنُ وَأَنَّىٰ لَهُ ٱلذِّكْرَىٰ ﴿٢٣﴾	wa jī’a yawma’idhiṁ bi-jahannama, yawma’idhiẏ yatadhakkaru-l insānu wa annā lahu-dh dhikra.	23. and on that Day He will bring forth hell; that Day man will remember, but how will the remembrance avail him?
يَقُولُ يَٰلَيْتَنِى قَدَّمْتُ لِحَيَاتِى ﴿٢٤﴾	Yaqūlu yā laytanī qaddamtu li-ḥayātī;	24. He will say: “I wish I had sent forward for my living!
فَيَوْمَئِذٍ لَّا يُعَذِّبُ عَذَابَهُۥٓ أَحَدٌ ﴿٢٥﴾	fa-yawma’idhiḷ lā yu‘adhdhibu ‘adhābahū aḥad,—	25. But on that Day no one can chastise like His chastising,
وَلَا يُوثِقُ وَثَاقَهُۥٓ أَحَدٌ ﴿٢٦﴾	-wa lā yūthiqu wathāqahū aḥad.	26. and no one can bind like His binding.

يَٰٓأَيَّتُهَا ٱلنَّفْسُ ٱلْمُطْمَئِنَّةُ ﴿٢٧﴾	Yā ayyatuha-n nafsu-l muṭma'innah,—	27. "O you the tranquil soul!
ٱرْجِعِىٓ إِلَىٰ رَبِّكِ رَاضِيَةً مَّرْضِيَّةً ﴿٢٨﴾	-rji'ī ilā rabbiki rāḍiyatam marḍiyyah;	28. "come back to your Rabb well-pleased, well-pleasing.
فَٱدْخُلِى فِى عِبَٰدِى ﴿٢٩﴾	fadkhulī fī 'ibādī,	29. "So, you enter among My servants;
وَٱدْخُلِى جَنَّتِى ﴿٣٠﴾	wa-dkhulī jannatī.	30. "and enter into My Garden!"

Explanation:

1-2. The sūrah derives its title from the mention of *fajr* (*lit.* dawn, daybreak) in the first verse. The dawn and night are two contrasting features of a 24-hour day. The dawn indicates the gradual waking up of a sleeping world and the night indicates falling back into the darkness. The second verse mentions ten nights, indicating that these 'ten nights' bear special significance in human spirituality. These ten nights could be the last ten nights of *Ramadān*, or the first ten nights of *Dhu al-Hijjah* when the rites of the pilgrimage are performed.

3. The odds and even are two variations that refer to odd and even numbered prayers. They may also refer to the even and odd days of the month of Ramadān, or 9th (Arafat) and 10th (sacrifice) day of Hajj.

4. The night departs, indicating that the world is brightened spiritually with the light of Islam.

5. All the above variations provide clear sign of Oneness of Allāh.

6-8. These verses refer to the fate of powerful nations from the past. The people of 'Ād built houses on firm pillars. Their famous city was Iram, now buried in sand dunes in the area between Uman and Hadramawt in southern Arabia. Despite their massive power and reputation, Allāh severely punished them for their wrongdoing.

9-14. The Thamūd were the powerful nation of their time. They built houses curved out in mountainous rocks. The Pharaohs were rulers well-known for their might and glory. Yet, due to their rebellion and rejection of truth, Allāh punished them. He always watches and records what the wrongdoers do. When the corruption increases, He lets a diverse punishment fall upon them.

15-16. Allāh often tests human beings with comfort or difficulties in life. When Allāh favors someone and gives them honor, some people become proud, thinking that they are special. This is a test to see if these people are humble and thankful or arrogant. On the other hand, when Allāh tests someone with difficulties and hardship, the ungrateful person complains and loses all hope. Allāh does not like either of these type of attitudes.

17-20. Four types of evil conduct of ungrateful and arrogant people are mentioned in this set of verses. They are: (i) not caring for orphans, (ii) not feeding the poor, (iii) stealing the rights of weak, women, children and orphans, and (iv) becoming greedy and materialistic, as if collecting wealth is their only goal in life.

21-24. A day will come when the earth will be crushed, the Day of Judgment will be set off and the Justice of Rabb will come down. Angels will come down in row after row to execute the Divine command. On that Day, Hell will be brought near the sinners. At that time, they will begin to remember their past deeds. They will realize that during their earthly lives, they threw away the opportunities to do good deeds. They will regret that they did not send anything good for the Hereafter. But such regret and late realization will not benefit the sinners.

25-26. The sinners will be punished with a severity that no one had ever witnessed. No one can bind them to their sins like Allāh will, without giving them any hope of escape.

27-30. Amid all the punishment and suffering of the sinners, the reward for the pious will also be of the highest level. The righteous will be content with their Rabb because they will get their promised reward. They will enter the Jannah, since they had been loyal to Allāh and followed His commands.

Words to know

Hijr: understanding or intelligence (that stops from doing bad), barrier. *Hajara*: to prevent. *Hujurāt*: private chamber, apartment. *Hujūr*: Guardian.
'Imād: lofty structure, pillar. *'Amada*: to support, place pillars. *'Amūd*: support, base, pillar.
Fasād: mischief-making corruption. *Fasada*: to be evil, to make mischief. *Mufsid*: wrongdoer. *Tufsidū*: you will make mischief.
Mirsād: watch, look out. *Rasada*: to watch, lay in wait. *Irsād*: hiding or lurking space.
Akrama: he has honored. *Karīm*: honorable. *Al-Karīm*: Most Honorable, one of the most excellent names of Allāh.
Miskīn: poor, submissive, humble. *Sakana*: to rest, quiet. *Sakīnat*: security, tranquility.
Rādiyatam: well-pleased. *Radiya*: satisfied. *Mardiyah*: well-pleasing. *Ridwān*: Good pleasure

Sūrah Al-Fajr
Word-by-word meaning

ٱلرَّحِيمِ	ٱلرَّحْمَـٰنِ	ٱللَّهِ	بِسْمِ
the Most-Rewarding	the Most-Kind	Allāh	In the name of
وَٱلشَّفْعِ	عَشْرٍ ٢	وَلَيَالٍ	وَٱلْفَجْرِ ١
and even	ten	and nights	By the Dawn
يَسْرِ ٤	إِذَا	وَٱلَّيْلِ	وَٱلْوَتْرِ ٣
departs	when	and night	and odd

هَلْ	فِى	ذَٰلِكَ	قَسَمٌ
is there	in	those things	an oath
لِّذِى	حِجْرٍ ٥	أَلَمْ	تَرَ
who has	understanding	have you not	seen
كَيْفَ	فَعَلَ	رَبُّكَ	بِعَادٍ ٦
how	dealt	your Rabb	with 'Ad
إِرَمَ	ذَاتِ	ٱلْعِمَادِ ٧	ٱلَّتِى
Iram	having	lofty structures	these
لَمْ	يُخْلَقْ	مِثْلُهَا	فِى
not	was created	like it	in
ٱلْبِلَٰدِ ٨	وَثَمُودَ	ٱلَّذِينَ	جَابُوا۟
in cities	and Thamud	who	carved
ٱلصَّخْرَ	بِٱلْوَادِ ٩	وَفِرْعَوْنَ	ذِى
the rocks	in the valley	and Fir'awn	lord
ٱلْأَوْتَادِ ١٠	ٱلَّذِينَ	طَغَوْا۟	فِى
hosts	who	rebelled	in
ٱلْبِلَٰدِ ١١	فَأَكْثَرُوا۟	فِيهَا	ٱلْفَسَادَ ١٢
the cities	so increased	therein	mischief-making
فَصَبَّ	عَلَيْهِمْ	رَبُّكَ	سَوْطَ
poured	upon them	your Rabb	diverse

لَبِٱلْمِرْصَادِ ١٤ on watch	رَبَّكَ your Rabb	إِنَّ Surely	عَذَابٍ ١٣ punishment
مَا ever	إِذَا when	ٱلْإِنسَٰنُ the man	فَأَمَّا then as for
وَنَعَّمَهُۥ and favors him	فَأَكْرَمَهُۥ honors him	رَبُّهُۥ his Rabb	ٱبْتَلَىٰهُ disciplines him
وَأَمَّآ and as for	أَكْرَمَنِ ١٥ honored me	رَبِّىٓ my Rabb	فَيَقُولُ then he says
عَلَيْهِ upon him	فَقَدَرَ measures out	ٱبْتَلَىٰهُ disciplines him	إِذَا مَا when ever
أَهَٰنَنِ ١٦ disgraced me.	رَبِّىٓ my Rabb	فَيَقُولُ then he says	رِزْقَهُۥ his provision
تُكْرِمُونَ you honor	لَّا no	بَل but	كَلَّا ۖ no
عَلَىٰ to	تَحَٰٓضُّونَ urge on	وَلَا and no	ٱلْيَتِيمَ ١٧ the orphan
ٱلتُّرَاثَ inheritance	وَتَأْكُلُونَ and you devour	ٱلْمِسْكِينِ ١٨ the poor	طَعَامِ feed
ٱلْمَالَ the wealth	وَتُحِبُّونَ and you love	لَّمًّا ١٩ entire	أَكْلًا devouring

إِذَا	كَلَّآ	جَمًّا (٢٠)	حُبًّا
when	no	exceeding	love
دَكًّا (٢١)	دَكًّا	ٱلْأَرْضُ	دُكَّتِ
crushing	crushing	the earth	crushed
صَفًّا	وَٱلْمَلَكُ	رَبُّكَ	وَجَآءَ
row	and the angels	your Rabb	and come
بِجَهَنَّمَ ۚ	يَوْمَئِذٍۭ	وَجِاْىٓءَ	صَفًّا (٢٢)
Hell	that day	and brought	row
وَأَنَّىٰ	ٱلْإِنسَـٰنُ	يَتَذَكَّرُ	يَوْمَئِذٍ
and how	the man	remember	that day
يَـٰلَيْتَنِى	يَقُولُ	ٱلذِّكْرَىٰ (٢٣)	لَهُ
I wish I had	he will say	the remembrance	for him
لَّا	فَيَوْمَئِذٍ	لِحَيَاتِى (٢٤)	قَدَّمْتُ
none	that day	for my living	sent forth
وَلَا	أَحَدٌ (٢٥)	عَذَابَهُۥٓ	يُعَذِّبُ
and none	any one	His chastising	can chastise
يَـٰٓأَيَّتُهَا	أَحَدٌ (٢٦)	وَثَاقَهُۥٓ	يُوثِقُ
O you	any one	His binding	will bind
إِلَىٰ	ٱرْجِعِىٓ	ٱلْمُطْمَئِنَّةُ (٢٧)	ٱلنَّفْسُ
to	come back	tranquil	soul

فَٱدۡخُلِي	مَّرۡضِيَّةٗ ٢٨	رَاضِيَةٗ	رَبِّكِ
enter	well-pleasing	well-pleased	your Rabb
جَنَّتِي ٣٠	وَٱدۡخُلِي	عِبَٰدِي ٢٩	فِي
My Garden.	and enter	My servants	among

A few applications of the message:

We should remember that our lives have contrasting events—ups and down, good and bad. How we deal with each event will ultimately decide where we will be in the Hereafter. If we are righteous, we can very well hope for the reward. Allāh gives us good and takes away good to test us. The sūrah reminds us that Allāh surely watches all—whether we are grateful and thankful for His blessings or we have lost hope in life when faced with a setback.

In the past Allāh made 'Ād, Thamūd and Pharaoh powerful. However, due to their rejection of the truth and rebellion against Allāh, they were punished on a massive scale. We do not want to be like the people who will regret on the Day of Judgment for not doing enough good work. We do not want to be like the people who will suffer an unheard of punishment. We should learn lessons from the fate of past nations and take precautions. Our lives are short. We should make sure that in the Hereafter we will not have regrets.

We want to be like the people who will be rewarded with entrance to the Garden, and like those who will be well pleased. This will be possible only when we obey Allāh and follow His guidance.

Questions:

1. What is the name of the city of 'Ād mentioned in the first part of Sūrah *al-Fajr*?
2. Two different ancient tribes are mentioned in Sūrah *al-Fajr*. What are their names?
3. In Sūrah *al-Fajr* what does Man say when Allāh tests by giving him honor and favor?
4. In Sūrah *al-Fajr* when Allāh tests Man by limiting his blessings, he says that Allāh has humiliated him. Why does he think this way?
5. In Sūrah *al-Fajr*, four things are mentioned that bad people do. What are these four things? Write in your own words.
6. Sūrah *al-Fajr* says that when Hell will be brought near the sinner, they will regret not doing something. What will they say? Write in your own words.
7. Sūrah *al-Fajr* says that the pious people will be at peace. They will be told three things about their achievements. What are the three things that will be told to them? Write in your own words.

Sūrah 88

Revealed in Makkah

Al-Ghāshiyah

The Overwhelming Event

Introduction:

The sūrah deals with the condition of two types of people—the disbelievers and the believers. On the Day of Awakening, a Severe and Overwhelming Event will happen. On that Day the disbelievers will suffer hardship and punishment, while the believers will experience blissful conditions. The sūrah also tells us to think about some of the signs of Allāh that we can see in the nature. These signs remind us of the Power and Wisdom of Allāh.

بِسۡمِ ٱللَّهِ ٱلرَّحۡمَٰنِ ٱلرَّحِيمِ

Bismi-llāhi-r raḥmāni-r raḥīm

In the name of Allah, the Most-Kind, the Most-Rewarding.

هَلۡ أَتَىٰكَ حَدِيثُ ٱلۡغَٰشِيَةِ ١	Hal atāka ḥadīt̲h̲u-l ghāshiyah.	1. Has there come to you the news of the Overwhelming Event?
وُجُوهٞ يَوۡمَئِذٍ خَٰشِعَةٌ ٢	Wujūhuẏ yawma'id̲h̲iṅ khāshi'ah,	2. Faces on that Day will be downcast;
عَامِلَةٞ نَّاصِبَةٞ ٣	'āmilatuṅ nāṣibah,	3. laboring, weary;
تَصۡلَىٰ نَارًا حَامِيَةٗ ٤	taṣlā nāraṅ ḥāmiyah,	4. undergoing roasting in scorching Fire.
تُسۡقَىٰ مِنۡ عَيۡنٍ ءَانِيَةٖ ٥	tusqā min 'ayniṅ āniyah.	5. They will be made to drink from a boiling spring.
لَّيۡسَ لَهُمۡ طَعَامٌ إِلَّا مِن ضَرِيعٖ ٦	Laysa lahum ṭa'āmun illā min ḍarī'i,—	6. They will have no food but from a thorny bush,—

لَّا يُسْمِنُ وَلَا يُغْنِى مِن جُوعٍ ٧	lā yusminu wa lā yughnī min jū'i.	7. it is neither nourishing nor satisfying from hunger.
وُجُوهٌ يَوْمَئِذٍ نَّاعِمَةٌ ٨	Wujūhuy yawma'id̲h̲iṅ nā'imah,—	8. Faces on that Day will be joyful,
لِّسَعْيِهَا رَاضِيَةٌ ٩	Li sa'yihā rāḍiyah,	9. well-satisfied with their striving,
فِى جَنَّةٍ عَالِيَةٍ ١٠	fī jannatiṅ 'āliyah,—	10. in a highly-placed Garden,
لَّا تَسْمَعُ فِيهَا لَٰغِيَةً ١١	lā tasma'u fīhā lāghiyah.	11. you will not hear in it any idle talk.
فِيهَا عَيْنٌ جَارِيَةٌ ١٢	Fīhā 'aynuṅ jāriyah.	12. In it is a flowing spring.
فِيهَا سُرُرٌ مَّرْفُوعَةٌ ١٣	Fīhā sururuṁ marfū'ah,—	13. In it are thrones raised high.
وَأَكْوَابٌ مَّوْضُوعَةٌ ١٤	-wa akwābuṁ mawḍū'ah,—	14. and drinking-cups ready-at-hand,
وَنَمَارِقُ مَصْفُوفَةٌ ١٥	-wa namāriqu maṣfūfah,—	15. and cushions set in rows,
وَزَرَابِىُّ مَبْثُوثَةٌ ١٦	-wa jharābiyyu mabt̲h̲ut̲h̲ah.	16. and carpets spread out.
أَفَلَا يَنظُرُونَ إِلَى ٱلْإِبِلِ كَيْفَ خُلِقَتْ ١٧	A-fa-lā yanzurūna ila-l ibili kayfa khuliqat,	17. Do they not then look at the camels, how they are created;
وَإِلَى ٱلسَّمَآءِ كَيْفَ رُفِعَتْ ١٨	wa ila-s samā'i kayfa rufi'at,	18. and at the sky how it is raised high,
وَإِلَى ٱلْجِبَالِ كَيْفَ نُصِبَتْ ١٩	wa ila-l jibāli kayfa nuṣibat,	19. and at the mountains how they are erected;
وَإِلَى ٱلْأَرْضِ كَيْفَ سُطِحَتْ ٢٠	wa ila-l arḍi kayfa suṭiḥat.	20. and at the earth how it is spread out?
فَذَكِّرْ إِنَّمَآ أَنتَ مُذَكِّرٌ ٢١	Fa d̲h̲akkir; innamā anta mud̲h̲akkir.	21. So go on reminding; you are certainly a reminder.

لَّسْتَ عَلَيْهِم بِمُصَيْطِرٍ ﴿٢٢﴾	Lasta ‘alayhim bi-musayṭir,	22. You are not a warden over them;
إِلَّا مَن تَوَلَّىٰ وَكَفَرَ ﴿٢٣﴾	illā man tawallā wa kafar,	23. but whoever turns back and disbelieves,
فَيُعَذِّبُهُ ٱللَّهُ ٱلْعَذَابَ ٱلْأَكْبَرَ ﴿٢٤﴾	fa-yu‘adh͟dh͟ibuhu-llāhu-l ‘adh͟āba-l akbar.	24. then Allāh will punish him with a great punishment.
إِنَّ إِلَيْنَآ إِيَابَهُمْ ﴿٢٥﴾	Inna ilaynā iyābahum,	25. Surely towards Us is their return;
ثُمَّ إِنَّ عَلَيْنَا حِسَابَهُم ﴿٢٦﴾	t͟humma inna ‘alaynā ḥisābahum.	26. then it is for Us indeed to take their account.

Explanation:

1. Al-Ghāshiyah means the Overwhelming or Severe event. It refers to the Day of Awakening. The root word *ghashiya* means to cover something. The Day is called Overwhelming because it will overcome the present world and a new world will appear.

2-7. For the sinners and disbelievers the Overwhelming Day will be a terrible day. Their faces will be gloomy, tired, and disappointed due to the shame of living a wicked life and from the fear of punishment. Their appearance will be sweaty and worn out, as they get ready to enter the punishment of the Fire. The difficulty of bearing the Hellfire will make them thirsty for cold water, but they will be given boiling water. They will feel hunger, but the only food will be a thorny, bitter, smelly fruit. The boiling water will not quench their thirst, neither will the food satisfy their hunger.

8-11. In contrast to the disbelievers, the believers will have a different experience. Their faces will be joyful. They will be happy from their past activities in the world. They will be in the Garden where there will be no idle or useless speech, but only greetings of peace. The Garden will be placed high—as it will be removed far from the Fire. It will be best place for the best people.

12-16. Compared to the hot boiling water for the disbelievers, the believers in the Garden will get spring water. They will also get drinking cups filled with refreshing drinks. They will sit on thrones raised high for them with cushions laid out to recline. Carpets will be spread out to welcome them as they are guests of honor.

17-20. This set of verses refers to four things that people in Arabia see in everyday life. In case people still deny the Hereafter, they are asked to (i) look at the camels—how they are created by providing them with flabby feet to walk easily on the sand, and with a sack in stomach to store water, and making them useful as the ships of the desert. (ii) Look at the heaven, or universe—how it is raised high without any supporting pillars. (iii) Look at the mountains—how majestically they are raised high. (iv) Look at the earth—how it is spread out. Allāh created all these objects with a definite purpose. All these objects testify to Allāh's Absolute Power.

21-22. The Prophet (S) was asked to go on reminding people about the importance of belief, and to warn them about the effect of disbelief. He was not responsible for what people did, since everyone is responsible for his or her own deeds.

23-26. After receiving the reminder and warning, if anybody turns back and disbelieves, then they will suffer great punishment. Ultimately everybody will return to Allāh when the Overwhelming Event will start. At that time Allāh will take an account of every person any pay them back according to their deeds.

Words to know

Hadīth: history, story, news. *Hadatha*: to report. *Ahādīth*: plural of *Hadīth*.
Ghāshiyatun: overwhelms, a thing that covers up. *Ghishāwatun*: covering. *Aghshā*: to cover, to overwhelm.
Khāshi'atun: (eyes) downcast, in a state of humility. *Khasha'a*: to be humble, submissive. *Khushū*: humility.
Nā'imatun: joyful, delighted. *Na'ama*: to enjoy, be joyful. *In'ām*: gift, favor to a person. *Al-Ni'mat*: bliss.
Jannatun: Garden, paradise, covered with plants. *Janna*: to cover, to wrap, to conceal. *Jinn*: hidden creatures. *Majnūn*: insane (whose mind is covered).
Mudhakkir: one who reminds, admonishes. *Dhikrā*: reminder, admonition. *Dhakara*: to remember. *Dhakir*: one who remembers.

Sūrah Al-Ghāshiyah
Word-by-word meaning

ٱلرَّحِيمِ	ٱلرَّحۡمَٰنِ	ٱللَّهِ	بِسۡمِ
the Most-Rewarding	the Most-Kind	Allāh	In the name of
ٱلۡغَٰشِيَةِ ١	حَدِيثُ	أَتَىٰكَ	هَلۡ
Overwhelming Event	news	come to you	has there
عَامِلَةٞ	خَٰشِعَةٌ ٢	يَوۡمَئِذٍ	وُجُوهٞ
laboring	downcast	that day	faces
حَامِيَةٗ ٤	نَارًا	تَصۡلَىٰ	نَّاصِبَةٞ ٣
scorching	fire	roasting	weary
ءَانِيَةٖ ٥	عَيۡنٍ	مِنۡ	تُسۡقَىٰ
boiling	spring	from	made to drink

لَيۡسَ not	لَهُمۡ for them	طَعَامٌ food	إِلَّا except
مِن from	ضَرِيعٖ (٦) thorny bush	لَّا no	يُسۡمِنُ nourishing
وَلَا and not	يُغۡنِي satisfying	مِن for	جُوعٖ (٧) hunger
وُجُوهٞ faces	يَوۡمَئِذٖ that day	نَّاعِمَةٞ (٨) joyful	لِّسَعۡيِهَا with their striving
رَاضِيَةٞ (٩) well-pleased	فِي in	جَنَّةٍ Garden	عَالِيَةٖ (١٠) highly placed
لَّا not	تَسۡمَعُ hear	فِيهَا in it	لَٰغِيَةٗ (١١) idle speech
فِيهَا it it	عَيۡنٞ a spring	جَارِيَةٞ (١٢) flowing	فِيهَا in it
سُرُرٞ thrones	مَّرۡفُوعَةٞ (١٣) raised high	وَأَكۡوَابٞ and cups	مَّوۡضُوعَةٞ (١٤) ready-at-hand
وَنَمَارِقُ and cushions	مَصۡفُوفَةٞ (١٥) set in rows	وَزَرَابِيُّ and carpets	مَبۡثُوثَةٌ (١٦) spread out
أَفَلَا do they not	يَنظُرُونَ look	إِلَى at	ٱلۡإِبِلِ the camels

ٱلسَّمَآءِ the sky	وَإِلَى and at	خُلِقَتْ ﴿١٧﴾ created	كَيْفَ how
ٱلْجِبَالِ the mountains	وَإِلَى and at	رُفِعَتْ ﴿١٨﴾ raised high	كَيْفَ how
ٱلْأَرْضِ the earth	وَإِلَى and at	نُصِبَتْ ﴿١٩﴾ erected	كَيْفَ how
إِنَّمَآ only	فَذَكِّرْ therefore remind	سُطِحَتْ ﴿٢٠﴾ spread out	كَيْفَ how
عَلَيْهِم upon them	لَّسْتَ you are not	مُذَكِّرٌ ﴿٢١﴾ reminder	أَنتَ you are
تَوَلَّىٰ turns away	مَن who	إِلَّا except	بِمُصَيْطِرٍ ﴿٢٢﴾ a warden
ٱلْعَذَابَ punishment	ٱللَّهُ Allāh	فَيُعَذِّبُهُ will punish him	وَكَفَرَ ﴿٢٣﴾ and disbelieves
إِيَابَهُمْ ﴿٢٥﴾ their return	إِلَيْنَآ towards Us	إِنَّ surely	ٱلْأَكْبَرَ ﴿٢٤﴾ the great
حِسَابَهُم ﴿٢٦﴾ their account	عَلَيْنَا for Us	إِنَّ indeed	ثُمَّ then

A few applications of the message:

The sūrah tells us with great detail about the condition of the sinners and the righteous people on the Day of Awakening. As we read the conditions in verses 2 to 11, we have to stop and think—which of the two groups do we want to be with. Walking on the wrong path can be fun, but what about roasting in the scorching Fire in consequence? No sensible person would want to suffer the agonizing conditions mentioned in verses 2 to 7. Then why are we not doing our best to be with the other group that will have joyous faces, those that will be in the Garden?

The sūrah gives us a fairly good description of the comfort and pleasure in Heaven. The sūrah also tells us what to do in order to go to Heaven—to believe and not to turn away from the truth. As long as we remember this in our lives and follow the commands of Allāh, we will not suffer. We should remember that surely, we will one day return to Allāh.

Questions:

1. Why is the Day of Awakening mentioned as an Overwhelming Event?
2. On the Day of the Overwhelming Event, what two things will be given to the disbelievers?
3. In the Garden, the believers will not hear a certain type of speech. What type of speech is that?
4. What four things are mentioned in Sūrah *al-Ghāshiyah* as an indication of the power of Allāh?
5. Towards the end of Sūrah *al-Ghāshiyah,* the Prophet (S) was asked to do something. What was he asked to do?
6. Why isn't the Prophet (S) or any Muslim responsible for another person's deeds?

Sūrah 87 | Revealed in Makkah

Al-A'lā

The Most High

Introduction:

This sūrah asks all believers to praise their Rabb who has the power to create and regulate the life cycle. He also guides the believers and helps them remember the Divine teachings. Those who obey the truth find peace in this world and in the Hereafter. On the other hand, those who ignore the truth will suffer a great punishment. The sūrah reminds us that the Hereafter is better than the present life. This absolute truth was taught by all past prophets, including Ibrāhīm (A) and Mūsā (A).

بِسۡمِ ٱللَّهِ ٱلرَّحۡمَٰنِ ٱلرَّحِيمِ

Bismi-llāhi-r raḥmāni-r raḥīm

In the name of Allah, the Most-Kind, the Most-Rewarding.

سَبِّحِ ٱسۡمَ رَبِّكَ ٱلۡأَعۡلَى ١	Sabbiḥi-sma rabbika-l a'la,—	1. Glorify the name of your Rabb, the most High,
ٱلَّذِى خَلَقَ فَسَوَّىٰ ٢	-lladhī khalaqa fa-sawwā;	2. Who creates, then He perfects;
وَٱلَّذِى قَدَّرَ فَهَدَىٰ ٣	wa-lladhī qaddara fa-hadā;	3. and Who measures, and guides;
وَٱلَّذِىٓ أَخۡرَجَ ٱلۡمَرۡعَىٰ ٤	wa-lladhī akhraja-l mar'ā;	4. and Who brings forth herbage,
فَجَعَلَهُۥ غُثَآءً أَحۡوَىٰ ٥	fa-ja'alahū ghuthā'an aḥwā.	5. then renders it dried up, grey-colored.
سَنُقۡرِئُكَ فَلَا تَنسَىٰٓ ٦	Sa-nuqri'uka fa-lā tansā,	6. We shall soon make you recite, so you will not forget—

إِلَّا مَا شَآءَ ٱللَّهُ ۚ إِنَّهُۥ يَعْلَمُ ٱلْجَهْرَ وَمَا يَخْفَىٰ ٧	illā mā shā'a-llāh. Innahū ya'lamu-l jahra wa mā yakhfā.	7. except whatever Allāh please. He indeed knows the exposed, and what is hidden.
وَنُيَسِّرُكَ لِلْيُسْرَىٰ ٨	Wa nuyassiruka lil yusrā;	8. And We shall ease for you with easing.
فَذَكِّرْ إِن نَّفَعَتِ ٱلذِّكْرَىٰ ٩	fa-dhakkir in nafa'ati-dh dhikrā.	9. So go on reminding; surely the Reminder brings benefit.
سَيَذَّكَّرُ مَن يَخْشَىٰ ١٠	Sa yadhdhakkaru man yakhshā,	10. He will be reminded who fears,
وَيَتَجَنَّبُهَا ٱلْأَشْقَى ١١	wa yatajannabuha-l ashqa,—	11. but the evil-minded will avoid it,
ٱلَّذِى يَصْلَى ٱلنَّارَ ٱلْكُبْرَىٰ ١٢	-lladhī yaṣla-n nāra-l kubrā;	12. who will undergo roasting in the great Fire.
ثُمَّ لَا يَمُوتُ فِيهَا وَلَا يَحْيَىٰ ١٣	thumma lā yamūtu fīhā wa lā yaḥyā.	13. And then he will not die in it, nor will he live.
قَدْ أَفْلَحَ مَن تَزَكَّىٰ ١٤	Qad aflaḥa man tazakkā,	14. He indeed succeeds who purifies himself,
وَذَكَرَ ٱسْمَ رَبِّهِۦ فَصَلَّىٰ ١٥	wa dhkara-sma rabbihī fa-ṣallā.	15. and remembers the name of his Rabb, and performs Salāt.
بَلْ تُؤْثِرُونَ ٱلْحَيَوٰةَ ٱلدُّنْيَا ١٦	Bal tu'thirūna-l ḥayāta-d dunyā,	16. In fact, you prefer the life of this world,
وَٱلْـَٔاخِرَةُ خَيْرٌ وَأَبْقَىٰٓ ١٧	wal ākhiratu khayruw wa abqā.	17. while the Hereafter is better and ever-lasting.
إِنَّ هَـٰذَا لَفِى ٱلصُّحُفِ ٱلْأُولَىٰ ١٨	Inna hādhā lafi-ṣ ṣuḥufi-l ūlā,	18. Surely this is in the earlier Scrolls—
صُحُفِ إِبْرَٰهِيمَ وَمُوسَىٰ ١٩	ṣuḥufi ibrāhīma wa mūsā	19. the Scrolls of Ibrahim and Musa.

Explanation:

1-3. This set of verses begins by asking all believers to glorify their Rabb. The best way we can glorify our Rabb is by performing salāt and obeying His commands. Our Rabb has created everything in due proportion, plan and order. He gives everyone according to a Divine plan. He guides but never forces anybody to believe. He leaves the decision to follow the guidance entirely up to us. However, He also tells us the consequences of following the good and bad paths—as we will later find in this sūrah.

4-5. Everything in the nature follows the laws established by Allāh. In the right season Allāh brings forth green vegetation and then in another season He makes the vegetation dry up. This cycle of birth and death is a proof of the Supreme Power that controls everything.

6. It is reported that the Prophet (S) used to worry that he might not remember the Divine revelation accurately, forget part of it, or fail to transmit it properly. He was told not to rush with the revelations or not to hurry to memorize them. Allāh assured him that He, Himself, would teach the Prophet (S) and make sure that he would not forget it.

7-8. The Prophet (S), as a normal human being, might have forgotten many worldly things over the course of time. Such things are not necessary for everyday living and it is alright to forget them. Therefore, Allāh says that the Prophet (S) might forget something. However, as mentioned in verse 6, by the Grace of Allāh, he will not forget any Divine revelation. Gradually, the process of remembering the Divine revelation will become easy for him.

9-11. The Prophet (S) was asked to continue delivering the Divine message. Only those who follow the Right Path will benefit from the message, but the evil-minded people will avoid the message.

12-13. The people who do not believe in the message of the Qur'ān will suffer punishment in the Great Fire. They will be in a strange condition between life and death. They will wish to die to end all their sufferings, but they will not die; instead they will be alive, but such a life would not be worth living as it is full of punishment in Fire.

14-15. Truly successful people are those who purify themselves by embracing Islam as a way of life. They always remember their Rabb. The best way to remember Allāh is through salāt—thus they perform salāt to give thanks and to receive blessings.

16-19. Most people love the present world. They live to enjoy this world. The pleasure and comfort of this life is everything to them. They know the present life does not last long, yet they do not care for the Hereafter. To them, the realities of the Hereafter are too far away to count. Some of them do not even believe in the Hereafter. Whereas, these are not new teachings. In the past, all prophets taught their people that Hereafter is permanent and much better than the present life. For example, Ibrāhīm (A) and Mūsā (A), both taught their people this message.

Words to know

Al-A'lā: The Most-High, one of the most excellent names of Allāh. *'Alā*: to be high, lofty. *'Illiyūn*: the highest of the places. *Ta'ālā*: high, above all. *'Ulā*: lofty ones.

Sawwa: to perfect, to proportion. *Sawāun*: same, alike.

Qaddara: he measured. *Qadara*: to measure, to be able to do. *Taqdīr*: measuring decree. *Muqtadir*: powerful. *Qādir*: The Capable, one of the Most Excellent names of Allāh.

Dhikrā: reminder, admonition. *Dhakara*: to remember. *Dhakir*: one who remembers. *Mudhakkir*: one who reminds, admonishes.

Sūrah Al-A'lā
Word-by-word meaning

ٱلرَّحِيمِ	ٱلرَّحْمَـٰنِ	ٱللَّهِ	بِسْمِ
the Most-Rewarding	the Most-Kind	Allāh	In the name of
ٱلْأَعْلَى ﴿١﴾	رَبِّكَ	ٱسْمَ	سَبِّحِ
the Most-High	your Rabb	name	Glorify
وَٱلَّذِى	فَسَوَّىٰ ﴿٢﴾	خَلَقَ	ٱلَّذِى
and who	perfects	creates	who
أَخْرَجَ	وَٱلَّذِىٓ	فَهَدَىٰ ﴿٣﴾	قَدَّرَ
brings forth	and who	guides	measures
أَحْوَىٰ ﴿٥﴾	غُثَآءً	فَجَعَلَهُۥ	ٱلْمَرْعَىٰ ﴿٤﴾
grey-colored	dried up	renders it	herbage
إِلَّا	تَنسَىٰٓ ﴿٦﴾	فَلَا	سَنُقْرِئُكَ
except	forget	will not	We make you recite
إِنَّهُۥ	ٱللَّهُ	شَآءَ	مَا
He indeed	Allāh	pleases	what
يَخْفَىٰ ﴿٧﴾	وَمَا	ٱلْجَهْرَ	يَعْلَمُ
hidden	and what	the exposed	knows
إِن	فَذَكِّرْ	لِلْيُسْرَىٰ ﴿٨﴾	وَنُيَسِّرُكَ
if	so remind	with easing	and We shall ease

نَّفَعَتِ	ٱلذِّكْرَىٰ ٩	سَيَذَّكَّرُ	مَن
benefits	the reminder	reminded	who
يَخْشَىٰ ١٠	وَيَتَجَنَّبُهَا	ٱلْأَشْقَى ١١	ٱلَّذِى
fears	and avoid it	the evil-minded	who
يَصْلَى	ٱلنَّارَ	ٱلْكُبْرَىٰ ١٢	ثُمَّ
undergo roasting	the fire	the great	then
لَا	يَمُوتُ	فِيهَا	وَلَا
no	die	in it	and not
يَحْيَىٰ ١٣	قَدْ	أَفْلَحَ	مَن
live	indeed	succeeds	who
تَزَكَّىٰ ١٤	وَذَكَرَ	ٱسْمَ	رَبِّهِۦ
purifies	and remembers	name	his Rabb
فَصَلَّىٰ ١٥	بَلْ	تُؤْثِرُونَ	ٱلْحَيَوٰةَ
performs salat	but	you prefer	life
ٱلدُّنْيَا ١٦	وَٱلْءَاخِرَةُ	خَيْرٌ	وَأَبْقَىٰٓ ١٧
the world	and the Hereafter	better	and ever-lasting
إِنَّ	هَـٰذَا	لَفِى	ٱلصُّحُفِ
surely	this	in	the Scrolls
ٱلْأُولَىٰ ١٨	صُحُفِ	إِبْرَٰهِيمَ	وَمُوسَىٰ ١٩
earlier	Scrolls	Ibrāhīm	and Mūsā.

A few applications of the message:

One of the key messages of this sūrah is in verses 16 and 17 where it says that while people prefer the life of this world, the Hereafter is better and longer lasting. As we read the verses, do we truly grasp the meaning? Do we truly understand the significance of the message?

If we look around ourselves, we will see most people love the life of this world. This love of *dunya* derails them from the path of Allāh. The pleasure and comfort of this life is all that matters to them. They know everyone will die one day, yet they do not care for the Hereafter.

This sūrah tells us how we can achieve the best in the Hereafter. We have to remember Allāh and perform salāt. These two duties when done in the most sincere manner, and in true spirit of the word, can purify our souls. These simple duties will make us successful.

Questions:

1. In the first verse of Sūrah *al-Ālā,* what did Allāh tell us to do?
2. In Sūrah *al-'Ālā* what six things does Allāh, most High, do? These are mentioned in the first five verses.
3. In Sūrah *al-Ālā,* the Prophet (S) was asked to go on reminding people. What type of people will pay attention to the reminder?
4. Sūrah *al-'Ālā* mentions that the disbelievers will be in a peculiar condition in the Hereafter. What is the condition mentioned in the sūrah?
5. Based on Sūrah *al-'Ālā,* what do you think the scrolls of Ibrāhīm (A) and Mūsā (A) mention?

Sūrah 86

Revealed in Makkah

At-Tāriq

The Night Visitor

Introduction:

The Qur'ān defines *tāriq* as a brilliant star with a piercing radiance. Just as a bright star watches over dark night, someone keeps an eye over what people do. The sūrah reminds people to think about their own creation. On the Day of Awakening Allāh will recreate human beings again. The evil people think that the Awakening is just a joke; so they plot against Islam and the Qur'ān. They plot against Allāh, but Allāh also plans against them. They enjoy for a while, but, ultimately, they will find there is no one to help them on the Day their thoughts and bad deeds will be disclosed.

بِسۡمِ ٱللَّهِ ٱلرَّحۡمَٰنِ ٱلرَّحِيمِ

Bismi-llāhi-r raḥmāni-r raḥīm
In the name of Allah, the Most-Kind, the Most-Rewarding.

وَٱلسَّمَآءِ وَٱلطَّارِقِ ١	Was samāi' waṭ-ṭāriq,	1. By the heaven and the Night-Visitor!
وَمَآ أَدۡرَىٰكَ مَا ٱلطَّارِقُ ٢	wa mā adrāka maṭ ṭāriq,—	2. And what will make you know what the Night-Visitor is?
ٱلنَّجۡمُ ٱلثَّاقِبُ ٣	Annajmu-th̲ th̲āqib,	3. The Star of piercing radiance.
إِن كُلُّ نَفۡسٖ لَّمَّا عَلَيۡهَا حَافِظٞ ٤	in kullu nafsil̤ lammā 'alayhā ḥāfiz.	4. There is no soul but has a guardian over it.
فَلۡيَنظُرِ ٱلۡإِنسَٰنُ مِمَّ خُلِقَ ٥	Fal yanzuri-l insānu mimma khuliq.	5. So let man consider from what he is created.

خُلِقَ مِن مَّآءٖ دَافِقٖ ٦	Khuliqa miṅ māi'ṅ dāfiq,—	6. He is created out of a liquid gushing forth,—
يَخۡرُجُ مِنۢ بَيۡنِ ٱلصُّلۡبِ وَٱلتَّرَآئِبِ ٧	-yakhruju miṅ bayni-ṣ ṣulbi wat tarā'ib.	7. coming out from between the backbone and the breastbone.
إِنَّهُۥ عَلَىٰ رَجۡعِهِۦ لَقَادِرٞ ٨	Innahū 'alā raj'ihī la-qādir.	8. Surely, He is capable of bringing him back.
يَوۡمَ تُبۡلَى ٱلسَّرَآئِرُ ٩	Yawma tubla-s sarā'ir,	9. The Day when secrets will be exposed,
فَمَا لَهُۥ مِن قُوَّةٖ وَلَا نَاصِرٖ ١٠	fa-mā lahū min quwwatiẇ wa lā nāṣir.	10. then he will not have any strength, nor any helper.
وَٱلسَّمَآءِ ذَاتِ ٱلرَّجۡعِ ١١	Was samā'i dẖāti-r raj'i,	11. Consider the cloud which keeps coming back,
وَٱلۡأَرۡضِ ذَاتِ ٱلصَّدۡعِ ١٢	wal arḍi dẖāti-ṣ ṣad'i,	12. and the earth which splits asunder.
إِنَّهُۥ لَقَوۡلٞ فَصۡلٞ ١٣	innahū la-qawluṅ faṣl,—	13. Certainly this is a conclusive statement,
وَمَا هُوَ بِٱلۡهَزۡلِ ١٤	-wa mā huwa bil hazl.	14. and it is not a joke.
إِنَّهُمۡ يَكِيدُونَ كَيۡدٗا ١٥	Innahum yakīdūna kayda,—	15. Surely they plot a plot,
وَأَكِيدُ كَيۡدٗا ١٦	-wa akīdu kaydā;	16. and I plan a plan.
فَمَهِّلِ ٱلۡكَٰفِرِينَ أَمۡهِلۡهُمۡ رُوَيۡدَۢا ١٧	fa mahhili-l kāfirīna amhilhum ruwaydā.	17. So leave the disbelievers; leave them for awhile.

Explanation:

1-3. The sūrah derives its title from the word *tāriq*, which means night visitor. *Tāriq* is one who comes by night and knocks on the door since the doors are closed. The Qur'ān defines *tāriq* as a star of piercing radiance. *At-tāriq* is used as a symbol of brilliant Divine guidance appearing in midst of spiritual darkness across Arabia. It seems that *at-tāriq* is watching people with its piercing radiance when it is dark everywhere.

4. Just as *at-tāriq* is watching over people, so also does the human soul have a guardian over it. No one can escape the consequence of his actions because Allāh is the Ultimate Guardian over every soul.

5-7. If people think that Allāh cannot be the Guardian of every soul, let them think about their own creation. Allāh created every human being from life giving cells that have their early biological origins between the backbone and ribs. This fact can be further understood by studying the embryonic and evolutionary origin of cells in any animal, including human being.

8-10. The Creator who created human from life giving cells is also able to cause his return to life in the Hereafter. At that time, his good and evil deeds will be uncovered and brought to clear memory. At that time, the disbelievers will not be able to defend themselves or find any helper to guide them.

11-12. Two natural incidents are mentioned here to explain Allāh's power: (a) clouds or rain coming back, and (b) earth splitting by its herbage and springs. Timely rain helps germination of seedlings on dry land. In the Qur'ān, rain is often symbolically used to signify Divine guidance, and the germination of seeds is used as proof of the Awakening.

13-14. The disbelievers may reject the message of the Qur'ān, but this Book singles out the right from the wrong. The prophecy of the Awakening may appear false to the disbelievers, but let them remember that the message of the Qur'ān is not a funny story or useless speech.

15-17. The disbelievers want to stop the progress of Islam. They make plots not knowing that Allāh's plan is the best plan. Allāh is asking the Prophet (S) and all of us to leave the disbelievers alone. Allāh wants to give the disbelievers a small interval so that they may realize their mistakes. Those who do not utilize time or misuse it, will find Allāh's judgment is quick and unavoidable.

Words to know

Tāriq: visitor of night, morning star. *Taraqa*: to come by night, knock, strike. *Tariqan*: way, path.
Nafsun: soul. *Nafas*: breathing, gust. *Nafsī*: myself. *Nufūsun* and *Anfusu*: plural of *Nafsun*.
Hāfizun: guardian, protector. *Hafiza*: to guard, protect.
Khuliqa: was created. *Khalaqa*: to create, to proportion. *Khallāq*: Great Creator. *Khulq*: character, nature, habit.
Qādir: The Capable, one of the Most Excellent names of Allāh. *Qadara*: to be able to do, to measure.
Taqdīr: measuring decree, knowledge. *Muqtadir*: powerful.
Kaida: to plot, to plan. *Akīdu*: I plan, I devise. *Makīdūna*: victim of their own plot.

Sūrah At-Tāriq
Word-by-word meaning

ٱلرَّحِيمِ	ٱلرَّحۡمَٰنِ	ٱللَّهِ	بِسۡمِ
the Most-Rewarding	the Most-Kind	Allāh	In the name of
أَدۡرَىٰكَ	وَمَآ	وَٱلطَّارِقِ ١	وَٱلسَّمَآءِ
will make you know	and what	and the Night Visitor	By the heaven
ٱلثَّاقِبُ ٣	ٱلنَّجۡمُ	ٱلطَّارِقُ ٢	مَا
piercing radiance	the Star	the Night Visitor	what
لَّمَّا	نَفۡسٖ	كُلُّ	إِن
but	soul	every	no
ٱلۡإِنسَٰنُ	فَلۡيَنظُرِ	حَافِظٞ ٤	عَلَيۡهَا
the man	so let consider	a guardian	over it
مِن	خُلِقَ	خُلِقَ ٥	مِمَّ
from	created	created	from what
مِنۢ	يَخۡرُجُ	دَافِقٖ ٦	مَّآءٖ
from	coming out	gushing forth	fluid
إِنَّهُۥ	وَٱلتَّرَآئِبِ ٧	ٱلصُّلۡبِ	بَيۡنِ
surely	and the breastbone	the backbone	between
يَوۡمَ	لَقَادِرٞ ٨	رَجۡعِهِۦ	عَلَىٰ
day	indeed Capable	return	upon

لَهُۥ	فَمَا	ٱلسَّرَآئِرُ ﴿٩﴾	تُبْلَى
for him	so no	the secrets	exposed
نَاصِرٍ ﴿١٠﴾	وَلَا	قُوَّةٍ	مِن
helper	and no	strength	any
وَٱلْأَرْضِ	ٱلرَّجْعِ ﴿١١﴾	ذَاتِ	وَٱلسَّمَآءِ
by the earth	coming back	which	by the sky
لَقَوْلٌ	إِنَّهُۥ	ٱلصَّدْعِ ﴿١٢﴾	ذَاتِ
statement	Certainly	splits asunder	which
بِٱلْهَزْلِ ﴿١٤﴾	هُوَ	وَمَا	فَصْلٌ ﴿١٣﴾
joke	it is	and not	conclusive
وَأَكِيدُ	كَيْدًا ﴿١٥﴾	يَكِيدُونَ	إِنَّهُمْ
and I plan	a plot	they plot	Surely they
أَمْهِلْهُمْ	ٱلْكَٰفِرِينَ	فَمَهِّلِ	كَيْدًا ﴿١٦﴾
leave them	the disbelievers	so leave	a plan
			رُوَيْدًۢا ﴿١٧﴾
			a little while

A few applications of the message:

All the examples in the sūrah point to the power of a Supreme Creator. He is ever watchful over us. He has sent the Qur'ān as a Book that distinguishes truth from falsehood, right from wrong. We Muslims, therefore, should always follow the teachings of the Qur'ān carefully and honestly. We should not take the message of the Qur'ān lightly—the way disbelievers do. We should also remember that Allāh is the Master Planner. Under His Master Plan, bad peoples' evil plots can never become successful.

As believers, when we plan, we should remember that nothing can happen unless Allāh wills. His plan might be different from our plans. We should try our best, but trust His plan and surrender to His will. Allāh also advises us to leave the disbelievers alone – we are not judges to punish them or anybody for their disbelief. We should remember the disbelievers cannot harm Islam or the Muslims since Allāh is the Master Planner.

Questions:

1. What is the nature of the star mentioned in Sūrah *at-Tāriq*?
2. Based on Sūrah *at-Tāriq,* what does every human soul always have?
3. In Sūrah *at-Tāriq,* what argument did Allāh mention to prove that it is easy for Him to create us again on the Day of Awakening?
4. Why do the disbelievers think the Qur'ān is a matter of amusement?
5. Sūrah *at-Tāriq* says that Allāh is planning against the disbelievers. What should the Muslims do about them?

Sūrah 85

Revealed in Makkah

Al-Burūj

The Constellations

Introduction:

This early Makkan sūrah increased the morale of the early believers who were tortured by the polytheist Arabs. The sūrah encourages the believers to practice perseverance. The sūrah also promises them victory. Examples from history are mentioned to show that Allāh destroyed powerful nations that were arrogant and ruthless. The righteous people were given victory. This sūrah rightly serves as a message for the Muslims in all periods of time.

بِسْمِ ٱللَّهِ ٱلرَّحْمَـٰنِ ٱلرَّحِيمِ

Bismi-llāhi-r raḥmāni-r raḥīm

In the name of Allah, the Most-Kind, the Most-Rewarding.

وَٱلسَّمَآءِ ذَاتِ ٱلْبُرُوجِ ﴿١﴾	Was samā'i dẖāti-l burūj,	1. By the sky full of the Constellations,
وَٱلْيَوْمِ ٱلْمَوْعُودِ ﴿٢﴾	wal yawmi-l maw'ūd;	2. and the Promised Day,
وَشَاهِدٍ وَمَشْهُودٍ ﴿٣﴾	wa shāhidiẇ wa mashhūd.	3. and the witness, and the witnessed.
قُتِلَ أَصْحَـٰبُ ٱلْأُخْدُودِ ﴿٤﴾	Qutila aṣḥābu-l ukhdūd,	4. Destroyed are the companions of the Ditch,—
ٱلنَّارِ ذَاتِ ٱلْوَقُودِ ﴿٥﴾	Annāri dẖāti-l waqūd,	5. the fire supplied with fuel;
إِذْ هُمْ عَلَيْهَا قُعُودٌ ﴿٦﴾	idẖ hum 'alayhā qu'ūd,	6. when they sat by it,

وَهُمْ عَلَىٰ مَا يَفْعَلُونَ بِٱلْمُؤْمِنِينَ شُهُودٌ ٧	wa hum ‘alā mā yaf‘alūna bil mu’minīna shuhūd.	7. and they witnessesd what they were doing to the Believers.
وَمَا نَقَمُوا۟ مِنْهُمْ إِلَّآ أَن يُؤْمِنُوا۟ بِٱللَّهِ ٱلْعَزِيزِ ٱلْحَمِيدِ ٨	Wa mā naqamū minhum illā aṅ yu’minū bi-llāhi-l ‘ajhījhi-l ḥamīd,	8. And they did not have a grudge against them except that they believed in Allāh— the Exalted in Might, the most Praised,—
ٱلَّذِى لَهُۥ مُلْكُ ٱلسَّمَـٰوَٰتِ وَٱلْأَرْضِ ۚ وَٱللَّهُ عَلَىٰ كُلِّ شَىْءٍ شَهِيدٌ ٩	Alladh̲ī lahū mulkus samāwāti wal arḍ. Wa-llāhu ‘alā kulli shay’iṅ shahīd.	9. to Whom belongs the sovereignty of the heavens and the earth. And Allāh is a Witness over all things.
إِنَّ ٱلَّذِينَ فَتَنُوا۟ ٱلْمُؤْمِنِينَ وَٱلْمُؤْمِنَـٰتِ ثُمَّ لَمْ يَتُوبُوا۟ فَلَهُمْ عَذَابُ جَهَنَّمَ وَلَهُمْ عَذَابُ ٱلْحَرِيقِ ١٠	Inna-lladh̲īna fatanu-l mu’minīna wal mu’mināti t̲humma lam yatūbū fa-lahum ‘adh̲ābu jahannama wa lahum ‘adh̲ābu-l ḥarīq.	10. Surely, as to those who persecute the believing men and the believing women, and then do not repent, for them then is the chastisement of Hell, and they will have the punishment of burning.
إِنَّ ٱلَّذِينَ ءَامَنُوا۟ وَعَمِلُوا۟ ٱلصَّـٰلِحَـٰتِ لَهُمْ جَنَّـٰتٌ تَجْرِى مِن تَحْتِهَا ٱلْأَنْهَـٰرُ ۚ ذَٰلِكَ ٱلْفَوْزُ ٱلْكَبِيرُ ١١	Inna-l ladh̲īna āmanū wa ‘amilu-ṣ ṣāliḥāti lahum jannātuṅ tajrī min taḥtiha-l anhār. Dh̲ālika-l fawjhu-l kabīr.	11. Surely, as to those who believe and do good, for them are Gardens beneath which rivers flow. That is the great Achievement.
إِنَّ بَطْشَ رَبِّكَ لَشَدِيدٌ ١٢	Inna baṭsha rabbika la-shadīd.	12. Surely the seizing of your Rabb is indeed severe.

إِنَّهُۥ هُوَ يُبْدِئُ وَيُعِيدُ ﴿١٣﴾	Innahū huwa yubdi’u wa yu‘īd;	13. Surely He it is Who originates, and He reproduces;
وَهُوَ ٱلْغَفُورُ ٱلْوَدُودُ ﴿١٤﴾	wa huwa-l ghafūru-l wadūd,	14. and He is the most Forgiving, the Loving,
ذُو ٱلْعَرْشِ ٱلْمَجِيدُ ﴿١٥﴾	dhu-l ‘arshi-l majīd,	15. Master of the Throne of power, the Glorious,
فَعَّالٌ لِّمَا يُرِيدُ ﴿١٦﴾	fa‘-‘āluḷ limā yurīd.	16. Doer of what He intends.
هَلْ أَتَىٰكَ حَدِيثُ ٱلْجُنُودِ ﴿١٧﴾	Hal atāka ḥadīthu-l junūd,	17. Has not there come to you the story of the hosts—
فِرْعَوْنَ وَثَمُودَ ﴿١٨﴾	fir‘awna wa thamūd.	18. of Fir‘awn and Thamud?
بَلِ ٱلَّذِينَ كَفَرُوا۟ فِى تَكْذِيبٍ ﴿١٩﴾	Bali-lladhīna kafarū fī takdhīb,	19. Of course, those who disbelieve are in denial;
وَٱللَّهُ مِن وَرَآئِهِم مُّحِيطٌۢ ﴿٢٠﴾	wa-llāhu min warā’ihim muḥīṭ;	20. but Allāh is encompassing from behind them.
بَلْ هُوَ قُرْءَانٌ مَّجِيدٌ ﴿٢١﴾	bal huwa qur’ānum majīd,	21. But, it is a glorious Qur’ān,
فِى لَوْحٍ مَّحْفُوظٍۭ ﴿٢٢﴾	fī lawḥim maḥfūẓ.	22. in a Tablet guarded.

Explanation:

1-3. The sūrah begins with an oath in the name of three things: (a) *burūj*, (b) the Promised Day and (c) witness and those who witnessed. The term *burūj* (lit. castle, tower) means star, a sign of the Zodiac or a group of stars called a constellation. The Promised Day refers to the Day of Judgment. On that Day, people will bear witness against each other. Our organs will bear witness. All prophets will bear witness and Allāh, Himself, will bear witness against our good and bad deeds.

4-5. The verses refer to a bad ruler who killed thousands of people because they believed in One God. The ruler is traditionally mentioned as *Dhu Nuwās* of Yemen. He dug a deep pit and lit an enormous fire in it. He threw all the people who refused to give up their faith in One God.

6-9. The ruler and his followers threw the believers in the pit of fire and watched them burn in it. The ruler was angry with the believers because they believed in Allāh, and that the Heaven and the earth belongs to Allāh and that He watches everything.

10. The verse states a clear message that applies at all periods of time. The message is that whoever tortures believing men or women will burn in the fire of Hell. However, if they repent to Allāh, they may avoid the punishment. The ruler in Yemen tortured the believers and never repented, therefore, he will burn in fire of Hell.

11. Whoever believes in Allāh and does good deeds will be admitted in the gardens of Heaven. Whoever enters the Garden, will realize it is surely a great achievement.

12-16. This set of verses present some of the attributes of Allāh. The grip of Allāh is indeed very severe. The evil people who torture believing men and women cannot escape Allāh's grip. Allāh is also most Forgiving and Loving. Allāh originates the creation and, after that, He makes sure the creation reproduces itself in accordance to His law. He has the power to do everything, as He is the Master of the Throne of Power. He does what He plans to do as He is not answerable to anyone.

17-20. The well-known accounts of two past nations are mentioned here. The people of Fir'awn and the tribes of Thamūd were very powerful in their times. These people had rejected the truth and disbelieved in Allāh. They tortured the believing men and women. Both nations were ultimately destroyed in a very dramatic manner. Their power, superiority and wealth did not come to any use when Allāh gripped them severely.

21-22. The principle of punishing the evil people and rewarding the believing people are mentioned in the Qur'ān. The teachings of the Qur'ān are preserved by Allāh against any corruption, manipulation or destruction. It is like a tablet well guarded by Allāh. A tablet is like a slab on which someone writes and the writings cannot be deleted because they are permanently inscribed.

Words to know

Shahida: he bore witness. *Mashhūd:* which is witnessed. *Shahādat:* to give witness, to testify.
'Arsh: Throne, Power, Sovereignty. *'Arasha*: to build, raise a roof.
Hadīth: history, story, news. *Hadatha*: to report. *Ahādīth*: plural of *Hadīth.*
Mahfūz: guarded one, protected one. *Hafiza*: to guard, protect. *Hafizun*: protector (one who memorizes the Qur'ān and protects from forgetting).

Sūrah Al-Burūj
Word-by-word meaning

ٱلرَّحِيمِ	ٱلرَّحْمَٰنِ	ٱللَّهِ	بِسْمِ
the Most-Rewarding	the Most-Kind	Allāh	In the name of
وَٱلْيَوْمِ	ٱلْبُرُوجِ ١	ذَاتِ	وَٱلسَّمَآءِ
and the day	the Constellations	with	By the sky

قُتِلَ	وَمَشْهُودٍ ٣	وَشَاهِدٍ	ٱلْمَوْعُودِ ٢
destroyed	and the witnessed	and witness	promised
ذَاتِ	ٱلنَّارِ	ٱلْأُخْدُودِ ٤	أَصْحَٰبُ
with	the fire	the ditch	fellows
عَلَيْهَا	هُمْ	إِذْ	ٱلْوَقُودِ ٥
upon it	they	when	fuel
مَا	عَلَىٰ	وَهُمْ	قُعُودٌ ٦
what	to	and they	sat
وَمَا	شُهُودٌ ٧	بِٱلْمُؤْمِنِينَ	يَفْعَلُونَ
and not	witnesses	to the Believers	they do
أَن	إِلَّآ	مِنْهُمْ	نَقَمُوا۟
that	except	against them	grudge
ٱلْحَمِيدِ ٨	ٱلْعَزِيزِ	بِٱللَّهِ	يُؤْمِنُوا۟
the Most-Praised	the Exalted in Might	in Allāh	they believed
ٱلسَّمَٰوَٰتِ	مُلْكُ	لَهُۥ	ٱلَّذِى
the heavens	sovereignty	for him	who
كُلِّ	عَلَىٰ	وَٱللَّهُ	وَٱلْأَرْضِ ۚ
all	over	and Allāh	and earth

ٱلَّذِينَ those	إِنَّ Surely	شَهِيدٌ ﴿٩﴾ Witness	شَىْءٍ things
ثُمَّ then	وَٱلْمُؤْمِنَٰتِ and believing women	ٱلْمُؤْمِنِينَ the believing men	فَتَنُوا۟ persecute
عَذَابُ chastisement	فَلَهُمْ for them	يَتُوبُوا۟ repent	لَمْ not
ٱلْحَرِيقِ ﴿١٠﴾ burning	عَذَابُ punishment	وَلَهُمْ and for them	جَهَنَّمَ Hell
وَعَمِلُوا۟ and do	ءَامَنُوا۟ believe	ٱلَّذِينَ those	إِنَّ Surely
تَجْرِى flow	جَنَّٰتٌ Gardens	لَهُمْ for them	ٱلصَّٰلِحَٰتِ good deeds
ذَٰلِكَ that	ٱلْأَنْهَٰرُ ۚ the rivers	تَحْتِهَا beneath	مِن which
بَطْشَ seizing	إِنَّ Surely	ٱلْكَبِيرُ ﴿١١﴾ great	ٱلْفَوْزُ achievement
هُوَ He	إِنَّهُۥ surely	لَشَدِيدٌ ﴿١٢﴾ indeed severe	رَبِّكَ your Rabb

ٱلْغَفُورُ	وَهُوَ	وَيُعِيدُ ﴿١٣﴾	يُبْدِئُ
the Most-Forgiving	and He	and reproduces	originates
ٱلْمَجِيدُ ﴿١٥﴾	ٱلْعَرْشِ	ذُو	ٱلْوَدُودُ ﴿١٤﴾
the Glorious	the Throne of Power	Master	the Loving.
هَلْ	يُرِيدُ ﴿١٦﴾	لِّمَا	فَعَّالٌ
has	intends	of what	Doer
فِرْعَوْنَ	ٱلْجُنُودِ ﴿١٧﴾	حَدِيثُ	أَتَىٰكَ
Fir'awn	the hosts	the story	reached you
كَفَرُوا۟	ٱلَّذِينَ	بَلِ	وَثَمُودَ ﴿١٨﴾
disbelieve	those	of course	and Thamud
مِن	وَٱللَّهُ	تَكْذِيبٍ ﴿١٩﴾	فِى
from	and Allāh	denial	in
هُوَ	بَلْ	مُّحِيطٌۢ ﴿٢٠﴾	وَرَآئِهِم
this	but	encompassing	behind them
لَوْحٍ	فِى	مَّجِيدٌ ﴿٢١﴾	قُرْءَانٌ
Tablet	in	Glorious	Qur'ān
			مَّحْفُوظٍۭ ﴿٢٢﴾
			guarded

A few applications of the message:

After reading the sūrah we need to remember two things: (a) not to become like those nations who torture people, and (b) not to disbelieve and deny the truth. We may think that because we are not rulers of a country, we cannot do large scale torture. Participating or allowing torture of any scale angers Allāh. In verse 4, Allāh says that He destroyed the companions of the Trenches. In verse 18, Allāh says He destroyed the nations of Pharaoh and Thamūd. The super powers of that time became powerless when Allāh gripped them. In verse 12 Allāh says He grips the sinners very severely. They were punished because they rejected truth and tortured believers. Be it a super power or a single individual, bullies will never be successful. If we make a mistake we should repent to avoid punishment (see verse 10). Once we repent, we should never go back to the same sin again. We should remember Allāh is Forgiving and Loving (verse 14). If Allāh forgives us, we will enter the Garden beneath which rivers flow. This will be our supreme achievement (verse 11). We should try to achieve the best in the Hereafter.

Questions:

1. In the beginning of Sūrah *al-Burūj*, an oath is taken in the name of three things. What are the three things?
2. Why did the evil ruler kill people in his country?
3. What will happen to anyone who tortures believing men and women?
4. Some of the beautiful names of Allāh are mentioned in verses 8, 14 and 15? Write the Arabic names and English meanings.
5. What is the significance of the Qur'ān being a Tablet well preserved? Explain in a few sentences.

Sūrah 84

Revealed in Makkah

Al-Inshiqāq

The Ripped Apart

Introduction:

This sūrah begins with scenes of a great disturbance that will happen all over the universe at the time of the Awakening. During all these disturbances, the universe and the earth will completely submit to Allāh. Man, too, will completely submit to Allāh because he will return to his Lord for a full accounting. The sūrah shows certain scenes of life on the earth. Some people reject faith and do not care about the Awakening. The sūrah then shows the position of these people at the time of Judgment and compares their condition to the righteous people.

بِسۡمِ ٱللَّهِ ٱلرَّحۡمَـٰنِ ٱلرَّحِيمِ

Bismi-llāhi-r raḥmāni-r raḥīm

In the name of Allah, the Most-Kind, the Most-Rewarding.

إِذَا ٱلسَّمَآءُ ٱنشَقَّتۡ ۝١	Idha-s samā'u-nshaqqat,	1. When the sky is ripped apart,
وَأَذِنَتۡ لِرَبِّهَا وَحُقَّتۡ ۝٢	wa adhinat li-rabbihā wa ḥuqqat,	2. and it listens to its Rabb, and it rightly must—
وَإِذَا ٱلۡأَرۡضُ مُدَّتۡ ۝٣	wa idha-l arḍu muddat.	3. and when the earth is stretched out,
وَأَلۡقَتۡ مَا فِيهَا وَتَخَلَّتۡ ۝٤	Wa alqat mā fīhā wa takhallat,	4. and casts forth what is in it, and becomes empty,
وَأَذِنَتۡ لِرَبِّهَا وَحُقَّتۡ ۝٥	wa adhinat li-rabbihā wa ḥuqqat.	5. and it listens to its Rabb,— and it rightly must.

يَٰٓأَيُّهَا ٱلۡإِنسَٰنُ إِنَّكَ كَادِحٌ إِلَىٰ رَبِّكَ كَدۡحٗا فَمُلَٰقِيهِ ٦	Yā ayyuha-l insānu innaka kādiḥuṅ ilā rabbika kadḥaṅ fa-mulāqīh;	6. O you man! surely you have to labor towards your Rabb laboriously, then you will meet Him.
فَأَمَّا مَنۡ أُوتِيَ كِتَٰبَهُۥ بِيَمِينِهِۦ ٧	fa ammā man ūtiya kitābahū bi-yamīnih,	7. Then whoever is given his Book in his right hand,
فَسَوۡفَ يُحَاسَبُ حِسَابٗا يَسِيرٗا ٨	fa sawfa yuḥāsabu ḥisābaṅ yasīra,—	8. then he will soon be accounted for with an easy accounting;
وَيَنقَلِبُ إِلَىٰٓ أَهۡلِهِۦ مَسۡرُورٗا ٩	-wa yanqalibu ilā ahlihī masrūrā.	9. then he will return to his people joyfully.
وَأَمَّا مَنۡ أُوتِيَ كِتَٰبَهُۥ وَرَآءَ ظَهۡرِهِۦ ١٠	Wa ammā man ūtiya kitābahū warā'a zahrih,	10. But as to him who is given his Book behind his back,
فَسَوۡفَ يَدۡعُواْ ثُبُورٗا ١١	fa sawfa yad'ū thubūra—	11. then he will soon call for destruction,
وَيَصۡلَىٰ سَعِيرًا ١٢	-wa yaṣlā sa'īrā.	12. and enter the burning Fire.
إِنَّهُۥ كَانَ فِيٓ أَهۡلِهِۦ مَسۡرُورًا ١٣	Innahū kāna fī ahlihī masrūrā.	13. surely, he used to be joyful among his people.
إِنَّهُۥ ظَنَّ أَن لَّن يَحُورَ ١٤	Innahū zanna aṅ laṅ yaḥūra;—	14. He indeed thought that he would never return.
بَلَىٰٓۚ إِنَّ رَبَّهُۥ كَانَ بِهِۦ بَصِيرٗا ١٥	balā;— inna rabbahū kāna bihī baṣīrā.	15. Yes! surely his Rabb is ever Seeing him.
فَلَآ أُقۡسِمُ بِٱلشَّفَقِ ١٦	Fa lā uqsimu bish shafaq,	16. Then no! I swear by the evening twilight,—
وَٱلَّيۡلِ وَمَا وَسَقَ ١٧	wa-llayli wa mā wasaq,	17. and the night and what it collects,
وَٱلۡقَمَرِ إِذَا ٱتَّسَقَ ١٨	wal qamari idha-t tasaq,	18. and the moon when it grows full,

لَتَرْكَبُنَّ طَبَقًا عَن طَبَقٍ ١٩	la-tarkabunna ṭabaqaṅ ‘an ṭabaq.	19. you will surely progress from stage to stage.
فَمَا لَهُمْ لَا يُؤْمِنُونَ ٢٠	Fa-mā lahum lā yu’minūn,	20. Then what is with them that they do not believe,
وَإِذَا قُرِئَ عَلَيْهِمُ ٱلْقُرْءَانُ لَا يَسْجُدُونَ ۩ ٢١	wa idẖā quri’a ‘alayhimu-l Qur’ānu lā yasjudūn. **(Sajdah)**	21. and when the Qur’ān is recited to them they do not perform SAJDAH?
بَلِ ٱلَّذِينَ كَفَرُوا۟ يُكَذِّبُونَ ٢٢	Bali-lladẖīna kafarū yukadẖdẖibūn;	22. Rather, those who disbelieve deny.
وَٱللَّهُ أَعْلَمُ بِمَا يُوعُونَ ٢٣	wa-llāhu a‘lamu bimā yū‘ūn;	23. But Allāh knows best what they conceal.
فَبَشِّرْهُم بِعَذَابٍ أَلِيمٍ ٢٤	fa-bashshirhum bi-‘adẖābiṅ alīm,	24. So, inform them of a painful chastisement.
إِلَّا ٱلَّذِينَ ءَامَنُوا۟ وَعَمِلُوا۟ ٱلصَّٰلِحَٰتِ لَهُمْ أَجْرٌ غَيْرُ مَمْنُونٍۭ ٢٥	illa-lladẖīna āmanū wa ‘amiluṣ ṣāliḥāti lahum ajruṅ ghayru mamnūn.	25. Except those who believe and do good,—for them is a reward never to be cut off.

Explanation:

1-5. The beginning of the Awakening is narrated in this section with a series of dreadful events happening in the universe. The sky will split and the earth will flatten and throw out all its contents. Everything in the heavens and earth will obey the Divine command. Obeying the Divine command means following the laws of Allāh.

6. The word *kadh* (meaning toil, labor, strive hard) used twice in this verse points to certain realities in life. Our lives are a mixture of pain, labor, sorrow, sacrifice, disappointment as well as pleasure and happiness. Allāh wants everyone to walk the path to Him with their due share of pain and labor until they come to ‘meet’ the Judgment of Allāh.

7-9. The Qur'ān often uses the right hand and left hand to contrast people engaged in righteous deeds versus corrupt deeds. On the Day of Judgment people who will receive their books of deeds in their right hands means Allāh will approve their deeds. They will return happily to those members of their families who received their books in their right hands.

10-15. The sinners will receive their books of deeds in their left hands, behind their backs. At that time, they will realize that their deeds have been wasted. Due to shame and dishonor, the sinners will wish to die rather than face the Judgment. During their earthly lives, these sinners lived with pride and pleasure without caring for spiritual principles. They thought they would never be held accountable for their deeds. They failed to understand that their Lord watches every action of every individual.

16-18. Three signs of nature are mentioned in the verses. They are the sunset, nightfall and a full moon—all of which point towards some of the conclusive realities of the nature. These natural events illustrate that nothing on this earth is static; everything is ever changing and progressing to the next stage.

19. Those who follow the Divine teachings will progress spiritually from one stage to another. The stages of human progression can be understood as *ammarah,* or animal stage, to *lawwamah,* or human stage, and, finally, to *mutma'innah,* or heavenly stage.

20-23. After observing the natural signs all over the universe, it is clear that there is One Creator who regulates, administers, shapes, and evolves His creation. The Qur'ān then exclaims: what is the problem with these people that they don't believe! They do not bring their bodies and mind to prostrate to the Lord! They do not believe in the message of the Qur'ān! Allāh knows their thoughts and motives as to why they constantly reject the truth. (When you recite verse 21, make an actual Sajdah).

24-25. The disbelievers are given the tragic news of a painful punishment for rejecting the truth. On the other hand, the believers are given the good news of a reward that will never end. The declaration of faith alone will not be enough. We must also perform good deeds. Therefore, the Qur'ān always emphasizes the importance of belief *and* doing good deeds.

Words to know

Inshaqqa: He split. *Shaqqa:* to split, place under difficulty. *Shiqāq:* chism, cleavage. *Shiqqin:* great difficulty.
Adhinat: listened. *Adhina*: listen, respond. *Adhdhana*: announced. *Adhānun*: announcement.
Huqqat: rightly must do, obligated. *Haqqa*: to be right. *Al-Haqqu*: The most Truthful—one of the Most Excellent names of Allāh.
Masrūran: joyful, delighted. *Sarra*: to be glad. *Surūr*: heartfelt happiness.
Mamnūn: cutting off (of benefit). *Manna*: he showed grace or benefit. *Al-Mannān*: The Great Benefactor—one of the Most Excellent names of Allāh.

Sūrah Al-Inshiqāq
Word-by-word meaning

ٱلرَّحِيمِ	ٱلرَّحْمَٰنِ	ٱللَّهِ	بِسْمِ
the Most-Rewarding	the Most-Kind	Allāh	In the name of
وَأَذِنَتْ	ٱنشَقَّتْ ١	ٱلسَّمَآءُ	إِذَا
and listen	ripped apart	the sky	When

لِرَبِّهَا its Rabb	وَحُقَّتْ ﴿٢﴾ and it rightly must	وَإِذَا and when	ٱلْأَرْضُ the earth
مُدَّتْ ﴿٣﴾ stretched out	وَأَلْقَتْ and cast forth	مَا what	فِيهَا in it
وَتَخَلَّتْ ﴿٤﴾ and become empty	وَأَذِنَتْ and listens	لِرَبِّهَا to its Rabb	وَحُقَّتْ ﴿٥﴾ and it rightly must
يَٰٓأَيُّهَا O you	ٱلْإِنسَٰنُ the man	إِنَّكَ surely you	كَادِحٌ labor
إِلَىٰ towards	رَبِّكَ your Rabb	كَدْحًا laboriously	فَمُلَٰقِيهِ ﴿٦﴾ will meet Him.
فَأَمَّا then as to	مَنْ who	أُوتِىَ given	كِتَٰبَهُۥ his Book
بِيَمِينِهِۦ ﴿٧﴾ in his right hand	فَسَوْفَ then soon	يُحَاسَبُ be accounted	حِسَابًا accounting
يَسِيرًا ﴿٨﴾ easy	وَيَنقَلِبُ and return	إِلَىٰٓ to	أَهْلِهِۦ his people
مَسْرُورًا ﴿٩﴾ joyfully	وَأَمَّا and as for	مَنْ who	أُوتِىَ given
كِتَٰبَهُۥ his Book	وَرَآءَ behind	ظَهْرِهِۦ ﴿١٠﴾ his back	فَسَوْفَ soon

يَدۡعُواْ call for	ثُبُورًا ١١ destruction	وَيَصۡلَىٰ and enter	سَعِيرًا ١٢ burning Fire
إِنَّهُۥ Surely he	كَانَ was	فِيٓ in	أَهۡلِهِۦ people
مَسۡرُورًا ١٣ in happiness	إِنَّهُۥ He indeed	ظَنَّ thought	أَن that
لَّن never	يَحُورَ ١٤ return	بَلَىٰٓ yes	إِنَّ surely
رَبَّهُۥ his Rabb	كَانَ was	بِهِۦ with him	بَصِيرًا ١٥ Seer
فَلَآ then, no	أُقۡسِمُ I call to witness	بِٱلشَّفَقِ ١٦ by evening twilight	وَٱلَّيۡلِ and the night
وَمَا and what	وَسَقَ ١٧ collects	وَٱلۡقَمَرِ and the moon	إِذَا when
ٱتَّسَقَ ١٨ grows full	لَتَرۡكَبُنَّ surely progress	طَبَقًا stage	عَن to
طَبَقٍ ١٩ stage	فَمَا then what	لَهُمۡ with them	لَا not
يُؤۡمِنُونَ ٢٠ they believe	وَإِذَا and when	قُرِئَ is recited	عَلَيۡهِمُ to them

بَلِ rather	يَسْجُدُونَ ۩ ﴿٢١﴾ they prostrate (SAJDAH)	لَا not	ٱلْقُرْءَانُ the Qur'ān
وَٱللَّهُ and Allāh	يُكَذِّبُونَ ﴿٢٢﴾ deny	كَفَرُوا۟ disbelieve	ٱلَّذِينَ those
فَبَشِّرْهُم inform them	يُوعُونَ ﴿٢٣﴾ they conceal	بِمَا what	أَعْلَمُ knows best
ٱلَّذِينَ those	إِلَّا except	أَلِيمٍ ﴿٢٤﴾ painful	بِعَذَابٍ chastisement
لَهُمْ for them	ٱلصَّٰلِحَٰتِ good deeds	وَعَمِلُوا۟ and do	ءَامَنُوا۟ believe
	مَمْنُونٍۭ ﴿٢٥﴾ cut off	غَيْرُ without	أَجْرٌ reward

A few applications of the message:

One of the lessons we learn from the sūrah is how to receive the "Book" in our right hands. If we can receive the book in our right hands our lives in the Hereafter will be easy and rewarding. In contrast, if we have to receive the book in our left hands, our lives in the Hereafter will be miserable. We should seek the guidance of the Qur'ān, so that we can receive the book in our right hands.

This sūrah, and the Qur'ān in general, tells us how we can avoid misery in the Hereafter. The simplest and easiest process is to believe in Allāh and demonstrate our faith through good deeds. If we do this, Allāh assures our reward will never be cut off.

The sūrah also reminds us our life is a mixture of pain, labor, sorrow, sacrifice, disappointment as well as pleasure and happiness. Even the life of the Prophet (S) was full of pain, labor, sacrifice, but with full contentment and blessings. No matter what happens to us in our lives, we should never forget Allāh. The Qur'ān reminds us that with due share of pain and labor in this life, we will come to 'meet' the Judgment of Allāh.

Questions:

1. Compare verse 4 of Sūrah *inshiqāq* with verse 2 of Sūrah *Az-Zalzalah* and verse 9 of Sūrah *Al-'Ādiyat*. What is the common message in all these verses?
2. What will happen to the people who will receive their record in their right hands?
3. Compare the message of verse 7 with verses 17:71 and 69:19. What conclusion can you draw from reading these verses?
4. Compare the message of verse 7 to verse 10 and then to 69:25. Which offer is better and why?
5. What should a person do in this life to get his records in the right hand?

Sūrah 83

Revealed in Makkah

Al-Mutaffifin

The Cheating

Introduction:

This sūrah illustrates a social environment where the righteous versus the sinners, and good versus evil people interact. The sūrah explains what will ultimately happen to each group of people. In this process, the sūrah emphasizes that everyone is accountable for his or her own actions. The records of our deeds are maintained carefully and they will be brought out on the Day of Judgment. In summary the sūrah has four parts—(a) dealing with the cheaters, (b) condemning the cheaters, (c) giving an account of the righteous and (d) dealing with how the sinners taunted the righteous people and how the righteous people will respond to their taunting.

بِسْمِ ٱللَّهِ ٱلرَّحْمَٰنِ ٱلرَّحِيمِ

Bismi-llāhi-r raḥmāni-r raḥīm
In the name of Allah, the Most-Kind, the Most-Rewarding.

وَيْلٌ لِّلْمُطَفِّفِينَ ﴿٢﴾	Wayluḷ lil muṭaffifīn,—	1. Woe be to the cheaters—
ٱلَّذِينَ إِذَا ٱكْتَالُوا۟ عَلَى ٱلنَّاسِ يَسْتَوْفُونَ ﴿٢﴾	Alladhīna idhā-ktālū ‘ala-n nāsi yastawfūn.	2. who, when they take measure from people, they demand full measure,
وَإِذَا كَالُوهُمْ أَو وَّزَنُوهُمْ يُخْسِرُونَ ﴿٣﴾	Wa idhā kālūhum aw wajhanūhum yukhsirūn.	3. but when they give measure to them or weigh out for them, they give less.
أَلَا يَظُنُّ أُو۟لَٰٓئِكَ أَنَّهُم مَّبْعُوثُونَ ﴿٤﴾	A-lā yaẓunnu ulā’ika an-nahum mab‘ūthūn,	4. Do they not think— these— that they will surely be raised again,
لِيَوْمٍ عَظِيمٍ ﴿٥﴾	li-yawmiṅ ‘azīm,—	5. on a terrible Day:

يَوْمَ يَقُومُ ٱلنَّاسُ لِرَبِّ ٱلْعَٰلَمِينَ ٦	-yawma yaqūmu-n nāsu li-rabbi-l ʻālamīn.	6. the Day when mankind will stand up before the Rabb of all the worlds?
كَلَّآ إِنَّ كِتَٰبَ ٱلْفُجَّارِ لَفِى سِجِّينٍ ٧	Kallā inna kitāba-l fujjāri lafī sijjīn.	7. No! Surely the record of the wicked will indeed be in Sijjin.
وَمَآ أَدْرَىٰكَ مَا سِجِّينٌ ٨	Wa mā adrāka mā sijjīn.	8. And what will make you know what the Sijjin is?
كِتَٰبٌ مَّرْقُومٌ ٩	Kitābuṁ marqūm.	9. A written Register.
وَيْلٌ يَوْمَئِذٍ لِّلْمُكَذِّبِينَ ١٠	Wayluỷ yawma'idẖiḷ lil mukadẖdẖibīn,—	10. Woe be on that Day to those who deny,—
ٱلَّذِينَ يُكَذِّبُونَ بِيَوْمِ ٱلدِّينِ ١١	Alladẖīna yukadẖdẖibūna bi-yawmi-d dīn.	11. who deny the Day of Judgment.
وَمَا يُكَذِّبُ بِهِۦٓ إِلَّا كُلُّ مُعْتَدٍ أَثِيمٍ ١٢	Wa mā yukadẖdẖibu bihī illā kullu muʻtadiṅ atẖīm,	12. And no one rejects it except every immoderate sinner,
إِذَا تُتْلَىٰ عَلَيْهِ ءَايَٰتُنَا قَالَ أَسَٰطِيرُ ٱلْأَوَّلِينَ ١٣	idẖā tutlā ʻalayhi āyātunā qāla asāṭīru-l awwalīn.	13. when Our Messages are recited to him, he says: "Stories of the ancients."
كَلَّا ۖ بَلْ ۜ رَانَ عَلَىٰ قُلُوبِهِم مَّا كَانُوا۟ يَكْسِبُونَ ١٤	Kallā bal, rāna ʻalā qulūbihim mā kānū yaksibūn.	14. No! rather, what they had been earning has rusted upon their hearts.
كَلَّآ إِنَّهُمْ عَن رَّبِّهِمْ يَوْمَئِذٍ لَّمَحْجُوبُونَ ١٥	Kallā innahum ʻan rab-bihim yawma'idẖiḷ la-maḥjūbūn.	15. No! certainly they will, that Day, indeed be veiled from their Rabb.
ثُمَّ إِنَّهُمْ لَصَالُوا۟ ٱلْجَحِيمِ ١٦	Tẖumma innahum la-ṣālu-l jaḥīm.	16. And then they will, of course, be roasted in the fierce Fire.

ثُمَّ يُقَالُ هَـٰذَا ٱلَّذِى كُنتُم بِهِۦ تُكَذِّبُونَ ١٧	Thumma yuqālu hādha-lladhī kuntum bihī tukadhdhibūn.	17. Then it will be said: "This is about that which you used to deny."
كَلَّآ إِنَّ كِتَـٰبَ ٱلْأَبْرَارِ لَفِى عِلِّيِّينَ ١٨	Kallā inna kitāba-l abrāri lafī ‘illiyyīn.	18. No! surely the record of the pious will be in the Zenith.
وَمَآ أَدْرَىٰكَ مَا عِلِّيُّونَ ١٩	Wa mā adrāka mā ‘illiyyūn.	19. And what will make you know what the Zenith is?
كِتَـٰبٌ مَّرْقُومٌ ٢٠	Kitābuṁ marqūm,—	20. A written Register,—
يَشْهَدُهُ ٱلْمُقَرَّبُونَ ٢١	-yashhaduhu-l muqarrabūn.	21. those drawn near will witness it.
إِنَّ ٱلْأَبْرَارَ لَفِى نَعِيمٍ ٢٢	Inna-l abrāra lafī na‘īm,	22. Surely, the pious will, of course, be in bliss,
عَلَى ٱلْأَرَآئِكِ يَنظُرُونَ ٢٣	‘ala-l arā’iki yanzurūn,	23. on high couches, gazing.
تَعْرِفُ فِى وُجُوهِهِمْ نَضْرَةَ ٱلنَّعِيمِ ٢٤	ta‘rifu fī wujūhihim naḍrata-n na‘īm;	24. You will recognize in their faces the brightness of bliss.
يُسْقَوْنَ مِن رَّحِيقٍ مَّخْتُومٍ ٢٥	yusqawna miṅ raḥīqiṁ makhtūm,	25. They will be given to drink a pure sealed beverage.
خِتَـٰمُهُۥ مِسْكٌ ۚ وَفِى ذَٰلِكَ فَلْيَتَنَافَسِ ٱلْمُتَنَـٰفِسُونَ ٢٦	khitāmuhū misku. Wa fī dhālika fal-yatanāfasi-l mutanāfisūn.	26. Its sealing will be musk. And to this let the aspirers aspire.
وَمِزَاجُهُۥ مِن تَسْنِيمٍ ٢٧	Wa mijhājuhū min tasnīm,	27. And its mixing will be with Tasnim,—
عَيْنًا يَشْرَبُ بِهَا ٱلْمُقَرَّبُونَ ٢٨	‘aynaẏ yashrabu biha-l muqarrabūn.	28. a spring from which those drawn near will drink.

إِنَّ ٱلَّذِينَ أَجْرَمُوا۟ كَانُوا۟ مِنَ ٱلَّذِينَ ءَامَنُوا۟ يَضْحَكُونَ ﴿٢٩﴾	Inna-lladhīna ajramū kānū mina-lladhīna āmanū yaḍḥakūn;	29. Surely, those who transgress used to laugh at those who believed;
وَإِذَا مَرُّوا۟ بِهِمْ يَتَغَامَزُونَ ﴿٣٠﴾	wa idhā marrū bihim yataghāmajhūn;	30. and when they passed by them, they winked at one another;
وَإِذَا ٱنقَلَبُوٓا۟ إِلَىٰٓ أَهْلِهِمُ ٱنقَلَبُوا۟ فَكِهِينَ ﴿٣١﴾	wa idha-nqalabū ilā ahlihimu-nqalabū fakihīn;	31. and when they, returned to their people, they returned jesting.
وَإِذَا رَأَوْهُمْ قَالُوٓا۟ إِنَّ هَٰٓؤُلَآءِ لَضَآلُّونَ ﴿٣٢﴾	wa idhā ra'awhum qālū inna hāulā'i la-ḍāllūn,	32. And when they saw them they said: "Certainly these are indeed the lost ones",
وَمَآ أُرْسِلُوا۟ عَلَيْهِمْ حَٰفِظِينَ ﴿٣٣﴾	wa mā ursilū 'alayhim ḥāfizīn.	33. though they have not been sent as guardians over them.
فَٱلْيَوْمَ ٱلَّذِينَ ءَامَنُوا۟ مِنَ ٱلْكُفَّارِ يَضْحَكُونَ ﴿٣٤﴾	Fal yawma-lladhīna āmanū mina-l kuffāri yaḍḥakūn;	34. So this Day those who believed will be laughing at the disbelievers,—
عَلَى ٱلْأَرَآئِكِ يَنظُرُونَ ﴿٣٥﴾	'ala-l arā'iki, yanzurūn.	35. on high couches, while gazing.
هَلْ ثُوِّبَ ٱلْكُفَّارُ مَا كَانُوا۟ يَفْعَلُونَ ﴿٣٦﴾	Hal thuwwiba-l kuffāru mā kānū yaf'alūn.	36. "Are not the disbelievers awarded according to what they used to do?"

Explanation:

1-3. The term *mutaffifin* means one who gives short measure. The word is based on *tatfif* which means he deceived, he made defective. The verses condemn the cheaters who cheat people in their business transactions. For example, the cheaters tamper the scale to weigh fewer goods in the transaction, or give fewer items for the money they charged or give bad or rotten items without people knowing about it. In short, the verses condemn any type of illegal or fraudulent business transactions.

4-6. People have illegal and deceptive business practices because they think that they can get away with cheating. They think they will never be held responsible. They think the world is everything to them. They forget that Day of Judgment will happen when everyone will have to answer for his or her actions.

7-9. The deeds of every person are carefully recorded. The record of the wicked people will be in a book called *Sijjīn*. The term *sijjin* is derived from the root word *sijn* which means prison, anything hard, the bottom of Hell. All these meanings indicate the record books have everything recorded in them, thus making the wicked people prisoners of their own deeds.

10- 13. The disbelievers do not want to be held accountable for their deeds. Therefore, they say the Day of Judgment will never happen. They think that after they die, it is not possible that they could be revived. All past prophets told their people about the Awakening and the Day of Judgment. When Prophet Muhammad (S) told his community about the Awakening, they laughed at him. They thought the warning about the Awakening was nothing other than the same old stories told by their forefathers.

14-17. Over a period of time, the wicked peoples' deeds cast a layer of rust over their hearts. As such, they cannot see or understand that they are doing wrong. They cannot understand the truth. On the Day of Judgment, the wicked people will be shut out from receiving mercy from Allāh. Separation from Allāh will be their most painful experience because they will be sent to suffer punishment in fierce Fire. They will then realize how unwise it was for them to deny this Judgment.

18-21. In contrast to the destiny of the wicked, here the destiny of the righteous people is mentioned. The records of the good people will be in a separate register called *'illiyīn*. The term *'illiyīn* is the plural form of *'illi* or *'illiyah*, which means high places, a person who sits on high place, or loftiness. People who did righteous deeds will be happy to show the examples of their deeds. They will be drawn near to their Rabb and they will witness the *'illiyīn* with a great satisfaction.

22-24. The righteous people will surely be in a blissful condition. Their dignity and honor will be similar to the kings. They will be seated on royal thrones or highly decorated couches as a mark of their dignity. Their faces will look bright and joyous as a reflection of complete happiness.

25-28. The righteous people will have many types of drinks. One such drink will be a pure sealed beverage. The seal on the beverage emphasizes its purity and approval from Allāh. The seal on the beverage will have the fragrance of musk. The beverage will be flavored with *tasnīm*—a heavenly pure drink. The fountain of *tasnīm* is placed in the highest part of Paradise, for those who earn the highest status.

29-32. Think of the ultimate reward of the righteous people mentioned above. During their earthly lives, the wicked people used to laugh at the righteous people. The wicked people passed sarcastic remarks about the righteous people. They used to think the righteous people were crazy and losers.

33-36. The wicked people believed that they have a right to guide the righteous people who they thought were losers. Allāh did not sent the wicked people with any authority to supervise the righteous people. On the Day of Judgment the righteous people will have the last laugh. They will sit on high and dignified couches, enjoying the reward for their good deeds. They will watch the wicked people suffer for their misdeeds. It will become obvious that the disbelievers got their punishment in accordance to the misdeeds they had been doing in their earthly lives.

Words to know

Sijjīn: prison. Sajana: to imprison. *Masjūn*: prisoner.
'Illiyūn: the highest of the places, zenith. *Alā:* to be high, lofty. *Al-A'lā*: The Most-High, one of the most excellent names of Allāh. *'Ta'ālā:* high, above all. *'Ulā:* lofty ones.
Tasnīm: water coming from above. *Sanima*: to raise. *Sanam*: camel's hump, prominent.

Sūrah Al-Mutaffifīn
Word-by-word meaning

ٱلرَّحِيمِ	ٱلرَّحْمَـٰنِ	ٱللَّهِ	بِسْمِ
the Most-Rewarding	the Most-Kind	Allāh	In the name of
إِذَا	ٱلَّذِينَ	لِّلْمُطَفِّفِينَ ﴿٢﴾	وَيْلٌ
when	those	to the cheaters	woe
يَسْتَوْفُونَ ﴿٢﴾	ٱلنَّاسِ	عَلَى	ٱكْتَالُوا۟
take full measure	people	against	measure
وَّزَنُوهُمْ	أَو	كَالُوهُمْ	وَإِذَا
weigh them	or	measure them	and when
أُو۟لَـٰٓئِكَ	يَظُنُّ	أَلَا	يُخْسِرُونَ ﴿٣﴾
those	think	do they not	give less
عَظِيمٍ ﴿٥﴾	لِيَوْمٍ	مَّبْعُوثُونَ ﴿٤﴾	أَنَّهُم
terrible	for a day	be raised	that they
لِرَبِّ	ٱلنَّاسُ	يَقُومُ	يَوْمَ
for Rabb	mankind	stand up	Day
كِتَـٰبَ	إِنَّ	كَلَّآ	ٱلْعَـٰلَمِينَ ﴿٦﴾
record	surely	no	the worlds
وَمَآ	سِجِّينٍ ﴿٧﴾	لَفِى	ٱلْفُجَّارِ
and what	Sijjin	in	the wicked

كِتَٰبٌ register	سِجِّينٌ ٨ Sijjin	مَا what is	أَدْرَىٰكَ do you know
لِّلْمُكَذِّبِينَ ١٠ who deny	يَوْمَئِذٍ that day	وَيْلٌ woe	مَّرْقُومٌ ٩ written
ٱلدِّينِ ١١ Judgment	بِيَوْمِ Day	يُكَذِّبُونَ deny	ٱلَّذِينَ those (who)
إِلَّا except	بِهِۦٓ it	يُكَذِّبُ the deny	وَمَا and not
إِذَا when	أَثِيمٍ ١٢ sinful	مُعْتَدٍ immoderate	كُلُّ every
قَالَ said	ءَايَٰتُنَا our Messages	عَلَيْهِ to him	تُتْلَىٰ recited
بَلْ ۜ rather	كَلَّا ۖ no, not	ٱلْأَوَّلِينَ ١٣ the ancients	أَسَٰطِيرُ stories
مَّا what	قُلُوبِهِم their hearts	عَلَىٰ on	رَانَ rust
إِنَّهُمْ they indeed	كَلَّآ no, certainly	يَكْسِبُونَ ١٤ they earning	كَانُوا۟ were
لَّمَحْجُوبُونَ ١٥ veiled	يَوْمَئِذٍ that Day	رَّبِّهِمْ their Rabb	عَن from

ٱلْجَحِيمِ (١٦)	لَصَالُوا۟	إِنَّهُمْ	ثُمَّ
the fierce Fire	will enter	of course they	then
ٱلَّذِى	هَـٰذَا	يُقَالُ	ثُمَّ
what	this is	is said	then
إِنَّ	كَلَّآ	تُكَذِّبُونَ (١٧)	كُنتُم بِهِۦ
indeed	no, surely	deny	you used to
عِلِّيِّينَ (١٨)	لَفِى	ٱلْأَبْرَارِ	كِتَـٰبَ
Zenith	in	the pious	record
عِلِّيُّونَ (١٩)	مَا	أَدْرَىٰكَ	وَمَآ
Zenith	what is	do you know	and what
ٱلْمُقَرَّبُونَ (٢١)	يَشْهَدُهُ	مَّرْقُومٌ (٢٠)	كِتَـٰبٌ
the drawn near	witness it	written	register
نَعِيمٍ (٢٢)	لَفِى	ٱلْأَبْرَارَ	إِنَّ
bliss	of course in	the pious	surely
تَعْرِفُ	يَنظُرُونَ (٢٣)	ٱلْأَرَآئِكِ	عَلَى
you recognize	gazing	high couches	on
ٱلنَّعِيمِ (٢٤)	نَضْرَةَ	وُجُوهِهِمْ	فِى
the bliss	brightness of	their faces	in
مَّخْتُومٍ (٢٥)	رَّحِيقٍ	مِن	يُسْقَوْنَ
sealed	pure beverage	out of	given to drink

خِتَـٰمُهُۥ sealing of it	مِسْكٌ ۚ musk	وَفِى and in	ذَٰلِكَ that
فَلْيَتَنَافَسِ let aspire	ٱلْمُتَنَـٰفِسُونَ ٢٦ the aspirers	وَمِزَاجُهُۥ and its mixture	مِن of/from
تَسْنِيمٍ ٢٧ Tasnim	عَيْنًا spring	يَشْرَبُ they drink	بِهَا with it
ٱلْمُقَرَّبُونَ ٢٨ the near ones	إِنَّ indeed	ٱلَّذِينَ those (who)	أَجْرَمُوا۟ transgress
كَانُوا۟ they were	مِنَ at	ٱلَّذِينَ those (who)	ءَامَنُوا۟ believed
يَضْحَكُونَ ٢٩ laughing	وَإِذَا and when	مَرُّوا۟ pass	بِهِمْ by them
يَتَغَامَزُونَ ٣٠ wink	وَإِذَا and then	ٱنقَلَبُوٓا۟ they returned	إِلَىٰٓ to
أَهْلِهِمُ their people	ٱنقَلَبُوا۟ returned	فَكِهِينَ ٣١ jesting	وَإِذَا and when
رَأَوْهُمْ saw them	قَالُوٓا۟ they say	إِنَّ indeed	هَـٰٓؤُلَآءِ those
لَضَآلُّونَ ٣٢ surely lost	وَمَآ and not	أُرْسِلُوا۟ sent	عَلَيْهِمْ upon them

ءَامَنُوا۟	ٱلَّذِينَ	فَٱلْيَوْمَ	حَـٰفِظِينَ ٣٣
believed	those (who)	so today	guardians
عَلَى	يَضْحَكُونَ ٣٤	ٱلْكُفَّارِ	مِنَ
on	laughing	the disbelievers	at
ثُوِّبَ	هَلْ	يَنظُرُونَ ٣٥	ٱلْأَرَآئِكِ
awarded	have been	gazing	high couches
يَفْعَلُونَ ٣٦	كَانُوا۟	مَا	ٱلْكُفَّارُ
do	they used	what	the disbelievers

A few applications of the message:

In everyday life we will get many opportunities, big or small, to prove our actual merit. Sometimes nobody watches us or nobody notices if we do wrong. The question is, can we get away with it by doing wrong. The tricksters cheat people thinking that they can get away with cheating. They think they will never have to answer for their actions. They forget that the Day of Judgment will happen when everyone will have to answer for his or her action. We should remember, even if we think nobody is watching us, Allāh is actually watching us and having all our deeds recorded.

On the Day of Judgment, all of us will receive our books of records. Whatever we do during this life will come back to haunt us. If we reject the truth, participate in evil, laugh at people, we are doing something wrong. We are sure to earn the displeasure of Allāh. Our record books will show it. On the other hand, if we do good deeds, our record books will show that too. We have to decide what we want to see in our record books. We have the control. Let us plan and act accordingly so we won't have regrets on the Day of Judgment.

Questions:

1. What is the meaning of the word *tatfif*? Who is a *mutaffifin*?
2. How do the cheaters do business with the good and honest people?
3. What is *Sijjīn*? What is the root word of *sijjīn*?
4. What was one of the answers of the wicked people when the divine message was about the Awakening was mentioned to them?
5. Based on the Sūrah *al-Mutaffifīn*, mention some of the pleasures and bliss of the pious people in the Hereafter.

Sūrah 82

Revealed in Makkah

Al-Infitār

The Splitting Apart

Introduction:

The sūrah reminds us about the events before the Awakening and asks us to prepare for it. The sūrah has four parts to it—(a) it reminds us about some major events prior to the Awakening, (b) it reminds us about our own creation, (c) it criticizes people who deny the Awakening, and (d) it tells us how awful the Day of Judgment will be.

بِسۡمِ ٱللَّهِ ٱلرَّحۡمَٰنِ ٱلرَّحِيمِ

Bismi-llāhi-r raḥmāni-r raḥīm
In the name of Allah, the Most-Kind, the Most-Rewarding.

إِذَا ٱلسَّمَآءُ ٱنفَطَرَتۡ ﴿١﴾	Idha-s samāu'-nfaṭarat,	1. When the sky is split apart,
وَإِذَا ٱلۡكَوَاكِبُ ٱنتَثَرَتۡ ﴿٢﴾	wa idha-l kawākibu-ntatharat,	2. and when the planets are scattered,
وَإِذَا ٱلۡبِحَارُ فُجِّرَتۡ ﴿٣﴾	wa idha-l biḥāru fujjirat,	3. and when the rivers are made to flow;
وَإِذَا ٱلۡقُبُورُ بُعۡثِرَتۡ ﴿٤﴾	wa idha-l qubūru bu'thirat,	4. and when the graves are laid open—
عَلِمَتۡ نَفۡسٞ مَّا قَدَّمَتۡ وَأَخَّرَتۡ ﴿٥﴾	'alimat nafsuṁ mā qaddamat wa akhkharat.	5. a soul will know what it has sent forward, and left behind.
يَٰٓأَيُّهَا ٱلۡإِنسَٰنُ مَا غَرَّكَ بِرَبِّكَ ٱلۡكَرِيمِ ﴿٦﴾	Yā ayyuha-l insānu mā gharraka bi rabbika-l karīm,—	6. O you men! what has deceived you about your Rabb, the most Gracious,

ٱلَّذِى خَلَقَكَ فَسَوَّىٰكَ فَعَدَلَكَ ٧	Alladhī khalaqaka fa-sawwāka fa-‘adalak,	7. Who has created you, then fashioned you, then gave you the right proportion—
فِىٓ أَىِّ صُورَةٍ مَّا شَآءَ رَكَّبَكَ ٨	fī ayyi ṣūratiṁ mā shā’a rakkabak.	8. in whatever shape He pleased He moulded you?
كَلَّا بَلْ تُكَذِّبُونَ بِٱلدِّينِ ٩	Kallā bal tukadhdhibūna bi-ddīn,	9. No, you of course deny the Judgment.
وَإِنَّ عَلَيْكُمْ لَحَـٰفِظِينَ ١٠	wa inna ‘alaykum la-ḥāfiẓīn,	10. And surely over you there are guardians,
كِرَامًا كَـٰتِبِينَ ١١	kirāmaṅ kātibīn,	11. honored ones, recorders,
يَعْلَمُونَ مَا تَفْعَلُونَ ١٢	ya‘lamūna mā taf‘alūn.	12. they know what you do.
إِنَّ ٱلْأَبْرَارَ لَفِى نَعِيمٍ ١٣	Inna-l abrāra lafī na‘īm;	13. Surely the virtuous will indeed be in a bliss,
وَإِنَّ ٱلْفُجَّارَ لَفِى جَحِيمٍ ١٤	wa inna-l fujjāra lafī jaḥīm,—	14. and surely the wicked will be in the fierce Fire;
يَصْلَوْنَهَا يَوْمَ ٱلدِّينِ ١٥	-yaṣlawnahā yawma-d dīn.	15. they will enter it on the Day of Judgment.
وَمَا هُمْ عَنْهَا بِغَآئِبِينَ ١٦	Wa mā hum ‘anhā bi-ghā’ibīn.	16. And they will not be absent from there.
وَمَآ أَدْرَىٰكَ مَا يَوْمُ ٱلدِّينِ ١٧	Wa mā adrāka mā yaw-mu-d dīn,	17. And what will make you realize what the day of Judgment is?
ثُمَّ مَآ أَدْرَىٰكَ مَا يَوْمُ ٱلدِّينِ ١٨	thumma mā adrāka mā yawmu-d dīn.	18. Again, what will make you realize what the day of Judgment is?
يَوْمَ لَا تَمْلِكُ نَفْسٌ لِّنَفْسٍ شَيْـًٔا ۖ وَٱلْأَمْرُ يَوْمَئِذٍ لِّلَّهِ ١٩	Yawma lā tamliku nafsuḷ li-nafsiṅ shay’ā. Wal amru yawma’idhiḷ li-llāh.	19. The Day when a soul will not be able to do anything for another soul. And the command on that Day will belong to Allāh.

Explanation:

1-4. The first four verses of the sūrah tell us some events at the time of the Awakening. The sūrah derives its title from the mention of *'infitār* in the first verse. The word means to cleave or split something. On the Day of Awakening, the sky will split—indicating that the entire cosmic structure will collapse. The earth will be in devastating turmoil. The oceans will overflow and submerge the dry land. The graves will be laid open and the dead will be brought back to life.

5-6. At the time of the Awakening, people will have complete knowledge and full understanding of his or her deeds. The deeds of people include all the duties they were required to do and those duties that they forgot or ignored. "What it has left behind" refers to the duties man had ignored in the earthly life by committing sins and/or rejecting the good deeds expected of him. Then Allāh asks people why they got distracted and deceived from remembrance of Allāh, the most-Merciful.

7-8. It is Allāh who has created us, and after the creation He fashioned us in due proportion through stages of creation. Allāh knew best the ideal physical shape of human beings and He proportioned us in that fashion.

9-12. When a question arises about the Awakening, particularly about our responsibility for all deeds, most people deny it will ever happen. Human beings cannot avoid the accountability. This is because angels are writing down all our deeds as well as those righteous deeds that we forget or ignore. The angels record everything we do.

13-16. On the Day of Judgment there will be two groups of people—the righteous and the sinners. The righteous will be in state of bliss, whereas the sinners will be in a fierce Fire.

17-19. In this passage, the same question is asked twice: "what will make you realize what the day of Judgment is?" The repetition of the statement creates a suspense, while makes it clear that the reality of the Hereafter is absolutely certain. On the Day of Judgment, every person will stand trial without getting any type of help from any corner. Allāh will have the absolute power and control of every proceeding on that Day.

Words to know

Bihār: bodies of water, seas. *Bahara*: to slit, make wide cut. *Bahr*: sea, great river. *Bahrain*: two bodies of water.

Qubūr: graves. *Qabara*: to bury the dead. *Maqābir*: graveyard, cemetery.

Q*addamat*: sent forward, brought forward. *Qadama*: to precede, come forward. *Qadamun*: human foot.

Akhkhara: put behind, delayed. *Akhara*: to put back. *Akhirat*: next life, hereafter.

Hāfizīn: guardians, protectors. *Hafiza:* to guard, to protect. *Mahfūz:* protected, guarded.

Fujjār: wicked, evil one. *Fajara:* to break up, to split, to pour water. *Fajrun:* daybreak.

Amrun: command, authority. *Amara:* to command, to order. *Āmirūn:* those who command.

Sūrah Al-Infitār
Word-by-word meaning

ٱلرَّحِيمِ	ٱلرَّحۡمَـٰنِ	ٱللَّهِ	بِسۡمِ
the Most-Rewarding	the Most-Kind	Allāh	In the name of
وَإِذَا	ٱنفَطَرَتۡ ١	ٱلسَّمَآءُ	إِذَا
and when	split apart	the sky	when
ٱلۡبِحَارُ	وَإِذَا	ٱنتَثَرَتۡ ٢	ٱلۡكَوَاكِبُ
the rivers	and when	scattered	the planets
بُعۡثِرَتۡ ٤	ٱلۡقُبُورُ	وَإِذَا	فُجِّرَتۡ ٣
laid open	the graves	and when	made to flow
قَدَّمَتۡ	مَّا	نَفۡسٌ	عَلِمَتۡ
sent forth	what	soul	know
مَا	ٱلۡإِنسَـٰنُ	يَـٰٓأَيُّهَا	وَأَخَّرَتۡ ٥
what	the mankind	O you	and left behind
ٱلَّذِى	ٱلۡكَرِيمِ ٦	بِرَبِّكَ	غَرَّكَ
who	the most Gracious	with your Rabb	deceived you
فِىٓ	فَعَدَلَكَ ٧	فَسَوَّىٰكَ	خَلَقَكَ
in	proportioned you	fashioned you	created you
شَآءَ	مَّا	صُورَةٍ	أَىِّ
pleased	whatever	shape	whatever

رَكَّبَكَ ﴿٨﴾	كَلَّا	بَلْ	تُكَذِّبُونَ
moulded you	no	of course	you deny
بِٱلدِّينِ ﴿٩﴾	وَإِنَّ	عَلَيْكُمْ	لَحَـٰفِظِينَ ﴿١٠﴾
judgment	and surely	over you	guardians
كِرَامًا	كَـٰتِبِينَ ﴿١١﴾	يَعْلَمُونَ	مَا
honored ones	recorders	they know	what
تَفْعَلُونَ ﴿١٢﴾	إِنَّ	ٱلْأَبْرَارَ	لَفِى
you do	surely	the virtuous	indeed in
نَعِيمٍ ﴿١٣﴾	وَإِنَّ	ٱلْفُجَّارَ	لَفِى
bliss	and surely	the wicked	in
جَحِيمٍ ﴿١٤﴾	يَصْلَوْنَهَا	يَوْمَ	ٱلدِّينِ ﴿١٥﴾
fierce Fire	enter it	day	judgment
وَمَا	هُمْ	عَنْهَا	بِغَآئِبِينَ ﴿١٦﴾
and not	they	from it	absent
وَمَآ	أَدْرَىٰكَ	مَا	يَوْمُ
and what	do you know	what	day
ٱلدِّينِ ﴿١٧﴾	ثُمَّ	مَآ	أَدْرَىٰكَ
judgement	then	what	do you know
مَا	يَوْمُ	ٱلدِّينِ ﴿١٨﴾	يَوْمَ
what	Day	judgement	Day

لِّنَفْسٍ	نَفْسٌ	تَمْلِكُ	لَا
for soul	soul	possess	not
لِّلَّهِ ١٩	يَوْمَئِذٍ	وَٱلْأَمْرُ	شَيْـًٔا
for Allah	that Day	and the command	anything

A few applications of the message:

This sūrah gives us a serious warning about the Day of Awakening and tells us what will happen to the righteous and the sinners. No one can avoid the Day, and no one can bypass the Day. Every single thing we do on this earth and every single good deed that we avoid or ignore on this earth will be accounted for. Angels are writing these down and the records will be produced as evidence against us.

Towards the end of the sūrah we are reminded of the terrible consequences of the sinners. They will have no one to assist them and they will have no power to rescue them. Their destiny will be in the Fire. By all means, we want to avoid this consequence. How can we avoid it? The only way we can avoid it is by being mindful of our duties towards Allāh. We do not want to be like those people who forget or ignore Allāh. After all, our very existence was made possible by Him, who created and fashioned us in the best proportions. After that, how can we become distracted from the remembrance of Allāh? When we think of this, we must try to be mindful of our duties towards Allāh.

Questions:

1. What four things will happen on the Day of Awakening as mentioned in first four verses of Sūrah *al-'Infitār*?
2. What does a soul send forward for life after death?
3. What are some of the things that distract people away from the remembrance of Allāh?
4. What will the evil people be unable to do on the Day of Judgment?
5. Where will the righteous and the sinners be in the Hereafter?

Sūrah 81

Revealed in Makkah

At-Takwīr

The Folding Up

Introduction:

This sūrah, similar to Sūrah *al-Infitār*, tells us about the dramatic events at the time of the Awakening. It uses striking images drawn from the universe and the earth and presents them in astonishing rhythms, end-rhymes and fine expressions. The sūrah has two major themes— (a) the onset of Awakening, (b) the truth in Divine revelation, and the integrity of the Prophet (S).

بِسۡمِ ٱللَّهِ ٱلرَّحۡمَـٰنِ ٱلرَّحِيمِ

Bismi-llāhi-r raḥmāni-r raḥīm
In the name of Allah, the Most-Kind, the Most-Rewarding.

إِذَا ٱلشَّمۡسُ كُوِّرَتۡ ١	Idẖa-sh shamsu kuwwirat,	1. When the sun is folded up,
وَإِذَا ٱلنُّجُومُ ٱنكَدَرَتۡ ٢	wa idẖa-n nujūmu-nkadarat,	2. And when the stars are dust-covered,
وَإِذَا ٱلۡجِبَالُ سُيِّرَتۡ ٣	wa idẖa-l jibālu suyyirat,	3. and when the mountains are made to pass away,
وَإِذَا ٱلۡعِشَارُ عُطِّلَتۡ ٤	wa idẖa-l ʻishāru ʻuṭṭilat,	4. and when the ten-month-pregnant camels are abandoned;
وَإِذَا ٱلۡوُحُوشُ حُشِرَتۡ ٥	wa idẖa-l uḥushu ḥushirat,	5. and when the wild beasts are gathered together,
وَإِذَا ٱلۡبِحَارُ سُجِّرَتۡ ٦	wa idẖa-l biḥāru sujjirat,	6. and when the seas are made to swell,
وَإِذَا ٱلنُّفُوسُ زُوِّجَتۡ ٧	wa idẖa-n nufūsu zuwwijat,	7. and when the souls are united,

وَإِذَا ٱلْمَوْءُۥدَةُ سُئِلَتْ ٨	wa id̲h̲a-l maw’ūdatu su’ilat,	8. and when the girl-child buried alive is questioned:
بِأَىِّ ذَنۢبٍ قُتِلَتْ ٩	bi-ayyi d̲h̲anbiṅ qutilat.	9. “For what sin she was killed?”
وَإِذَا ٱلصُّحُفُ نُشِرَتْ ١٠	Wa id̲h̲a-ṣ ṣuḥufu nushirat,	10. And when the pages are spread open;
وَإِذَا ٱلسَّمَآءُ كُشِطَتْ ١١	wa id̲h̲a-s samā’u kushiṭat,	11. and when the sky is uncovered,
وَإِذَا ٱلْجَحِيمُ سُعِّرَتْ ١٢	wa id̲h̲a-l jaḥīmu su‘-‘irat,	12. and when Hell-fire is ignited;
وَإِذَا ٱلْجَنَّةُ أُزْلِفَتْ ١٣	wa id̲h̲a-l jannatu uzlifat,	13. and when the Garden is brought near,—
عَلِمَتْ نَفْسٌ مَّآ أَحْضَرَتْ ١٤	‘alimat nafsuṁ mā aḥḍarat.	14. every soul will know what it has brought forward.
فَلَآ أُقْسِمُ بِٱلْخُنَّسِ ١٥	Fa-lā uqsimu bil khunnas,—	15. Therefore no, I swear by al-Khunnas,
ٱلْجَوَارِ ٱلْكُنَّسِ ١٦	Al jawāri-l kunnas,	16. al-Jawar, al-Kunnas.
وَٱلَّيْلِ إِذَا عَسْعَسَ ١٧	wal layli id̲h̲ā ‘as‘asa,	17. And the night when it departs,
وَٱلصُّبْحِ إِذَا تَنَفَّسَ ١٨	waṣ ṣubḥi id̲h̲ā tanaffas,	18. and the dawn when it brightens;
إِنَّهُۥ لَقَوْلُ رَسُولٍ كَرِيمٍ ١٩	innahū la-qawlu rasūliṅ karīm,	19. surely this is indeed the word of a noble Rasul—
ذِى قُوَّةٍ عِندَ ذِى ٱلْعَرْشِ مَكِينٍ ٢٠	d̲h̲ī quwwatiṅ ‘inda d̲h̲il ‘arshi makīn,—	20. the possessor of strength, established in the presence of the Master of the Throne,—
مُّطَاعٍ ثَمَّ أَمِينٍ ٢١	-muṭā‘iṅ t̲h̲amma amīn.	21. one obeyed, and trustworthy!

وَمَا صَاحِبُكُم بِمَجْنُونٍ ٢٢	Wa mā ṣāḥibukum bi-majnūn.	22. And your Companion is not a mad man.
وَلَقَدْ رَءَاهُ بِٱلْأُفُقِ ٱلْمُبِينِ ٢٣	Wa la-qad ra'āhu bil ufuqil mubīn.	23. And surely he has seen him in the clear horizon.
وَمَا هُوَ عَلَى ٱلْغَيْبِ بِضَنِينٍ ٢٤	Wa mā huwa 'ala-l ghaybi bi-ḍanīn.	24. he does not withhold about the unseen;
وَمَا هُوَ بِقَوْلِ شَيْطَٰنٍ رَّجِيمٍ ٢٥	Wa mā huwa bi-qawli shayṭāni-r rajīm,	25. and this is not the word of Shaitān, the driven away,
فَأَيْنَ تَذْهَبُونَ ٢٦	fa-ayna tadhhabūn.	26. then where will you be going?
إِنْ هُوَ إِلَّا ذِكْرٌ لِّلْعَٰلَمِينَ ٢٧	In huwa illā dhikruḷ lil 'ālamīn,	27. This is nothing but a Reminder to all the worlds,—
لِمَن شَآءَ مِنكُمْ أَن يَسْتَقِيمَ ٢٨	liman shā'a minkum aṅ yastaqīm.	28. for him among you who wishes to walk straight;
وَمَا تَشَآءُونَ إِلَّآ أَن يَشَآءَ ٱللَّهُ رَبُّ ٱلْعَٰلَمِينَ ٢٩	Wa mā tashā'ūna illā aṅ yashā'a-llāhu rabbu-l 'ālamīn.	29. and you will not wish except as Allah wishes,— the Rabb of all the worlds.

Explanation:

1-3. The sūrah derives its title from the mention of *kuwwirat*, derived from *takwir,* meaning the act of folding up, rolling, or wrapping up (like a carpet or turban). Folding up of the sun will result in intense darkness during the daytime. The stars would lose their light, turning the night into total darkness. Simultaneously, the foundations of the mountains will start to crumble. These three short verses bring the sense of total chaos and destruction.

4-5. A pregnant camel in her 10th month of pregnancy is very valuable since the young camel would add to the owner's wealth; along with the mother-camel providing plenty of milk—another source of income. Only during serious catastrophes would someone abandon such a valuable animal. Even the wild beasts will gather together. Out of terror, these beasts will forget their mutual hostility.

6. The chaos will spread to the seas, which swell up causing unseen destruction. This unforeseen flooding from the seas will inundate the land masses.

7-9. At the time of Awakening, all human souls irrespective of caste, creed, color, or nationality, will be united. One of the old sinful customs in Arabia was to bury the girl children alive. The Arabs used to feel ashamed if a girl child was born to them. Islam abolished this custom, and reminds the people that they will be brought to justice. People who committed such sinful acts will be questioned.

10-14. On the Day of Judgment the Books of Records will be laid open. The secrets of the universe will be known as if the universe had been revealed. The Hell-fire will be kindled up. Simultaneously, the Garden will be brought near the righteous people as a mercy from Allāh. Every soul will then realize all the deeds they have brought forward with them. Based on the merits of these deeds, people will either suffer in the Hell-fire or enter the Garden.

15-18. The second theme mentioned in the introduction of the sūrah begins here. The authenticity of the Qur'ān and the process of its revelation are emphasized with Divine oath. The oaths are uttered in the name of stars and other natural phenomenon on the earth.

19-22. This passage gives the description of our Prophet (S). He is noble and illustrious messenger of Allāh. About him Allāh says the Prophet (S) is mighty, in the sense that significant power and efforts are needed to carry on his mission. He enjoys a special position with the Master of the Throne—who will grant the Prophet (S) success in future and supremacy over the enemies. His position is such that he should be obeyed and trusted. There is nothing wrong about him. Disbelievers in Arabia thought he was an insane person, whereas he was not insane nor was he possessed by jinn.

23-25. It is reported in hadīth that the Prophet (S) saw Jibril on the night of the first revelation and at another occasion in the horizon. As the revelations kept coming, the Prophet (S) did not withhold any of the Messages. He delivered the message exactly as it was revealed to him. At the time of the Prophet (S), many well-known poets claimed they were possessed by jinn. Many people thought Muhammad (S), too, was possessed by jinn. However, such an authentic message of the Qur'ān could not have come from Shaitān, jinn or other evil sources.

26-29. This passage asks about the choices that people make—to walk on the Right Path or to get lost on the wrong path. The message of the Qur'ān is nothing but a reminder for all the worlds; it is not exclusively for those who follow it. Those who wish to walk on the Right Path will be rewarded. Those who wish to follow a different path are at liberty to do so. However, the Prophet (S) will not be responsible for their actions. Ultimately, it is the Will of Allāh that prevails.

Words to know

Jibāl: mountains, chiefs. *Jabala*: to make or create. *Jabal*: mountain.

'Ishār: ten-month pregnant camel, she-camels that are milked. *'Ashara*: tenth. *'Ashara Mubashara*: the ten who received good news.

Bihār: bodies of water, seas. *Bahara*: to slit, make a wide cut. *Bahr*: sea, great river. *Bahrain*: two bodies of water.

Suhufun: sheets, scrolls, scriptures. *Sahafa*: to write or read. *Sihāf*: hollow dish or bowl. *Sahīfa*: surface of the earth.

Khunnas: stars, those who move away when they advance. *Khannas*: one who hides.

Majnun: mad person, whose mind is covered. *Janna*: covered, to be dark. *Jinn*: hidden or covered creatures.

Sūrah At-Takwīr
Word-by-word meaning

بِسۡمِ In the name of	ٱللَّهِ Allāh	ٱلرَّحۡمَٰنِ the Most-Kind	ٱلرَّحِيمِ the Most-Rewarding
إِذَا When	ٱلشَّمۡسُ the sun	كُوِّرَتۡ ﴿١﴾ covered	وَإِذَا and when
ٱلنُّجُومُ the stars	ٱنكَدَرَتۡ ﴿٢﴾ dust-covered	وَإِذَا and when	ٱلۡجِبَالُ the mountains
سُيِّرَتۡ ﴿٣﴾ made to pass	وَ and	إِذَا when	ٱلۡعِشَارُ the pregnant camel
عُطِّلَتۡ ﴿٤﴾ abandoned	وَإِذَا and when	ٱلۡوُحُوشُ the beasts	حُشِرَتۡ ﴿٥﴾ gathered
وَإِذَا and when	ٱلۡبِحَارُ the seas	سُجِّرَتۡ ﴿٦﴾ filled with flames	وَإِذَا and when
ٱلنُّفُوسُ the souls	زُوِّجَتۡ ﴿٧﴾ paired	وَإِذَا and when	ٱلۡمَوۡءُۥدَةُ the buried alive baby girl
سُئِلَتۡ ﴿٨﴾ is questioned	بِأَيِّ with which	ذَنۢبٍ sin	قُتِلَتۡ ﴿٩﴾ she was killed
وَإِذَا and when	ٱلصُّحُفُ the pages	نُشِرَتۡ ﴿١٠﴾ spread	وَإِذَا and when

ٱلسَّمَآءُ the sky	كُشِطَتْ ﴿١١﴾ uncovered	وَإِذَا and when	ٱلْجَحِيمُ the hellfire
سُعِّرَتْ ﴿١٢﴾ ignited	وَإِذَا and when	ٱلْجَنَّةُ the Garden	أُزْلِفَتْ ﴿١٣﴾ brought near
عَلِمَتْ will know	نَفْسٌ the soul	مَّآ what	أَحْضَرَتْ ﴿١٤﴾ brought forward
فَلَآ so not that	أُقْسِمُ I swear	بِٱلْخُنَّسِ ﴿١٥﴾ by al-Khunnas	ٱلْجَوَارِ al-Jawar
ٱلْكُنَّسِ ﴿١٦﴾ al-Kunnas	وَٱلَّيْلِ and the night	إِذَا when	عَسْعَسَ ﴿١٧﴾ departs
وَٱلصُّبْحِ and the dawn	إِذَا when	تَنَفَّسَ ﴿١٨﴾ brightens	إِنَّهُۥ Surely this is
لَقَوْلُ a word	رَسُولٍ Rasul	كَرِيمٍ ﴿١٩﴾ noble	ذِى possessor
قُوَّةٍ strength	عِندَ with	ذِى possessor	ٱلْعَرْشِ the Throne
مَكِينٍ ﴿٢٠﴾ the position	مُّطَاعٍ obeyed	ثَمَّ thereby	أَمِينٍ ﴿٢١﴾ trustworthy
وَمَا and not	صَاحِبُكُم your companion	بِمَجْنُونٍ ﴿٢٢﴾ insane	وَلَقَدْ and has already

رَءَاهُ	بِٱلْأُفُقِ	ٱلْمُبِينِ ﴿٢٣﴾	وَمَا
seen him	horizon	clear	and not
هُوَ	عَلَى	ٱلْغَيْبِ	بِضَنِينٍ ﴿٢٤﴾
it is	of	the unseen	withholder
وَمَا	هُوَ	بِقَوْلِ	شَيْطَٰنٍ
and not	it is	word of	Shaitān
رَّجِيمٍ ﴿٢٥﴾	فَأَيْنَ	تَذْهَبُونَ ﴿٢٦﴾	إِنْ
driven away	so where	you going	not
هُوَ	إِلَّا	ذِكْرٌ	لِّلْعَٰلَمِينَ ﴿٢٧﴾
it	nothing	reminder	for the words
لِمَن	شَآءَ	مِنكُمْ	أَن
whoever	wills	among you	that
يَسْتَقِيمَ ﴿٢٨﴾	وَمَا	تَشَآءُونَ	إِلَّآ
walk rightly	and not	you will	except
أَن	يَشَآءَ	ٱللَّهُ	رَبُّ
that	wishes	Allah	Rabb
ٱلْعَٰلَمِينَ ﴿٢٩﴾			
the worlds			

A few applications of the message:

The climax of the sūrah is given in verse 14: "Every soul will know what it has brought forward." Prior to this verse, all the verses spoke of the tremendous events leading to the Awakening. The verses that follow verse 14 tell how we can bring forward acts that will lead us to the Garden. Our every action is recorded in a clear book. For almost every action, we may choose the right path or the wrong one. Our deeds are the biggest asset that we will carry with us to the Hereafter. We may choose to carry those assets that will ultimately benefit us or choose to carry those assets what will harm us. The choice is upon us, as mentioned in verse 28. The Qur'ān is only a reminder for those who wish to follow the guidance. The Qur'ān is not the word of Shaitān or an evil spirit. It is Divine. If we, as Muslims, can follow the teachings of the Qur'ān and the path shown by the Prophet (S), we will have no fear. The Awakening is real. The Day of Judgment is certain, and the life in Hereafter is real. We must ask ourselves, why can we not prepare ourselves for the real life in the Hereafter?

Questions:

1. Explain in your own words the significance of ten-month pregnant camels mentioned in the sūrah.
2. Explain why the Arabs used to bury their girl-children?
3. Explain why disbelievers used to say the revelations were words of Shaitān or soothsayer.

Sūrah 80

Revealed in Makkah

'Abasa

He Frowned

Introduction:

This sūrah was revealed when a blind man interrupted the Prophet (S) as he was discussing Islam with a group of Quraish leaders. The Prophet (S) was a little annoyed at the interruption. The sūrah criticizes the Prophet's (S) actions and points out that guidance is at the hands of Allāh. The Prophet's (S) responsibility was only to deliver the message. The rest of the sūrah calls our attention to the process of creation and to the signs in the nature. If we appreciate these signs, we will become aware of Allāh and prepare ourselves for the Day of Judgment.

بِسۡمِ ٱللَّهِ ٱلرَّحۡمَـٰنِ ٱلرَّحِيمِ

Bismi-llāhi-r raḥmāni-r raḥīm

In the name of Allah, the Most-Kind, the Most-Rewarding.

عَبَسَ وَتَوَلَّىٰٓ ﴿١﴾	'Abasa wa tawallā,	1. He frowned and turned aside, —
أَن جَآءَهُ ٱلۡأَعۡمَىٰ ﴿٢﴾	an jā'ahu-l a'mā.	2. because the blind man came to him.
وَمَا يُدۡرِيكَ لَعَلَّهُۥ يَزَّكَّىٰٓ ﴿٣﴾	Wa mā yudrīka la'allahū yazzakkā,	3. And how will you know that he might become pure,
أَوۡ يَذَّكَّرُ فَتَنفَعَهُ ٱلذِّكۡرَىٰٓ ﴿٤﴾	aw yadhdhakkaru fa-anfa'ahu-dh dhikrā.	4. or that he would receive a reminder and it would benefit him?
أَمَّا مَنِ ٱسۡتَغۡنَىٰ ﴿٥﴾	Ammā mani-staghnā,	5. But as for him who regarded himself without need,
فَأَنتَ لَهُۥ تَصَدَّىٰ ﴿٦﴾	fa-anta lahū taṣaddā.	6. to him you were then paying attention.

وَمَا عَلَيْكَ أَلَّا يَزَّكَّىٰ ٧	Wa mā ‘alayka allā yazzakkā.	7. And what is on you if he does not beome pure?
وَأَمَّا مَن جَآءَكَ يَسْعَىٰ ٨	Wa ammā man jā’aka yas‘ā,	8. Whereas, he who came to you striving,
وَهُوَ يَخْشَىٰ ٩	wa huwa yakhshā,	9. and he fears,
فَأَنتَ عَنْهُ تَلَهَّىٰ ١٠	fa-anta ‘anhu talahhā;	10. but you neglected him.
كَلَّآ إِنَّهَا تَذْكِرَةٌ ١١	kallā innahā tad͟hkirah,	11. By no means! Surely this is a Reminder,—
فَمَن شَآءَ ذَكَرَهُۥ ١٢	fa-man shā’a dhakarah.	12. so let whoever wishes, remember it.
فِى صُحُفٍ مُّكَرَّمَةٍ ١٣	Fi ṣuḥufiṁ mukarramah,—	13. On honored sheets,—
مَّرْفُوعَةٍ مُّطَهَّرَةٍۭ ١٤	-marfū‘atiṁ muṭahharah,	14. exalted, purified,
بِأَيْدِى سَفَرَةٍ ١٥	bi-aydī safarah,	15. with the hands of scribes,
كِرَامٍۭ بَرَرَةٍ ١٦	kirāmiṁ bararah.	16. honorable, virtuous.
قُتِلَ ٱلْإِنسَـٰنُ مَآ أَكْفَرَهُۥ ١٧	Qutila-l insānu mā akfarah.	17. May man be destroyed! how ungrateful he is!
مِنْ أَىِّ شَىْءٍ خَلَقَهُۥ ١٨	Min ayyi shay’iṅ khalaqah.	18. Out of what object He created him?
مِن نُّطْفَةٍ خَلَقَهُۥ فَقَدَّرَهُۥ ١٩	Min nuṭfatiṅ. Khalaqahū fa-qaddarah,	19. Out of a droplet! He created him, then proportioned him;
ثُمَّ ٱلسَّبِيلَ يَسَّرَهُۥ ٢٠	t͟humma-s sabīla yassarah,	20. then made the passage easy for him;
ثُمَّ أَمَاتَهُۥ فَأَقْبَرَهُۥ ٢١	t͟humma amātahū, fa-aqbarah,	21. then He causes him to die, and He provides him with a grave;
ثُمَّ إِذَا شَآءَ أَنشَرَهُۥ ٢٢	t͟humma id͟hā shā’a ansharah.	22. then when He pleases, He will raise him up.

كَلَّا لَمَّا يَقْضِ مَآ أَمَرَهُۥ ﴿٢٣﴾	Kallā lammā yaqḍi mā amarah.	23. No, he has not done what He commanded him.
فَلْيَنظُرِ ٱلْإِنسَـٰنُ إِلَىٰ طَعَامِهِۦٓ ﴿٢٤﴾	Fal yanzuri-l insānu ilā ṭa'āmih,	24. Then let man look at his food—
أَنَّا صَبَبْنَا ٱلْمَآءَ صَبًّا ﴿٢٥﴾	annā ṣabarna-l mā'a ṣabbā,	25. how We pour down the water in abundance;
ثُمَّ شَقَقْنَا ٱلْأَرْضَ شَقًّا ﴿٢٦﴾	t͟humma shaqaqna-l arḍa shaqqā,	26. and then We split the earth a splitting,
فَأَنۢبَتْنَا فِيهَا حَبًّا ﴿٢٧﴾	fa aṅbatnā fīhā ḥabba,—	27. so that We cause to grow in it grain,
وَعِنَبًا وَقَضْبًا ﴿٢٨﴾	-wa 'inabaẇ wa qaḍbaẇ,—	28. and grapes and vegetation,
وَزَيْتُونًا وَنَخْلًا ﴿٢٩﴾	-wa jhaytūnaẇ wa nakhlaẇ,—	29. and olives and dates,
وَحَدَآئِقَ غُلْبًا ﴿٣٠﴾	-wa ḥadā'iqa ghulbaẇ,—	30. and gardens thickly planted,
وَفَـٰكِهَةً وَأَبًّا ﴿٣١﴾	-wa fāhikataẇ wa abba,—	31. and fruits and pastures,—
مَّتَـٰعًا لَّكُمْ وَلِأَنْعَـٰمِكُمْ ﴿٣٢﴾	-matā'aḷ lakum wa li-an'āmikum.	32. a provision for you and for your cattle.
فَإِذَا جَآءَتِ ٱلصَّآخَّةُ ﴿٣٣﴾	Fa-id͟hā jā'ati-ṣ ṣākhkhah,	33. Then when the Terrible Blast comes—
يَوْمَ يَفِرُّ ٱلْمَرْءُ مِنْ أَخِيهِ ﴿٣٤﴾	yawma yafirru-l maru' min akhīh,	34. that Day man will flee from his brother,
وَأُمِّهِۦ وَأَبِيهِ ﴿٣٥﴾	wa ummihī wa abīh,	35. and his mother and his father,
وَصَـٰحِبَتِهِۦ وَبَنِيهِ ﴿٣٦﴾	wa ṣāḥibatihī wa banīh.	36. and his spouse and his children.
لِكُلِّ ٱمْرِئٍ مِّنْهُمْ يَوْمَئِذٍ شَأْنٌ يُغْنِيهِ ﴿٣٧﴾	Li kulli-mri'iṁ minhum yawma'id͟hiṅ sha'nuẏ yughnīh.	37. For every man that Day will have enough concern to make him indifferent.
وُجُوهٌ يَوْمَئِذٍ مُّسْفِرَةٌ ﴿٣٨﴾	Wujūhuẏ yawma'id͟hiṁ musfirah,	38. some faces that Day will be bright,

ضَاحِكَةٌ مُّسْتَبْشِرَةٌ ﴿٣٩﴾	ḍāḥikatuṁ mustabshirah;	39. laughing, rejoicing.
وَوُجُوهٌ يَوْمَئِذٍ عَلَيْهَا غَبَرَةٌ ﴿٤٠﴾	wa wujūhuẏ yawma'idh̲iṅ 'alayhā ghabarah,	40. And other faces that Day will have dust upon them;
تَرْهَقُهَا قَتَرَةٌ ﴿٤١﴾	tarhaquhā qatarah.	41. darkness covering them.
أُوْلَٰٓئِكَ هُمُ ٱلْكَفَرَةُ ٱلْفَجَرَةُ ﴿٤٢﴾	Ulā'ika humu-l kafaratu-l fajarah.	42. These are the disbelievers, the wicked.

Explanation

1-4. One day the Prophet (S) was speaking to a group of influential non-Muslim leaders of Makkah, hoping to convince them about the truth in his message. During that meeting, *Ibn Umm Maktūm*, who was also known as *'Abdullah ibn Surayh*, a blind early convert to Islam, approached him with a question. The Prophet (S) was annoyed by the sudden interruption and turned his attention away from the blind man. He thought his discussion with the elders of the Quraish needed greater attention. Immediately after this incidence, ten verses were revealed, disapproving the Prophet's (S) conduct. The blind man was already a Muslim and was seeking further guidance. Therefore, he deserved more attention from the Prophet (S) than those who did not want to be guided at all.

5-10. According to Allāh's principle, this blind person, who sincerely wanted to learn more about Islam, deserves to be guided. The blind person came to the Prophet (S) on his own, with a fear of Allāh in his heart. Yet the Prophet (S) ignored him. On the other hand, the rich Quraish leaders considered themselves to be self-sufficient. They did not feel there was any need to be guided. The Prophet (S), unaware of the true motives of the Quraish leaders, was hoping to guide them. Allāh reminded him that he was not responsible for guiding anyone. Guidance comes only from Allāh. Those who wish to be guided, are guided. Those who wish not to be guided, are left alone.

11-16. Allāh does not force anybody to believe in the truth. The message of the Qur'ān serves as a reminder for those who wish to be guided and pay attention to it. The Prophet (S) was not responsible for people believing in the Qur'ān. Before the Qur'ān was compiled into a formal book, the companions wrote down and memorized entire passage as these were revealed to the Prophet (S). The revelation was, thus, preserved from the very beginning. These passages were of the highest standard and purest in content. The companions were praised as they were honorable and virtuous.

17-23. Human beings may destroy themselves or they deserve to be destroyed because they are too proud to accept the Divine truth. They are ungrateful to Allāh. They do not realize that without Allāh's favor, they would not have existed. They forget that Allāh created them from insignificant germ cells, proportioned them in their mothers' wombs, brought them to life and made all their affairs in life easy and smooth. Allāh causes them to die, and Allāh will again bring them back to life at the time of the Awakening. Allāh controls the affairs of human beings, yet Allāh gives them the freedom of choice. As a result, human beings sometimes become engrossed in this life so much so that they forget to fulfill their duties in the life.

24-32. This set of verses asks people to look at their food. They are asked to think about how the food is made available to them—how the sky pours down rain, how the rainfall seeps in the ground and assists the seeds in splitting open the ground and germinating. From the seeds come varieties of fruits, vegetables and grasses providing nutrients and fodder for us and our cattle.

33-36. Then one day a terrible blast will set off the Day of Awakening. That Day everyone will be so scared and concerned for their own wellbeing that the family members will forget each other. Each person will have enough of his or her own worries that they will become indifferent to others.

37-42. The face of a person is an indication of his or her personality. On that Day there will be two types of faces. The believers will have happy, bright face—laughing and rejoicing because all their lives they believed in the Awakening and worked righteous deeds. They will know the time has come to get their reward. The disbelievers will have terrified, sad, downcast, gloomy faces because they denied the truth during their lives and neglected their duties.

Words to know

Abasa: he frowned. *'Abūsan*: frowning, grim.
Yazzakka: purify himself. *Zakāt*: purification, poor tax. *Zaka*: to be pure, to grow. *Azkā*: the purest.
Dhikrā: reminder. *Dhakara*: to remember. *Dhikr*: fame, admonition. *Mudhakkir*: admonisher, reminder.
Safaratin: scribes. *Safara*: to scribe, sweep, shine, travel. *Asfār*: large book. *Musfiratun*: shining, beaming.
Dzahikatun: laughing. *Dzahika*: to laugh, to wonder.

Sūrah 'Abasa
Word-by-word meaning

ٱلرَّحِيمِ	ٱلرَّحْمَٰنِ	ٱللَّهِ	بِسْمِ
the Most-Rewarding	the Most-Kind	Allāh	In the name of
جَآءَهُ	أَن	وَتَوَلَّىٰٓ ١	عَبَسَ
came to him	that	and turned away	frowned
لَعَلَّهُۥ	يُدْرِيكَ	وَمَا	ٱلْأَعْمَىٰ ٢
perhaps	make you know	and what	the blind man

يَزَّكَّىٰٓ ﴿٣﴾	أَوْ	يَذَّكَّرُ	فَتَنفَعَهُ
to purify	or	reminder	benefit him
ٱلذِّكْرَىٰٓ ﴿٤﴾	أَمَّا	مَنِ	ٱسْتَغْنَىٰ ﴿٥﴾
the remembrance	as for	who	without need
فَأَنتَ	لَهُۥ	تَصَدَّىٰ ﴿٦﴾	وَمَا
so you	to him	pay attention	and not
عَلَيْكَ	أَلَّا	يَزَّكَّىٰ ﴿٧﴾	وَأَمَّا
upon you	that not	be purified	and as for
مَن	جَآءَكَ	يَسْعَىٰ ﴿٨﴾	وَهُوَ
who	came to you	striving	and he
يَخْشَىٰ ﴿٩﴾	فَأَنتَ	عَنْهُ	تَلَهَّىٰ ﴿١٠﴾
fears	so you	from him	negligence
كَلَّآ	إِنَّهَا	تَذْكِرَةٌ ﴿١١﴾	فَمَن
No, certainly	this	reminder	so whoever
شَآءَ	ذَكَرَهُۥ ﴿١٢﴾	فِى	صُحُفٍ
wishes	remember it	in	sheets
مُّكَرَّمَةٍ ﴿١٣﴾	مَّرْفُوعَةٍ	مُّطَهَّرَةٍۭ ﴿١٤﴾	بِأَيْدِى
honored	exalted	purified	in the hands
سَفَرَةٍ ﴿١٥﴾	كِرَامٍۭ	بَرَرَةٍ ﴿١٦﴾	قُتِلَ
scribes	honorable	virtuous	is destroyed

مِنْ	أَكْفَرَهُۥ ﴿١٧﴾	مَآ	ٱلْإِنسَٰنُ
from	ungrateful	how	the man
مِنْ	خَلَقَهُۥ ﴿١٨﴾	شَىْءٍ	أَىِّ
out of	created him	object	what
ثُمَّ	فَقَدَّرَهُۥ ﴿١٩﴾	خَلَقَهُۥ	نُّطْفَةٍ
then	proportioned him	created him	droplet
أَمَاتَهُۥ	ثُمَّ	يَسَّرَهُۥ ﴿٢٠﴾	ٱلسَّبِيلَ
caused death	then	easy for him	the passage
شَآءَ	إِذَا	ثُمَّ	فَأَقْبَرَهُۥ ﴿٢١﴾
pleases	when	then	provided grave
يَقْضِ	لَمَّا	كَلَّا	أَنشَرَهُۥ ﴿٢٢﴾
done	not yet	no	raise him up
ٱلْإِنسَٰنُ	فَلْيَنظُرِ	أَمَرَهُۥ ﴿٢٣﴾	مَآ
the man	so let him look	commanded him	what
صَبَبْنَا	أَنَّا	طَعَامِهِۦٓ ﴿٢٤﴾	إِلَىٰ
We pour	that	his food	at
شَقَقْنَا	ثُمَّ	صَبًّا ﴿٢٥﴾	ٱلْمَآءَ
split	then	abundantly	the water
فِيهَا	فَأَنۢبَتْنَا	شَقًّا ﴿٢٦﴾	ٱلْأَرْضَ
in it	caused to grow	splitting	the earth

حَبًّا ﴿٢٧﴾ grain	وَعِنَبًا and grapes	وَقَضۡبًا ﴿٢٨﴾ and vegetation	وَزَيۡتُونًا and olive
وَنَخۡلًا ﴿٢٩﴾ and dates	وَحَدَآئِقَ and gardens	غُلۡبًا ﴿٣٠﴾ thickly planted	وَفَٰكِهَةً and fruit
وَأَبًّا ﴿٣١﴾ and pasture	مَّتَٰعًا provision	لَّكُمۡ for you	وَلِأَنۡعَٰمِكُمۡ ﴿٣٢﴾ and for your cattle
فَإِذَا so when	جَآءَتِ comes	ٱلصَّآخَّةُ ﴿٣٣﴾ the Terrible Blast	يَوۡمَ day
يَفِرُّ will flee	ٱلۡمَرۡءُ the man	مِنۡ from	أَخِيهِ ﴿٣٤﴾ his brother
وَأُمِّهِۦ and his mother	وَأَبِيهِ ﴿٣٥﴾ and his father	وَصَٰحِبَتِهِۦ and his spouse	وَبَنِيهِ ﴿٣٦﴾ and his children
لِكُلِّ for every	ٱمۡرِيٍٕ man	مِّنۡهُمۡ among them	يَوۡمَئِذٖ that day
شَأۡنٞ matter	يُغۡنِيهِ ﴿٣٧﴾ adequate for him	وُجُوهٞ faces	يَوۡمَئِذٖ that day
مُّسۡفِرَةٞ ﴿٣٨﴾ bright	ضَاحِكَةٞ laughing	مُّسۡتَبۡشِرَةٞ ﴿٣٩﴾ rejoicing	وَوُجُوهٞ and faces
يَوۡمَئِذٍ that day	عَلَيۡهَا upon them	غَبَرَةٞ ﴿٤٠﴾ dust	تَرۡهَقُهَا cover them

قَتَرَةٌ ﴿٤١﴾	أُوْلَـٰٓئِكَ	هُمُ	ٱلۡكَفَرَةُ
darkness	those	themselves	the disbelievers
ٱلۡفَجَرَةُ ﴿٤٢﴾			
the wicked			

A few applications of the message:

Allāh controls all the affairs of human beings, yet He gives them the freedom of choice. The freedom of choice allows us to choose between right and wrong. The message of the Qur'ān clearly points out what is right and what is wrong. The Qur'ān can inspire us if we pay attention to its message. However, we should remember that no one else but only Allāh can guide us, provided we seek the guidancc.

Guidance is one of Allāh's blessings. Other than guidance, Allāh has given us so many other things in life to make our lives good and worth living. Yet, most people are ungrateful to their Creator. Allāh dislikes people who are ungrateful. As we read this sūrah, we should remember to give thanks to Allāh for everything He does for us everyday. This will make us humble and help us submit to our Creator. If we remember Allāh through our faith and conduct, we will ultimately be successful in the Hereafter.

Questions:

1. Why did the Prophet (S) feel annoyed when the blind man interrupted him?
2. Based on the message of Sūrah *'Abasa,* who would benefit the most from the teachings of the Qur'ān?
3. In verse 24, why did Allāh ask people to look at their food?
4. On the Day of Awakening all men will run away from his relations. What relations are mentioned in the sūrah? Why will they run away?
5. Based on the narrations in Sūrah *'Abasa*, what will the condition of the disbelievers be on the Day of Judgment?

Sūrah 79

Revealed in Makkah

An-Nazi'āt

Those who Extract

Introduction:

This sūrah begins with a short narration about some of the scenes of Hereafter. There will be great commotion at the time of the Awakening. The sūrah then refers to the story of Mūsā (A) and Fir'awn. The story points out the utter destruction awaiting those who transgress, show pride, deny Allāh and self-glorify. The power, name and fame of a person will avail him no benefit. Finally, the sūrah highlights some of the natural events to draw our attention to the realities of the Awakening.

بِسۡمِ ٱللَّهِ ٱلرَّحۡمَـٰنِ ٱلرَّحِيمِ

Bismi-llāhi-r raḥmāni-r raḥīm

In the name of Allah, the Most-Kind, the Most-Rewarding.

وَٱلنَّـٰزِعَـٰتِ غَرۡقًا ﴿١﴾	Wan nāzi'āti gharqa,—	1. By the extractors proceeding violently;
وَٱلنَّـٰشِطَـٰتِ نَشۡطًا ﴿٢﴾	-wan nāshiṭāti nashṭaw,—	2. and those going forth in a steady going forth,
وَٱلسَّـٰبِحَـٰتِ سَبۡحًا ﴿٣﴾	-was sābiḥāti sabḥa,	3. and the swimmers in a swift swimming.
فَٱلسَّـٰبِقَـٰتِ سَبۡقًا ﴿٤﴾	fas sābiqāti sabqa,	4. Then the foremost go foremost!
فَٱلۡمُدَبِّرَٰتِ أَمۡرًا ﴿٥﴾	fal mudabbirāti amrā.	5. And consider those regulating the affairs!
يَوۡمَ تَرۡجُفُ ٱلرَّاجِفَةُ ﴿٦﴾	Yawma tarjufu-r rājifah,	6. The Day the quaking one will quake,
تَتۡبَعُهَا ٱلرَّادِفَةُ ﴿٧﴾	tatba'uha-r rādifah.	7. the consequence will follow it.

قُلُوبٌ يَوْمَئِذٍ وَاجِفَةٌ ٨	Qulūbuẏ yawma'idhiẇ wājifah,	8. Hearts on that Day will be trembling,
أَبْصَٰرُهَا خَٰشِعَةٌ ٩	abṣāruhā khāshi'ah.	9. their gaze will be downcast.
يَقُولُونَ أَءِنَّا لَمَرْدُودُونَ فِى ٱلْحَافِرَةِ ١٠	Yaqūlūna 'a-innā la-mardūdūna fil ḥāfirah.	10. They will say: "Shall we indeed be restored to our former state?
أَءِذَا كُنَّا عِظَٰمًا نَّخِرَةً ١١	A-'idhā kunnā 'izāmaṅ nākhirah.	11. "even after we shall become rotten bones?"
قَالُوا۟ تِلْكَ إِذًا كَرَّةٌ خَاسِرَةٌ ١٢	Qālū tilka idhaṅ karratuṅ khāsirah.	12. They say: "That then indeed would be a return with loss."
فَإِنَّمَا هِىَ زَجْرَةٌ وَٰحِدَةٌ ١٣	Fa-innamā hiya zajratuẇ wāḥidah,	13. So indeed, it will be a single blast,
فَإِذَا هُم بِٱلسَّاهِرَةِ ١٤	fa-idhā hum bis sāhirah.	14. they will then become awakened!
هَلْ أَتَىٰكَ حَدِيثُ مُوسَىٰٓ ١٥	Hal atāka ḥadīthu mūsā.	15. Did the story of Mūsā reach you?
إِذْ نَادَىٰهُ رَبُّهُۥ بِٱلْوَادِ ٱلْمُقَدَّسِ طُوًى ١٦	Idh nādāhu rabbuhu bi-l muqaddasi ṭuwā;	16. When his Rabb called out to him in the sacred valley, Tuwa,
ٱذْهَبْ إِلَىٰ فِرْعَوْنَ إِنَّهُۥ طَغَىٰ ١٧	idhhab ilā fir'awna innahū ṭaghā,	17. "You go to Fir'awn,—surely he has crossed the limits—
فَقُلْ هَل لَّكَ إِلَىٰٓ أَن تَزَكَّىٰ ١٨	fa-qul hal laka ilā an tazakkā;	18. "then say: 'Do you desire that you should purify yourself?
وَأَهْدِيَكَ إِلَىٰ رَبِّكَ فَتَخْشَىٰ ١٩	wa ahdiyaka ilā rabbika fa-takhshā;	19. 'I shall then guide you to your Rabb, so that you may fear'."
فَأَرَىٰهُ ٱلْءَايَةَ ٱلْكُبْرَىٰ ٢٠	fa arāhu-l āyata-l kubrā;	20. And he showed him the great Sign.
فَكَذَّبَ وَعَصَىٰ ٢١	fa kadhdhaba wa 'aṣā;	21. But he denied and disobeyed.
ثُمَّ أَدْبَرَ يَسْعَىٰ ٢٢	thumma adbara yas'ā;	22. Then he turned away striving;

فَحَشَرَ فَنَادَىٰ ﴿٢٣﴾	fa-ḥashara fa nādā;	23. and he gathered, and called out;
فَقَالَ أَنَا۠ رَبُّكُمُ ٱلْأَعْلَىٰ ﴿٢٤﴾	fa-qāla ana rabbukumu-l a‘lā;	24. then he said: “I am your lord, the most high.”
فَأَخَذَهُ ٱللَّهُ نَكَالَ ٱلْـَٔاخِرَةِ وَٱلْأُولَىٰٓ ﴿٢٥﴾	fa-akhadhahu-llāhu nakāla-l ākhirati wal ū!ā.	25. So Allāh seized him with an exemplary punishment of the Hereafter and of the former.
إِنَّ فِى ذَٰلِكَ لَعِبْرَةً لِّمَن يَخْشَىٰٓ ﴿٢٦﴾	26. Inna fī dhālika la-‘ibratan liman yakhshā.	26. Surely in that is a lesson for him who fears.
	Section 2	
ءَأَنتُمْ أَشَدُّ خَلْقًا أَمِ ٱلسَّمَآءُ ۚ بَنَىٰهَا ﴿٢٧﴾	’A antum ashaddu khalqan ami-s samāu. Banāhā;	27. Are you more difficult to create, or is the heaven? He has created it.
رَفَعَ سَمْكَهَا فَسَوَّىٰهَا ﴿٢٨﴾	rafa‘a samkahā fa-sawwāhā,	28. He has raised its height, and He made it perfect;
وَأَغْطَشَ لَيْلَهَا وَأَخْرَجَ ضُحَىٰهَا ﴿٢٩﴾	wa aghṭasha laylahā wa akhraja ḍuḥāhā.	29. and He has darkened its night, and brought out its sunshine.
وَٱلْأَرْضَ بَعْدَ ذَٰلِكَ دَحَىٰهَآ ﴿٣٠﴾	Wal arḍa ba‘da dhalika daḥāhā.	30. And the earth,— He spread it after that.
أَخْرَجَ مِنْهَا مَآءَهَا وَمَرْعَىٰهَا ﴿٣١﴾	Akhraja minhā mā’aha wa mar‘āhā.	31. He brought forth from it its water, and its pasture.
وَٱلْجِبَالَ أَرْسَىٰهَا ﴿٣٢﴾	Wal jibāla arsāhā,	32. And the mountains,— He set them firm,
مَتَٰعًا لَّكُمْ وَلِأَنْعَٰمِكُمْ ﴿٣٣﴾	matā‘an lakum wa li-an‘āmikum.	33. a provision for you and for your cattle.
فَإِذَا جَآءَتِ ٱلطَّآمَّةُ ٱلْكُبْرَىٰ ﴿٣٤﴾	Fa-idhā jā’ati-ṭ ṭāmmatu-l kubrā;	34. Then when the Great Calamity comes,
يَوْمَ يَتَذَكَّرُ ٱلْإِنسَٰنُ مَا سَعَىٰ ﴿٣٥﴾	yawma yatadhakkaru-l insānu mā sa‘ā,	35. on that Day man will remember what he strove for,

وَبُرِّزَتِ ٱلْجَحِيمُ لِمَن يَرَىٰ ٣٦	wa burrijhati-l jaḥīmu limaṅ yarā.	36. and Hell will be exposed to him whoever sees.
فَأَمَّا مَن طَغَىٰ ٣٧	Fa ammā man ṭaghā,	37. Then as to him who transgressed,
وَءَاثَرَ ٱلْحَيَوٰةَ ٱلدُّنْيَا ٣٨	wa āt͟hara-l ḥayāta-d dunyā,	38. and prefered the life of this world,
فَإِنَّ ٱلْجَحِيمَ هِىَ ٱلْمَأْوَىٰ ٣٩	fa-inna-l jaḥīma hiya-l ma'wā.	39. then surely the Hell— that is his home.
وَأَمَّا مَنْ خَافَ مَقَامَ رَبِّهِۦ وَنَهَى ٱلنَّفْسَ عَنِ ٱلْهَوَىٰ ٤٠	Wa ammā man khāfa maqāma rabbihī wa naha-n nafsa 'ani-l hawā,	40. But as to him who fears to stand before his Rabb, and restrains his soul from evil desires,
فَإِنَّ ٱلْجَنَّةَ هِىَ ٱلْمَأْوَىٰ ٤١	fa-inna-l jannata hiya-l ma'wā.	41. then surely the Garden— that is the home.
يَسْـَٔلُونَكَ عَنِ ٱلسَّاعَةِ أَيَّانَ مُرْسَىٰهَا ٤٢	Yas'alūnaka 'ani-s sā'ati ayyāna mursāhā.	42. They ask you about the Hour— "When will be its arrival?"
فِيمَ أَنتَ مِن ذِكْرَىٰهَآ ٤٣	Fīma anta min d͟hikrāhā.	43. What have you to declare it?
إِلَىٰ رَبِّكَ مُنتَهَىٰهَآ ٤٤	Ilā rabbika muntahāhā.	44. Towards your Rabb is its ultimate.
إِنَّمَآ أَنتَ مُنذِرُ مَن يَخْشَىٰهَا ٤٥	Innamā anta mund͟hiru maṅ yakhshāhā.	45. You are only a warner to him who fears it.
كَأَنَّهُمْ يَوْمَ يَرَوْنَهَا لَمْ يَلْبَثُوٓا۟ إِلَّا عَشِيَّةً أَوْ ضُحَىٰهَا ٤٦	Ka-annahum yawma yarawnahā lam yalbat͟hu illā 'ashiyyataṅ aw ḍuḥāhā.	46. The Day when they will see it, as if they had not stayed but an evening or a morning of it.

Explanation:

1-5. The sūrah derives its title from the mention of *nazi'at* (*lit.* who tear out, who yarned for) in the first verse. The set of five verses bear the Divine oath to confirm the realities of the Awakening. The commentators of the Qur'ān gave different interpretations as to who would be doing the actions mentioned in the verses. Some say the verses refer to angels who would pluck the souls of the wicked people violently, glide to the outer world and carry out Allāh's orders. Others say the verses refer to stars that run on their orbits and fulfill the commands of Allāh. Yet other commentators think the pluckers, runners, and swimmers are the stars, while those who regulate the affairs are the angels. Since the oaths do not identify the specifics of the participles, the interpretation of this passage continues to be different.

6-9. The above oaths emphasize the truth about the Awakening. On that Day, a violent commotion will follow one after another. The hearts of the sinners will be trembling and their eyes will be downcast. This is due to terror of the day and the realization that all their lives they were denying the realities of the Awakening.

10-12. The disbelievers always thought it was impossible that after they died and their bones became rotten, they would come back to life. They rejected the promise of the Awakening. They even mocked at the promise, saying that if ever the Awakening happened, it would put them at a loss. The Qur'ān repeats their mockery to make sure the loss they were ridiculing would truly turn into real loss.

13-14. A single blow on the Trumpet will begin the Awakening.

15-20. The story of Mūsā (A) and Fir'awn is mentioned in this section. When Mūsā (A) was in the valley of Tuwā, Allāh sent him revelation telling him to go back to Egypt. Fir'awn was the ruler in Egypt. He was a cruel ruler and he loved to torture the Israelites. He made his people worship him as a god. Mūsā (A) tried to bring him to the path of righteousness. In order to prove that he was speaking the truth, Mūsā (A) showed Fir'awn the many signs that Allāh gave him.

21-24. Fir'awn was not convinced. He refused to accept Mūsā (A) as a prophet. He assembled his skillful magicians to have a showdown with Mūsā (A). The Egyptians were already used to worshipping Fir'awn as a god, but then he declared himself as the Lord, the most high. This was an extreme example of disobedience.

25-26. As a result of his disobedience and arrogance, Allāh punished Fir'awn in a unique manner. He was drowned in the sea. His death in the sea was made an example for people for all time.

27-33. The disbelievers who think the Awakening can never happen are asked to think about their own creation. The human body has millions of complex mechanisms; the universe is even more complex. Allāh created everything. He made everything work in a perfect manner. Everything, from the system of day and night, the expansion of the earth, the formation of rain, the formation of vegetation and the mountains are blessings of Allāh that allow human beings and the animals to survive.

34-39. Nothing in creation is permanent. One day the Calamity will come and human beings will remember everything that they have been doing. Hell will be in full view of the wrongdoers, who thought that life on the earth was permanent. They are the ones who disobeyed Allāh and refused to accept the truth.

40-41. In contrast to the wrongdoers, the righteous people will have a different experience. They believed one day they would face judgment. So, they followed Allāh's guidance and avoided sins. They are the ones who will enter Paradise, which is the ultimate home.

42- 46. The disbelievers mockingly asked the Prophet (S) about the timing of the Awakening. The knowledge of the Hour is only with Allāh. The duty of the Prophet (S) was only to deliver the message and warn people. Those who deny the Awakening will soon see the Day with their own eyes. At that time, everyone will be brought back to life. The disbelievers will think they were waking up from an afternoon nap or morning sleep.

Words to know

Nāziat: those who extract, who perform their duty. *Naza'a*: to pluck, to withdraw.
Gharqan: violently, forcefully, swiftly. *Ghariqa*: to sink. *Aghraqa*: to sink, to pull a bow-string to the most.
Nāshitāt: who goes forth, who exerts. *Nashata*: to exert, to release.
Qulūbun: hearts. *Qalaba*: to return, change direction. *Munqalabin*: place or time of difficulty.
Khāshi'ah: downcast (eyes), in humility. *Khasha'a*: to be humble, cast down eyes. *Khushū*: humility.
Taghā: to transgress, to cross the limits. *Tāghūt*: transgressor. *Atghā:* most rebellious.
Banāhā: He created. *Banā*: to build, create. *Bannā*: builder, architect. *Bunyān*: building, structure.

Sūrah An-Nazi'āt
Word-by-word meaning

ٱلرَّحِيمِ	ٱلرَّحۡمَٰنِ	ٱللَّهِ	بِسۡمِ
the Most-Rewarding	the Most-Kind	Allāh	In the name of
نَشۡطٗا ٢	وَٱلنَّٰشِطَٰتِ	غَرۡقٗا ١	وَٱلنَّٰزِعَٰتِ
with steady going forth	and who go forth	violently	By the extractors
سَبۡقٗا ٤	فَٱلسَّٰبِقَٰتِ	سَبۡحٗا ٣	وَٱلسَّٰبِحَٰتِ
foremost	then foremost	swiftly swimming	and the swimmers
تَرۡجُفُ	يَوۡمَ	أَمۡرٗا ٥	فَٱلۡمُدَبِّرَٰتِ
quaking one	the day	affair	then regulating
قُلُوبٞ	ٱلرَّادِفَةُ ٧	تَتۡبَعُهَا	ٱلرَّاجِفَةُ ٦
hearts	the consequence	follow	the quake
خَٰشِعَةٞ ٩	أَبۡصَٰرُهَا	وَاجِفَةٌ ٨	يَوۡمَئِذٖ
downcast	their gaze	trembling	that day
فِي	لَمَرۡدُودُونَ	أَءِنَّا	يَقُولُونَ
to	indeed be restored	shall we	they say

ٱلْحَافِرَةِ ١٠	أَءِذَا	كُنَّا	عِظَـٰمًا
the former state	even after	we shall	bones
نَّخِرَةً ١١	قَالُوا۟	تِلْكَ	إِذًا
rotten	they say	that	then
كَرَّةٌ	خَاسِرَةٌ ١٢	فَإِنَّمَا	هِىَ
return	loosing	so indeed	it is
زَجْرَةٌ	وَٰحِدَةٌ ١٣	فَإِذَا	هُم
blast	one	then	they
بِٱلسَّاهِرَةِ ١٤	هَلْ	أَتَىٰكَ	حَدِيثُ
earth's surface	did it	reach you	story
مُوسَىٰٓ ١٥	إِذْ	نَادَىٰهُ	رَبُّهُۥ
Musa	when	called him	his Rabb
بِٱلْوَادِ	ٱلْمُقَدَّسِ	طُوًى ١٦	ٱذْهَبْ
valley	the sacred	Tuwa	go
إِلَىٰ	فِرْعَوْنَ	إِنَّهُۥ	طَغَىٰ ١٧
to	Fir'awn	he surely	cross the limit
فَقُلْ	هَل	لَّكَ	إِلَىٰٓ
then say	would it be	for you	towards
أَن	تَزَكَّىٰ ١٨	وَأَهْدِيَكَ	إِلَىٰ
that	you purify	and guide you	to

رَبِّكَ your Rabb	فَتَخْشَىٰ ﴿١٩﴾ so you may fear	فَأَرَىٰهُ so showed him	ٱلْـَٔايَةَ signs
ٱلْكُبْرَىٰ ﴿٢٠﴾ the great	فَكَذَّبَ then he denied	وَعَصَىٰ ﴿٢١﴾ and disobeyed	ثُمَّ then
أَدْبَرَ turned away	يَسْعَىٰ ﴿٢٢﴾ striving	فَحَشَرَ then gathered	فَنَادَىٰ ﴿٢٣﴾ then he called out
فَقَالَ then he said	أَنَا۠ I am	رَبُّكُمُ your lord	ٱلْأَعْلَىٰ ﴿٢٤﴾ the most high
فَأَخَذَهُ seized him	ٱللَّهُ Allāh	نَكَالَ exemplary punishment	ٱلْـَٔاخِرَةِ the Hereafter
وَٱلْأُولَىٰٓ ﴿٢٥﴾ and the former	إِنَّ surely	فِى in	ذَٰلِكَ that
لَعِبْرَةً a lesson	لِّمَن for who	يَخْشَىٰٓ ﴿٢٦﴾ fears	ءَأَنتُمْ are you
أَشَدُّ harder	خَلْقًا creation	أَمِ or	ٱلسَّمَآءُ ۚ the heaven
بَنَىٰهَا ﴿٢٧﴾ created it	رَفَعَ raised	سَمْكَهَا its height	فَسَوَّىٰهَا ﴿٢٨﴾ made it perfect
وَأَغْطَشَ and darkened	لَيْلَهَا its night	وَأَخْرَجَ and brought	ضُحَىٰهَا ﴿٢٩﴾ its sunshine

وَٱلْأَرْضَ and the earth	بَعْدَ after	ذَٰلِكَ that	دَحَىٰهَآ ٣٠ spread it
أَخْرَجَ brought forth	مِنْهَا from it	مَآءَهَا its water	وَمَرْعَىٰهَا ٣١ and pasture
وَٱلْجِبَالَ and the mountains	أَرْسَىٰهَا ٣٢ set firmly	مَتَٰعًا provision	لَّكُمْ for you
وَلِأَنْعَٰمِكُمْ ٣٣ and your cattle	فَإِذَا when	جَآءَتِ comes	ٱلطَّآمَّةُ the calamity
ٱلْكُبْرَىٰ ٣٤ the great	يَوْمَ the day	يَتَذَكَّرُ remember	ٱلْإِنسَٰنُ the man
مَا what	سَعَىٰ ٣٥ strove	وَبُرِّزَتِ and exposed	ٱلْجَحِيمُ the hell
لِمَن to him who	يَرَىٰ ٣٦ see	فَأَمَّا then as to	مَن who
طَغَىٰ ٣٧ crossed the limit	وَءَاثَرَ and prefers	ٱلْحَيَوٰةَ the life	ٱلدُّنْيَا ٣٨ the world
فَإِنَّ then surely	ٱلْجَحِيمَ the Hell	هِىَ that is	ٱلْمَأْوَىٰ ٣٩ the home
وَأَمَّا and as for	مَنْ who	خَافَ fear	مَقَامَ stand

رَبِّهِۦ	وَنَهَى	ٱلنَّفْسَ	عَنِ
his Rabb	and restrains	the soul	from

ٱلْهَوَىٰ ﴿٤٠﴾	فَإِنَّ	ٱلْجَنَّةَ	هِىَ
the evil desire	then surely	the Garden	that is

ٱلْمَأْوَىٰ ﴿٤١﴾	يَسْـَٔلُونَكَ	عَنِ	ٱلسَّاعَةِ
the home	they ask you	about	the hour

أَيَّانَ	مُرْسَىٰهَا ﴿٤٢﴾	فِيمَ	أَنتَ
when	its arrival	in what	you

مِن	ذِكْرَىٰهَآ ﴿٤٣﴾	إِلَىٰ	رَبِّكَ
from	its declare	towards	your Rabb

مُنتَهَىٰهَآ ﴿٤٤﴾	إِنَّمَآ	أَنتَ	مُنذِرُ
its ultimate	only	you	warner

مَن	يَخْشَىٰهَا ﴿٤٥﴾	كَأَنَّهُمْ	يَوْمَ
who	fears it	as though	day

يَرَوْنَهَا	لَمْ	يَلْبَثُوٓا۟	إِلَّا
they see it	not	they stayed	except

عَشِيَّةً	أَوْ	ضُحَىٰهَا ﴿٤٦﴾	
evening	or	morning	

A few applications of the message:

There is a saying that wise people learn from others' mistakes. The Qur'ān has narrated many past stories to point out the mistakes of other people. In the past, for example, Fir'awn rejected the truth and was severely punished. These stories are examples for those who pay attention.

What good is it if we read the sūrah but do not pay attention to how its message can improve our chances in the Hereafter? This sūrah reminds us about the Great Calamity when all living and dead people will be assembled to receive their rewards or punishments. The Day of Calamity will herald the news of a new beginning in the Hereafter. It is a certain event to happen.

Towards the end of the sūrah it tells us that for those who prefer the world, their ultimate destination will be the Fire. This is because the false appeal of this life misleads them from the path of righteousness and from the remembrance of Allāh. The sūrah also tells us that in order to enter Paradise, we should remember Allāh and restrain our evil desires. Remembering Allāh is not casual mental process, but includes doing everything He wants us to do. It also means remembering to avoid evil. After reading this sūrah, if we can sincerely remember Allāh through our righteous actions and avoid all evil, we will, insha-Allāh, be in our ultimate Home, Paradise.

Questions:

1. The disbelievers find it difficult to believe that they will be raised up at the time of the Awakening. What reasons do they mention about the impossibility of being raised up?
2. What is the name of the valley where Mūsā (A) received the instructions to go to Fir'awn?
3. How did Fir'awn respond when he saw the signs brought by Mūsā (A)?
4. What did Fir'awn declare about himself?
5. What does Allāh say about the complexity of the creation of human beings and the universe?
6. What does Allāh say about the timing of the Hour, when the Awakening will happen?

Sūrah 78

Revealed in Makkah

An-Naba'

The Information

Introduction:

This entire *Juz,* or the 30th part, of the Qur'ān is known as *Juz 'Amma*. The name of this *Juz* is based on the first word, *'amma,* mentioned in the first verse. The sūrah begins by asking what the disbelievers were inquiring about. They were inquiring about the possibility of the Awakening, but deep in their hearts they denied it. The sūrah then lists a number of Allāh's marvelous creation to demonstrate that if Allāh can create all these, He can easily cause the Awakening. The sūrah then narrates how the Awakening would happen. The purpose of the Hereafter is to reward or punish people according to their deeds on the earth. This section gives a graphic description of the conditions of the sinners and the righteous people.

بِسۡمِ ٱللَّهِ ٱلرَّحۡمَٰنِ ٱلرَّحِيمِ

Bismi-llāhi-r raḥmāni-r raḥīm

In the name of Allah, the Most-Kind, the Most-Rewarding.

عَمَّ يَتَسَآءَلُونَ ﴿١﴾	'Amma yatasā'alūn.	1. What are they asking one another?
عَنِ ٱلنَّبَإِ ٱلۡعَظِيمِ ﴿٢﴾	'Ani-n nabai-l 'aẓīm,—	2. About the tremendous Information,
ٱلَّذِي هُمۡ فِيهِ مُخۡتَلِفُونَ ﴿٣﴾	Alladhī hum fīhi mukhtalifūn.	3. about which they differ
كَلَّا سَيَعۡلَمُونَ ﴿٤﴾	Kallā sa-ya'lamūn,	4. No, they will soon know.
ثُمَّ كَلَّا سَيَعۡلَمُونَ ﴿٥﴾	thumma kallā sa-ya'lamūn.	5. Again, no! soon they will know.
أَلَمۡ نَجۡعَلِ ٱلۡأَرۡضَ مِهَٰدًا ﴿٦﴾	A-lam naj'ali-l arḍa mihādā,—	6. Have We not made the earth as a wide couch,
وَٱلۡجِبَالَ أَوۡتَادًا ﴿٧﴾	-wa-l jibāla awtādā,—	7. and the mountains as pegs?

وَخَلَقْنَٰكُمْ أَزْوَٰجًا ٨	-wa khalaqnākum azwājā,—	8. And We have created you in pairs
وَجَعَلْنَا نَوْمَكُمْ سُبَاتًا ٩	-wa ja'alnā nawmakum subātā,—	9. and We have made your sleep for rest
وَجَعَلْنَا ٱلَّيْلَ لِبَاسًا ١٠	-wa ja'alna-l layla libāsā,—	10. and We have made the night as a garment
وَجَعَلْنَا ٱلنَّهَارَ مَعَاشًا ١١	-wa ja'alna-n nahāra ma'āshā,—	11. and We have made the day for seeking livelihood
وَبَنَيْنَا فَوْقَكُمْ سَبْعًا شِدَادًا ١٢	wa banaynā fawqakum sab'an shidādā,—	12. And We have erected above you seven strong bodies.
وَجَعَلْنَا سِرَاجًا وَهَّاجًا ١٣	-wa ja'alnā sirājaẇ wahhājā,—	13. And We have placed a lamp brightly burning
وَأَنزَلْنَا مِنَ ٱلْمُعْصِرَٰتِ مَآءً ثَجَّاجًا ١٤	-wa anzalnā mina-l mu'ṣirāti mā'aṅ thajjājā,	14. and We bring down abundant water from dripping clouds
لِّنُخْرِجَ بِهِۦ حَبًّا وَنَبَاتًا ١٥	-li nukhrija bihī ḥabbaẇ wa nabātā,—	15. that We grow with it grains and vegetations
وَجَنَّٰتٍ أَلْفَافًا ١٦	-wa jannātiṅ alfāfa.	16. and gardens of vigorous growth
إِنَّ يَوْمَ ٱلْفَصْلِ كَانَ مِيقَٰتًا ١٧	Inna yawma-l faṣli kāna mīqātā,—	17. Surely the Day of Decision is of a fixed time
يَوْمَ يُنفَخُ فِى ٱلصُّورِ فَتَأْتُونَ أَفْوَاجًا ١٨	-yawma yunfakhu fiṣ ṣūri fa-ta'tūna afwājā,—	18. The Day when the Trumpet will be blown, you will then come in groups,
وَفُتِحَتِ ٱلسَّمَآءُ فَكَانَتْ أَبْوَٰبًا ١٩	-wa futiḥati-s samā'u fa-kānat abwābā,—	19. and the sky will be opened up, and it will then become doors;
وَسُيِّرَتِ ٱلْجِبَالُ فَكَانَتْ سَرَابًا ٢٠	-wa suyyirati-l jibālu fa-kānat sarābā.	20. and the mountains will be made to move,they then become a mirage

إِنَّ جَهَنَّمَ كَانَتْ مِرْصَادًا ٢١	Inna jahannama kānat mirṣādā,—	21. Surely, Hell is a place of ambush—
لِّلطَّٰغِينَ مَـَٔابًا ٢٢	-liṭ ṭāghīna maābā,—	22. a Destination for the rejectors
لَّٰبِثِينَ فِيهَآ أَحْقَابًا ٢٣	-lābithīna fīha aḥqābā;	23. staying in it for ages
لَّا يَذُوقُونَ فِيهَا بَرْدًا وَلَا شَرَابًا ٢٤	lā yadhūqūna fīha bardaẇ wa lā sharābā,	24. They will not taste in it coolness nor drink
إِلَّا حَمِيمًا وَغَسَّاقًا ٢٥	illā ḥamīmaẇ wa ghassāqā,	25. except boiling water and intensely cold fluid
جَزَآءً وِفَاقًا ٢٦	jazā'aẇ wifāqā.	26. an appropriate reward.
إِنَّهُمْ كَانُوا۟ لَا يَرْجُونَ حِسَابًا ٢٧	Innahum kānū lā yarjūna ḥisābā,—	27. Surely, they did not fear the accounting,
وَكَذَّبُوا۟ بِـَٔايَٰتِنَا كِذَّابًا ٢٨	-wa kadhdhabū bi āyātinā kidhdhābā.	28. and they denied Our Messages with a rejection.
وَكُلَّ شَىْءٍ أَحْصَيْنَٰهُ كِتَٰبًا ٢٩	Wa kulla shay'iṅ aḥṣaynāhu kitābā,	29. And everything— We have recorded it in writing,
فَذُوقُوا۟ فَلَن نَّزِيدَكُمْ إِلَّا عَذَابًا ٣٠	fa dhūqū fa-lan najhīdakum illā 'adhābā.	30. "So you taste; because We shall not increase you in anything except in torment."
	Section 2	
إِنَّ لِلْمُتَّقِينَ مَفَازًا ٣١	Inna lil muttaqīna mafāzā,	31. Certainly, for the reverent there is triumph—
حَدَآئِقَ وَأَعْنَٰبًا ٣٢	ḥadā'iqa wa a'nābā,—	32. orchards and vineyards;
وَكَوَاعِبَ أَتْرَابًا ٣٣	-wa kawā'iba atrābā,—	33. and youths of equal age,

وَكَأْسًا دِهَاقًا ﴿٣٤﴾	-wa ka'saṅ dihāqā.	34. and a cup filled up.
لَّا يَسْمَعُونَ فِيهَا لَغْوًا وَلَا كِذَّٰبًا ﴿٣٥﴾	Lā yasma'ūna fīhā laghwaẇ wa lā kidhdhābā;	35. They will not hear in it any idle talk, nor any falsehood.
جَزَآءً مِّن رَّبِّكَ عَطَآءً حِسَابًا ﴿٣٦﴾	jazā'aṁ miṅ rabbika 'aṭā'aṅ ḥisābā,—	36. A reward from your Rabb, a gift calculated—
رَّبِّ ٱلسَّمَٰوَٰتِ وَٱلْأَرْضِ وَمَا بَيْنَهُمَا ٱلرَّحْمَٰنِ ۖ لَا يَمْلِكُونَ مِنْهُ خِطَابًا ﴿٣٧﴾	-rabbi-s samāwāti wal arḍi wa mā baynahuma-r raḥmāni lā yamlikūna minhu khiṭābā;	37. the Rabb of the heavens and the earth and what is between them— from the Rahmān. They do not dare address Him.
يَوْمَ يَقُومُ ٱلرُّوحُ وَٱلْمَلَٰٓئِكَةُ صَفًّا ۖ لَّا يَتَكَلَّمُونَ إِلَّا مَنْ أَذِنَ لَهُ ٱلرَّحْمَٰنُ وَقَالَ صَوَابًا ﴿٣٨﴾	yawma yaqūmu-r rūḥu wal malā'ikatu ṣaffa-ḷ; lā yatakallamūna illā man adhina lahu-r raḥmānu wa qāla ṣawābā.	38. The Day when the Spirit and the angels will stand in rows; they will not speak except he whom the Rahmān permits, and who speaks rightly.
ذَٰلِكَ ٱلْيَوْمُ ٱلْحَقُّ ۖ فَمَن شَآءَ ٱتَّخَذَ إِلَىٰ رَبِّهِۦ مَـَٔابًا ﴿٣٩﴾	Dhālika-l yawmu-l ḥaqqu; fa-man shā'a-t takhadha ilā rabbihī ma'ābā.	39. This is the Certain Day; therefore whoever pleases chose a way back towards his Rabb.
إِنَّآ أَنذَرْنَٰكُمْ عَذَابًا قَرِيبًا يَوْمَ يَنظُرُ ٱلْمَرْءُ مَا قَدَّمَتْ يَدَاهُ وَيَقُولُ ٱلْكَافِرُ يَٰلَيْتَنِى كُنتُ تُرَٰبًۢا ﴿٤٠﴾	Innā andharnākum 'adhābaṅ qarībaẏ; yawma yanẓuru-l mar'u mā qaddamat yadāhu wa yaqūlu-l kāfiru yā laytanī kuntu turābā.	40. Surely We have warned you of a near punishment— the Day when man will see what his two hands have sent forward, and the disbeliever will say: "I wish I were dust!"

Explanation:

1-5. The title of the sūrah is derived from the mention of *nabā* in this verse. The word means news, tiding, information or prophecy. When the idol worshippers in Makkah heard about the Awakening, they were not sure how it would happen. They were questioning one another about it. The sūrah refers to Awakening, or Resurrection, as a Great News, or *nabāi-l 'azim* as it would be a tremendous event. People who have disagreement about the Awakening will soon come to know about it. Verses 4 and 5 emphasize the same statement that the Resurrection will invariably happen.

6-7. The argument as to how the Resurrection could happen is given in verses 6 through 16. The verses 6 and 7 speak about the formation of the earth and the mountains. The earth was spread wide for all life forms to originate and survive. The massive earth and the towering mountains are the signs of Allāh's extraordinary power to create. Similarly, He can recreate these and also cause the Awakening.

8-11. After the earth was created, all life forms originated. Allāh created all life forms, including human beings in pairs of males and females so that the life forms can reproduce and continue their races. Night and day, another form of pairs, testify Allāh's Supreme Power of creation. The night is created for us to rest and regain our energy. The night acts as a garmcnt since it covers the day and makes it dark. The day is created to help us seek our livelihoods.

12-16. Above us, Allāh has created the seven strong bodies (other seven planets of the solar system, or the seven layers of atmosphere). For us, the bright lamp in the sky is the sun. The light and warmth of sunshine, and abundant rain from the clouds, together, help growth of plants, crops and other vegetation. Allāh created these complex systems to support and sustain life. There is no doubt that He can also easily cause the Awakening.

17-20. The Day of Decision is when we will be judged by our deeds. The day will start when angel *'Israfīl* will blow the Trumpet. The blow will start a massive shake up of the universe. The sky will be opened up, and the mountains will disappear as they will be leveled flat.

21-23. Hell will lurk in ambush to take into it all the sinners. The mention of ambush indicates that the sinners continue to commit sin without realizing that Hell is close by and will be their ultimate destiny. They will live in there for a long time, for ages.

24-27. In contrast to the pure and wholesome drinks from the heavenly springs served to the righteous, the sinners will be served with horrific drinks— either boiling hot or bitter cold—unsuitable to drink. This 'reward' is appropriate for their sins committed during their earthly lives.

28-30. The sinners rejected the divine message. They thought and argued that Awakening would never happen. Their deeds are recorded in books. Their punishment would continue to increase since they continued to commit one sin after another during earthly life.

31-36. In contrast to the condition of the sinners, this section describes the condition of the righteous. The pleasure and comfort of Jannah are mentioned in physical terms so that people may relate to them. The actual nature of how these pleasures and comforts will be enjoyed is unknown, and their understanding is restricted by our limited knowledge. There will be no idle, senseless, false or useless speech in heaven. The sublime situation in Jannah will be the best environment to live in for our eternal lives. Allāh says that thic sublime environment will be a reward from Him.

37-38. In this section, we see, on the Day of Judgment Angel Jibril (the Spirit, or rūh) and other angels standing in ranks before Allāh. No one speaks without a permission from Allāh.

39-40. In the ending verses, Allāh again reminds us about this Day that will certainly come. There is no doubt about it. Allāh does not force anyone to accept or reject the certainty of that Day. He urges people to take the necessary precautions. We have a choice now—take a path to our Rabb or end up in the Hellfire. There is no doubt that Allāh has clearly warned us about the Day. On that Day everyone will see their own deeds. Those who sent too many bad deeds will be very fearful. They will be ashamed of their deeds. They will cry out with immense regret about what they have done during their earthly lives. Rather than facing this shameful and distressful condition, they will wish to become dust and bones again.

Words to know

Naba'a: news, information, great message. *Nabī:* prophet, to have a high position. *Nabūwwat*: a high position and to give a great message.
Mukhtalifūn: differ, vary. *Khalafa*: to follow, to take place, to be an agent. *Khilāf*: disagree, disobedience. *Khalīfah*: successor.
Libās: garment, clothing. *Labasa*: to cover, to obscure.
Sirāj: sun, lamp. *Sarija*: to shine, to glow, to be beautiful.
Sarābā: mirage, optical illusion. *Sāribun*: one who takes cover, lurks. *Sarāb*: mounds of loose sand.
Kadhdhaba: to reject outright, to deny, *Kadhaba*: to lie, to make up a lie. *Mukadhdhibun*: one who falsely denies.

Sūrah An-Naba'
Word-by-word meaning

ٱلرَّحِيمِ	ٱلرَّحْمَـٰنِ	ٱللَّهِ	بِسْمِ
the Most-Rewarding	the Most-Kind	Allāh	In the name of
ٱلنَّبَإِ	عَنِ	يَتَسَآءَلُونَ ١	عَمَّ
information	about	they are asking one another	about what
فِيهِ	هُمْ	ٱلَّذِى	ٱلْعَظِيمِ ٢
in it	they	which	tremendous

مُخْتَلِفُونَ ﴿٣﴾ differ	كَلَّا no	سَيَعْلَمُونَ ﴿٤﴾ soon they will now	ثُمَّ again
كَلَّا no	سَيَعْلَمُونَ ﴿٥﴾ soon they will know	أَلَمْ have not	نَجْعَلِ We made
ٱلْأَرْضَ the earth	مِهَٰدًا ﴿٦﴾ a couch	وَٱلْجِبَالَ and the mountains	أَوْتَادًا ﴿٧﴾ as pegs
وَخَلَقْنَٰكُمْ and We created you	أَزْوَٰجًا ﴿٨﴾ in pairs	وَجَعَلْنَا and We made	نَوْمَكُمْ your sleep
سُبَاتًا ﴿٩﴾ for rest	وَجَعَلْنَا and We made	ٱلَّيْلَ the night	لِبَاسًا ﴿١٠﴾ as a garment
وَجَعَلْنَا and We made	ٱلنَّهَارَ the day	مَعَاشًا ﴿١١﴾ livelihood	وَبَنَيْنَا and We have erected
فَوْقَكُمْ above you	سَبْعًا seven	شِدَادًا ﴿١٢﴾ strong bodies	وَجَعَلْنَا and We made
سِرَاجًا lamp	وَهَّاجًا ﴿١٣﴾ brightly burning	وَأَنزَلْنَا and We bring down	مِنَ from
ٱلْمُعْصِرَٰتِ the cloud	مَآءً water	ثَجَّاجًا ﴿١٤﴾ abundant	لِّنُخْرِجَ grow
بِهِۦ with it	حَبًّا grains	وَنَبَاتًا ﴿١٥﴾ and vegetation	وَجَنَّٰتٍ and gardens

أَلْفَافًا ﴿١٦﴾ vigorous growth	إِنَّ surely	يَوْمَ day	ٱلْفَصْلِ the decision
كَانَ is	مِيقَٰتًا ﴿١٧﴾ fixed	يَوْمَ on that day	يُنفَخُ blown
فِى in	ٱلصُّورِ the Trumpet	فَتَأْتُونَ then you will come	أَفْوَاجًا ﴿١٨﴾ in groups
وَفُتِحَتِ and will be opened	ٱلسَّمَآءُ the sky	فَكَانَتْ will become	أَبْوَٰبًا ﴿١٩﴾ doors
وَسُيِّرَتِ and move away	ٱلْجِبَالُ the mountains	فَكَانَتْ will be	سَرَابًا ﴿٢٠﴾ mirage
إِنَّ surely	جَهَنَّمَ hell	كَانَتْ is	مِرْصَادًا ﴿٢١﴾ in ambush
لِّلطَّٰغِينَ for rejectors	مَـَٔابًا ﴿٢٢﴾ destination	لَّٰبِثِينَ staying	فِيهَآ in it
أَحْقَابًا ﴿٢٣﴾ ages	لَّا not	يَذُوقُونَ taste	فِيهَا in it
بَرْدًا coolness	وَلَا and not	شَرَابًا ﴿٢٤﴾ drink	إِلَّا except
حَمِيمًا scalding water	وَغَسَّاقًا ﴿٢٥﴾ and cold fluid	جَزَآءً reward	وِفَاقًا ﴿٢٦﴾ appropriate

يَرْجُونَ expecting	لَا not	كَانُوا۟ were	إِنَّهُمْ surely they
كِذَّابًا ٢٨ rejecting	بِـَٔايَـٰتِنَا with our Messages	وَكَذَّبُوا۟ and rejected	حِسَابًا ٢٧ account
كِتَـٰبًا ٢٩ in writing	أَحْصَيْنَـٰهُ We recorded it	شَىْءٍ things	وَكُلَّ and all
إِلَّا except	نَّزِيدَكُمْ We increase you	فَلَن then never	فَذُوقُوا۟ so taste
مَفَازًا ٣١ success	لِلْمُتَّقِينَ for the reverent	إِنَّ surely	عَذَابًا ٣٠ torment
أَتْرَابًا ٣٣ of equal age	وَكَوَاعِبَ and youths	وَأَعْنَـٰبًا ٣٢ and vineyards	حَدَآئِقَ orchards
يَسْمَعُونَ they will hear	لَّا not	دِهَاقًا ٣٤ filled up	وَكَأْسًا and cups
كِذَّٰبًا ٣٥ falsehood	وَلَا and not	لَغْوًا idle talk	فِيهَا in it
عَطَآءً gift	رَّبِّكَ your Rabb	مِّن from	جَزَآءً reward
وَٱلْأَرْضِ and the earth	ٱلسَّمَـٰوَٰتِ the heavens	رَّبِّ Rabb	حِسَابًا ٣٦ account

لَا	ٱلرَّحْمَـٰنِ ۖ	بَيْنَهُمَا	وَمَا
not	the Rahmān	between them	and what
يَوْمَ	خِطَابًا ٣٧	مِنْهُ	يَمْلِكُونَ
the day	speech	for him	they dare
صَفًّا ۖ	وَٱلْمَلَـٰٓئِكَةُ	ٱلرُّوحُ	يَقُومُ
in rows	and the angels	the Spirit	stand
مَنْ	إِلَّا	يَتَكَلَّمُونَ	لَّا
whom	except	they will speak	not
وَقَالَ	ٱلرَّحْمَـٰنُ	لَهُ	أَذِنَ
and he speak	the Rahmān	to him	permitted
ٱلْحَقُّ ۖ	ٱلْيَوْمُ	ذَٰلِكَ	صَوَابًا ٣٨
the certain	day	that	rightly
إِلَىٰ	ٱتَّخَذَ	شَآءَ	فَمَن
towards	chose	pleases	then whoever
أَنذَرْنَـٰكُمْ	إِنَّآ	مَـَٔابًا ٣٩	رَبِّهِۦ
have warned you	surely	place of return	his Rabb
يَنظُرُ	يَوْمَ	قَرِيبًا	عَذَابًا
will see	day	near	punishment

يَدَاهُ	قَدَّمَتْ	مَا	ٱلْمَرْءُ
his hands	sent forth	what	the man
كُنتُ	يَٰلَيْتَنِى	ٱلْكَافِرُ	وَيَقُولُ
I were	I wish	the disbeliever	and will say
			تُرَٰبًۢا ﴿٤٠﴾
			dust.

A few applications of the message:

This long sūrah gives us two pictures—one about the punishment of the sinners and the other about the blissful condition of the righteous. Then towards the end of the sūrah Allāh tells us "whoever pleases chose a way back towards his Rabb." As we read the sūrah we have to ask ourselves—which of the two pictures we want to put ourselves in. If we truly want to be in Jannah, then we have to take a path back to our Rabb. How do we do that? The answer is given throughout the Qur'ān and throughout the Sunnah of our Prophet (S). We have to try our best to follow the guidance of Allāh and try our best to remain on the right path. Initially, it may appear difficult to stay on the right path, but the more we try, the more Allāh will make it easy for us.

Questions:

1. In Sūrah *an-Naba'* who are the people arguing? What are they arguing about?
2. In response to the argument in Sūrah *an-Naba'* Allāh mentioned 11 proofs in verses 6 to 16. List all the proofs.
3. What will happen to the sky and the earth when the Trumpet is blown?
4. List some of the experiences of the wicked people as mentioned in Sūrah *an-Naba'.*
5. Mention the condition of the righteous people as mentioned in Sūrah *an-Naba'.*

INDEX

Abū Lahab
Divine punishment for Abu Lahab 111:1-3.
wife of Abu Lahab meets her share of punishment 111:4-5.
'Ad
history of 'Ad 89:6-8.
Allāh
childless 112:3.
absolute Unity of Allāh 112:1-4.
created everything in pairs 78:8; 92:3.
independent of all— does not need help of others 112:2.
loves His creatures 85:14.
nothing is equal to Allāh 112:4.
One and the Only Allāh 112:1.
Angels
angels descend in Lailatul Qadr 97:4
recording of deeds done by angels 82:10-12.
'Arsh
Allāh is the Master of al-'Arsh 81:20, 85:15
Arabs— Pre-Islamic
daughters buried alive by pre-Islamic Arabs 81:8-9.
Awakening
disbelievers deny the Awakening by 79:10-11.
Awakening will take place out of dust and bones 79:11.
memory becomes clear on Awakening 79:35.
earth will be destroyed on Awakening 89:21.
earth will give out her contents on Awakening 84:4; 99:2.
heaven splits on Awakening 78:19; 84:1.
mountains crumble on Awakening 78:20; 101:5.
old order completely changed on 81:1-11.
Awakening will happen suddenly 79:46.
people terrified on Awakening 79:6-9; 101:1-4.
trumpet blown on Awakening 78:18; 79:13; 80:33.
Balance
in weighing, equity should be maintained 83:1-3.
heavy balance with good deeds brings success 101:6-7.
light balance with good deeds brings ruins 101:8-9.
Birds
birds destroyed the army of Abrahah 105:3.
Book of Deeds
everything recorded in as documentary evidence 78:29.
Book of Deeds is similar to prison for wicked 83:7-9.
Book of Deeds is similar to zenith for righteous 83:18-20.
Book of Deeds will be placed in left hand or back side of the wicked 84:10.
Book of Deeds will be placed in right hand of the righteous 84:7.
testimony of deeds in Book of Deeds 84:7-15.
Camel
creation of camels 88:17.
a she-camel as a sign of Allah 91:13
Charity
charity wipes away evil deeds 92:18.
charity should not be the motive of gain 74:6; 92:19.
show in charity disapproved 107:6.
avoiding charity is against the fundamental principles of Islam 107:7.
Cheating
cheaters are condemned 83:1-4.
punishment for cheating 83:4-10.

Day
night for rest and day for work 78:10-11.
Day of Judgment
Allāh is the Master of Day of Judgment 82:17-19.
Allāh possesses the knowledge of Day of Judgment 79:42-44.
balance will determine merits on Day of Judgment 101:6-9.
Day of Judgment is inevitable 79:13-14; 95:7.
disbelievers deny the Day of Judgment 84:14; 86:8; 95:7.
everyone will receive full dues on Day of Judgment 78:21,31,40; 80:38-42; 81:12-14; 82:5,13-14; 88:1-16; 89:23-30.
everything will be exposed on Day of Judgment 99:6; 100:10.
guilty cannot escape consequences on Day of Judgment 78:39-40.
guilty will want to return to earthly life on Day of Judgment 79:38.
no help on Day of Judgment 82:19; 86:10.
relations will not come to any help on Day of Judgment 80:34-37.
Deeds
smallest deeds also have effect 99:7-8.
deeds are recorded to shape the Hereafter 82:10-12.
Ditch
prophecy regarding companion of Ditch 85:4.
Earth
cradle is the nature of earth 78:6.
creation of earth after the heavens 79:27-30.
Elephant
Abrahah's army is called Fellows of Elephant 105:1.
crushing defeat for the army of Abrahah 105:1-5.
Face
brightness of faces 80:38; 83:24.
calmness of faces 88:8.
dust-covering on faces 80:40.
shame and gloom cover the faces of the guilty 80:40; 88:2.
Fir'awn
Fir'awn claimed to be god 79:24.
punished severely 89:13.
sin and disobedience of Fir'awn 89:12.
Garden
entering the Garden is a triumph 78:31.
Allāh's presence and pleasure is the highest bliss in Garden 83:21,28; 89:27-30; 92:20; 98:8.
filled-up cups presented in Garden 78:34; 88:14.
carpets laid in Garden 88:16.
companions in Garden are equal in age 78:33.
desires are fulfilled in Garden 83:26.
fountains in Garden 83:28; 88:12.
Lofty Garden 88:10.
musk— the fragrance of in Garden 83:26.
permanent stay in Garden 84:25.
pure drink given in Garden 78:34; 83:25.
Right-hand people will enter Garden 90:18.
Tasnim will be mixed in the blessed drink of the Garden 83:27.
couches and thrones provided in Garden 83:23,35; 88:13.
Grave
people in grave will be raised to life on the Day of Awakening 82:4.
Hell
fire of Hell scorching the entire body 88:4.
fire of Hell burns the heart 83:14; 104:6-7.
inmates of Hell are barred from the grace of Allāh 83:15.
Left-hand people will enter Hell 90:19.
Mother of sinners 101:8-11.
place of disappointment 88:7.

place of disgrace 88:2-3.
refuge for sinners is in Hell 79:39.
state in between life and death in Hell 87:13.
thorns as food in Hell 88:6.
boiling water given to drink in Hell 88:5.

Human beings
created from clot 96:2.
created out of water 86:6-7.
created from droplet 80:19.
created in the finest form 95:4.
creation of human being is simpler than that of heaven and earth 79:27.
cannot avoid death 80:18-21.
ungrateful to the bounties of Allāh 100:1-6.
ungrateful in good and bad times 89:15-16.

Ibrāhīm (A)
Arabs are descendants 90:3.
scripture of Ibrāhīm (A) 87:19.

Jinn
whispering of Jinn 114:6.

Lailat al-Qadr
angels descend in Lailatul Qadr 97:4.
better than thousand months 97:3.
Qur'ān revealed in Lailatul Qadr 44:3; 97:1.

Makkah
Secure City 95:3.

Mischief
seeking protection from mischief of created things 113:1-5; 114:4,6.

Mountains
passing away of mountains 78:20; 81:3; 101:5.
pegs of earth 78:7.
provision from mountains 79:32-33.

Muhammad (S)
allegations as madman 81:22.
anxiety for transforming humanity 94:2-3.
blind man's incident 80:1-10.
abundant good given 108:1.
heart of Muhammad (S) expanded 94:1.
being an orphan 93:6.
reading was commanded at the first revelation 96:1-5.
revelations gave relief 94:1-8.
search for guidance and reward of fulfillment 93:7.

Mūsā (A)
commanded to go to Fir'awn 79:15-17.
showed signs to Fir'awn 79:20.
received revelations at Sinai 95:2.
received revelations near mountain 79:16.
scripture given to Mūsā (A) 87:19.
received revelation in the valley of Tuwa 79:16.

Mutma'innah
highest stage of spiritual advancement is Mutma'innah 89:27-30.
soul should be developed to reach the stage of Mutma'innah 91:8-9.

Night
symbolic nature of night 79:29; 92:1; 93:2.

Orphans
guardian of orphans to take due care of them 89:17; 90:15; 107:1-2.
oppression of orphans strictly prohibited 93:9.
property of orphans should not be consumed 89:19.

Patience
patience and perseverance brings success 103:2-3.
Pen
Allāh taught the use of pen 96:4.
Poor
care of the poor 107:1-3.
Prayer
protection from evils 113:1-5; 114:1-6.
Quraish
advantages enjoyed by Quraish 106:1-4.
trade of Quraish in winter and summer 106:2.
Qur'ān
Tablet well-guarded 85:21-22.
explanation of the Qur'ān complete and perfect 86:13.
Reminder to the Right Path for the Believers 80:4,11; 81:27; 87:9.
revelation of the Qur'ān in Blessed Night 97:1.
scribes of the Qur'ān will be honored 80:13-16.
contains universal message 81:27.
Ramadan
Lailat al-Qadr falls in Ramadan 97:1.
Sālih (A)
she-camel put forward by Sālih (A) as a sign 91:13.
Slander
slanderer is condemned 104:1.
Soul
soul will meet Allāh 84:6.
contentment of soul rests in Allāh 89:27-28.
every soul will receive its full due 99:7-8.
every soul is responsible for its deeds 82:19.
soul will have no power to help 82:19.
soul should seek refuge in Allāh 113:1-2; 114:1-4.
three spiritual stages of soul 12:53; 75:2; 89:27-30.
Success
success awaits those who maintain purity 87:14.
Slaves
setting the slaves free without ransom is a deed of virtue 90:13.
Thamūd
carved mountain into houses 89:9.
punishment of Thamūd 85:18-20; 91:14.
three days of respite 1:65.
rejected Sālih 91:11,14.
slaying of she-camel 91:14.
Unbelievers
do not worship what Muslims worship 109:3-5.
Wealth
diverts from the path of Allāh 102;1-2.
hoarding of wealth condemned 104:2-3.
love of wealth leads people astray 89:20; 100:8.
disbelievers spend wealth to hinder progress of Islam 90:6.
Zakāt
obligatory nature of zakāt 98:5.